D0204950

FAULKNER:
MASKS AND METAPHORS

Faulkner
Masks and Metaphors

Lothar Hönnighausen

University Press of Mississippi
Jackson

In the process of writing sections of this book, I have significantly revised some previously published materials. One part of chapter 4 has been adapted from *The Artist and His Masks: William Faulkner's Metafiction*, ed. Agostino Lombardo; two other sections are based on a paper presented at the Vienna session of the *International Faulkner Symposium*, which appeared in *Faulkner, His Contemporaries, and His Posterity*, ed. Waldemar Zacharasiewicz. Part of chapter 5 draws on sections one and three of my article "The Imagery in Faulkner's *A Fable*," in *Faulkner: After the Nobel Prize*, ed. Michel Gresset and Kenzaburo Ohashi. The last section of chapter 7, in another form, was presented at the University of Mississippi Faulkner and Yoknapatawpha Conference (1986) and published in *Faulkner and Race*, ed. Doreen Fowler and Ann J. Abadie.

Copyright © 1997 by University Press of Mississippi
All rights reserved
Manufactured in the United States of America

00 99 98 97   4 3 2 1

The paper in this book meets the guidelines for permanence and durability of the Committee on Production Guidelines for Book Longevity of the Council on Library Resources.

Library of Congress Cataloging-in-Publication Data

Hönnighausen, Lothar.
    Faulkner : masks and metaphors / Lothar Hönnighausen.
        p.   cm.
    Includes bibliographical references (p.   ) and index.
    ISBN 0-87805-998-9 (cloth : alk. paper)
    1. Faulkner, William, 1897–1962—Style.   2. Metaphor.   3. Role playing in literature.   4. Disguise in literature.   I. Title.
PS3511.A86Z829   1997
813'.52—dc21   97-6952
                                                                            CIP

British Library Cataloging-in-Publication data available

FOR MY FRIENDS OF THE
INTERNATIONAL FAULKNER
SYMPOSIUM

CONTENTS

What then is truth? A mobile army of metaphors, metonymics, and anthropomorphism.
—Friedrich Nietzsche quoted in Jacques Derrida

Part of the fun of writing is putting on masks.
—Tom Whalen

Introduction

The pronouncement of the nineteenth century philosopher Friedrich Nietzsche as transmitted through the deconstructive spirit of Jacques Derrida and the casual remark of the contemporary American poet Tom Whalen on a writer's pleasure in role-playing mark the wide range of this book's theme. It contains cognitive, ethical, and aesthetic aspects, centering on masks and metaphors and comprising the sociopsychic implications for Faulkner's readers of his personae and his imagery. Nietzsche's replacement of truth by metaphor accords well with his conviction that the modern artist can best be understood as a wearer of masks ("around every complex spirit a mask continually grows" [*Beyond Good and Evil* 69–70]).[1] Indeed, Nietzsche's interrelated views on masks and metaphor constitute the threshold of my approach to Faulkner.[2]

The first part of the book, comprising chapters 1 and 2, is devoted to Faulkner's role-playing in his photos and interviews and to the theoretical grounding of the concepts of mask and metaphor. The second part (chapters 3 and 4) contains studies of specific masks and metaphors of the artist. Chapters 5–8, making up the third part, seek to utilize the aesthetics emerging in parts 1 and 2 by focusing on metaphoric strategies in Faulkner's major novels. The discussion in this third part proceeds from some specific aspects of the metaphoricity in *The Sound and the Fury, Light in August*, and *A Fable* to the center of the book, the more comprehensive studies of *Absalom, Absalom!* and particularly *The Hamlet*. The investigation of the interaction of the several modes of image making and image receiving, their psychoanalytic and sociopolitical, modernist and regionalist features, demonstrates that Faulkner's greatness lies as much in the creativeness of his metaphorics as in his narrative inventiveness.

Introduction

In recent years, the approach to metaphor has developed well beyond the taxonomic registering of rhetorical figures and the sensitive but essentially formalist image studies of the previous generation. Discourse theory, women's studies, and reader response criticism, as well as cultural studies, new historicism, and communication theory, have modified our sensibility and created a new awareness of the interrelationship between metaphoric forms and ideological contents. The idea inspiring my approach of an essential affinity between the transfer in role-playing and in metaphorizing opens up a new view of the processes of artistic imagination as well as of the functioning of metaphor. From this perspective, metaphor appears not so much as a single rhetorical device as a complex shaping power, as "metaphoricity," inspiring whole contexts and respective reader responses. Connected with these new concepts is the replacement of the work as ruling aesthetic metaphor by that of the illimitable text. Clearly, the new fascination with intertextuality and contextuality, with the logistics of role-playing, and with the transgression of categorical boundaries in metaphor is concomitant with a more comprehensive sociopolitical deconstruction of which the traditional notions of race and gender are the most prominent examples. While the romantics insisted on sincerity, we appreciate the aesthetics of role-play; while the New Critics focussed on the well-wrought urn and the definiteness of structure, we cherish the Bakhtinian "openness" of Faulkner's novels.

I had an epiphany of this development in observing a sculptor create a Faulkner bust for our garden. The first stage, in which my wife and I were to assist the artist in her Faulkner reading and to provide photographs and additional information on Faulkner's life and works, was pleasant enough, but then the artist entered into the next phase, in which she had to make up her mind which of the many Faulkner images we had discussed came closest to her or to our Faulkner. This decision-making process put all of us in a very postmodern situation. After it had emerged that it would be a bust of the old Faulkner, the problems did not go away, either for the artist or for us as witnesses. For me, who as a literary critic had been wont to communicate with several conveniently diverse Faulkner images, it was a painful experience to be asked by the artist whether I found specific emerging features of her sculpture authentic. Depending on the stage of the work, the material, the point of view, or the lighting, we were, between the rudimentary clay version, the wax form, and the finished bronze cast, confronted with a frightening multitude of possible Faulkners (plate 1).

In preparing this book's final draft, I have profited much from the valuable suggestions of Richard Gray, Peter Nicolaisen, Noel Polk, and Dorothy Scura, who very kindly read the manuscript. I should also like to acknowledge the expert advice of the publisher's readers. Ms. Natalie Kelemen was a conscientious research assistant. In the main phase of the work, the manuscript benefited very much from Katherine Burrell's intelligent and scrupulous copyediting. During my stay as visiting professor in the English Department of the University of Tennessee at Knoxville, I enjoyed the generous support of the chairman, Dr. Allen Carroll, and of the faculty and staff, particularly Lisa Lance, who was a great technical help in preparing the manuscript for the press. I would also like to acknowledge the thorough copyediting of Carol Cox, who provided me with some elegant solutions to potentially awkward phrases. I would also like to thank Ruth Piehl for her invaluable help in proofreading and preparing the text.

I have learned much from my European and American friends of the International Faulkner Symposium, who since 1983 have managed to organize scholarly meetings and to publish seven volumes of criticism. On the occasion of the centenary of Faulkner's birthday, I dedicate to them this book in grateful acknowledgment of their expertise and good fellowship.

Plate 1: Multitude of Faulkners and their transformation in the studio of sculptor Adelheid Bauer (private)

PRIMARY TEXTS: LIST OF ABBREVIATIONS

AA   *Absalom, Absalom!: William Faulkner, Novels 1936–1940.* New York: Library of America, 1990.

FAB   *A Fable: William Faulkner, Novels 1942–1954.* New York: Library of America, 1994.

AILD   *As I Lay Dying: William Faulkner, Novels 1930–1935.* New York: Library of America, 1985.

CS   *Collected Stories of William Faulkner.* New York: Random House, 1950.

ELM   *Elmer.* Ed. James B. Meriwether and Dianne L. Cox. *Mississippi Quarterly* 36 (Summer 1983): 337–460.

EPP   *Early Prose and Poetry.* Ed. Carvel Collins. Boston: Little, Brown, 1962.

ESPL   *Essays, Speeches and Public Letters.* Ed. James B. Meriwether. New York: Random House, 1966.

FD   *Flags in the Dust.* Ed. Douglas Day. New York: Random House, 1973.

FU   *Faulkner in the University: Class Conferences at the University of Virginia, 1957–1958.* Ed. Frederick L. Gwynn and Joseph Blotner. Charlottesville: U of Virginia P, 1959.

GDM   *Go Down, Moses: William Faulkner, Novels 1942–1954.* New York: Library of America, 1994.

HAM   *The Hamlet: William Faulkner, Novels 1936–1940.* New York: Library of America, 1990.

ID   *Intruder in the Dust: William Faulkner, Novels 1942–1954.* New York: Library of America, 1994.

ITJ   *If I Forget Thee, Jerusalem* [*The Wild Palms*]*: William Faulkner, Novels 1936–1940.* New York: Library of America, 1990.

Abbreviations

LA *Light in August: William Faulkner, Novels 1930–1935.* New York: Library of America, 1985.

LiG *Lion in the Garden: Interviews with William Faulkner, 1926–1962.* Ed. James B. Meriwether and Michael Millgate. Lincoln: Liveright, 1955.

MAY *Mayday.* Notre Dame and London: U of Notre Dame P, 1976.

MF & GB *The Marble Faun and A Green Bough.* New York: Random House, 1965.

MOS *Mosquitoes.* New York: Liveright, 1955.

NOS *New Orleans Sketches.* Ed. Carvel Collins. New York: Random House, 1968.

P *Pylon: William Faulkner, Novels 1930–1935.* New York: Library of America, 1985.

SAR *Sartoris.* New York: Random House, 1929.

SF *The Sound and the Fury, New, Corrected Edition.* New York: Random House, 1984.

SL *Selected Letters of William Faulkner.* Ed. Joseph Blotner. New York: Random House, 1977.

SP *Soldiers' Pay.* New York: Boni & Liveright, 1926.

T *The Town.* New York: Vintage, 1957.

U *The Unvanquished: William Faulkner, Novels 1936–1940.* New York: Library of America, 1990.

US *Uncollected Stories of William Faulkner.* Ed. Joseph Blotner. New York: Random House, 1979.

VS *Vision in Spring.* Austin: U of Texas P, 1984.

Preludes

And if you rightly look for it, you will almost always find that the author himself has somewhere furnished you with his own picture.

—Herman Melville, "Hawthorne and His Mosses"

But you, straying trustfully about this park of dark and rootless trees which Dr. Ellis and your Germans have recently thrown open to the public . . . A book is the writer's secret life, the dark twin of a man: you can't reconcile them. And with you, when the inevitable clash comes, the author's actual self is the one that goes down, for you are one of those for whom fact and fallacy gain verisimilitude by being in cold print.

—William Faulkner, *Mosquitoes*

O N E

Role-Play in Photos, Letters, and Interviews

Authors furnish us with pictures of themselves, but these are, as the epigraph from Faulkner's *Mosquitoes* indicates, not nearly as clear as Melville's remark would lead us to believe. Rather, they offer us, as both Melville's and Faulkner's examples illustrate, projections and distorted reflections of themselves. Noel Polk, in *Children of the Dark House*, illustrates a comic aspect of the problem by recounting how Faulkner, in the 1952 *Omnibus* television program about himself, says to the former editor of the Oxford *Eagle*, "Do your story," but then, putting on the mask of the writer as recluse, insists, "But no pictures" (242–43). The startling pronouncement of the Nobel Prize-winning author that he is not a writer at all but a grain and feed producing farmer (*LiG* 169) is another famous example of his role-play. The metaphors in the quotation from *Mosquitoes* and its eerie, psychoanalytic scenery uncover some of Faulkner's unconscious motifs in shaping his masks: an author's book is envisioned as his sinister *Doppelgänger* revealing the mysterious superiority of this other self.

As the study of Faulkner's masking practice will show, the elusive master employed not one but a multitude of masks to transform himself. This is not surprising if it is understood that a mask not only disguises but also constitutes an essential mode of living and writing. Consequently, to describe the entire diversity of Faulkner's roles, to assess their relatedness, and to evaluate their psychological motifs and literary functions, would involve a complete overview of his entire biography and work. As this could hardly be achieved in one book, my more modest goal is to provide an outline of such a project, discuss some examples, and offer a few methodological reflections. How does one reconcile the depressive side of Faulkner's personality and the respective role-playing (reckless horseman and ruthless drinker) with his human sympathy and humor, with his self-confidence and clear awareness of being one of the world's greatest novelists?[1] Do these oppositions, if they really are oppositions, resurface as particular masks which he assumed in his life or in his writing? It is these transformations and forms, particularly as they manifest themselves in Faulkner's photos, that I want to study in this chapter.

While it is tempting to dismiss Faulkner's dandyism as a means for him to compensate for his diminutive size, there is little doubt that such a simplistic approach would prove unsatisfactory. The dandy mask should not be viewed in isolation; it must be seen in relation to the opposing mask of the vagabond or bum. Furthermore, the coexistence of the dandy with the persona of the country boy, farmer, and country gentleman—all three having different symbolic implications—is worthy of consideration and evaluation. Finally, the differing appearances of the dandy and his close relative, the aesthete, must be discussed in both psychological and artistic terms, as they appear to be related to the polar features of the self-effacing minuteness of Faulkner's handwriting and its calligraphic elevation in his handcrafted art nouveau manuscripts. Critics have rarely taken these stylizing details of Faulkner's masks and the circumstances of their use into account. But the dandy mask, while serving compensatory and supplementary functions in Faulkner's life, also proved to be inspirational in his writing. Its élan and irony embodied the artist's creative buoyancy and his emerging sense of form.

If it is accepted that the reader's experience of Faulkner's fiction also involves considering the artist as "hero of the thousand faces," it is obviously necessary to consider the several media in which Faulkner cast images of himself. The example, in the introduction, of the transformation of the many Faulkners into one Faulkner sculpture illustrates how essential it is to differentiate between the impact of Faulkner's role-playing in his photos, letters, and interviews (chapter 1) and that of his artist personae in his fiction (chapters 3–8). Clearly, one must take into account the different media of Faulkner's self-projections, whether they be a group of drawings, a poetry volume, or a short story about a living or a marble faun. It does matter whether a portrayal as a fighter pilot is intended to impress some lady friend or whether two novelistic Quentins serve to express different sides of himself. But whether Faulkner poses for a photo in his new riding gear or identifies with suicidal flyers, these artist personae appear as historically and individually conditioned foci of the text and as aesthetically transforming its sociocultural contents. The awareness that fictionalizing plays as considerable a part in Faulkner's biography as in his literary works will lead to new approaches in biographical criticism as well as in the study of his works.

However, assessing the impact of the different personae of the artist on our reception of his art is complicated by several factors, particularly how the various media through which these several personae— the drawn faun or the photographed war veteran—are established and how they affect us simultaneously yet differently. Further, little is yet known about how these personae or images interact and in which ways their interaction influences our reception of Faulkner's writing. The following are a few observations and suggestions on how one may deal with the problem and in the practice of Faulkner criticism draw consequences from contemporary theory. Readers' encounters with Faulkner's literary self-portraits or masks constitute a very different kind of experience from their exposure to his images in sculpture, drawing, and photography. Above all, the personae of the author, whom readers help create by sensuously and intellectually realizing the metaphorics that constitute them, remain subordinate to the laws of the narrative cosmos within each story or novel.

In contrast, the masks conveyed through other media seem to affect us more directly. However, reflections on some of Faulkner's drawings and photographs will reveal that they, too, presuppose mask-building and metaphorizing processes and do not give us the real thing.

The publicity shot (plate 2) which the United Press needed for a write-up on *Sanctuary* (1931) provides an interesting example of the transformative activity involved in photography. From Jack Cofield's report, the different metaphorizing goals of Faulkner, Estelle, and himself on that occasion can be identified. While Faulkner intended to shock the viewing public by playing the bum ("On this occasion Bill wore an old, old brown tweed coat, red bandana hanky in his pocket, white seersucker pants smeared and spotted with paint, uncombed hair"[1,3]), both Estelle and Cofield favored a more conventional image of the young Mississippian as successful author. The two remarkable photos reprinted in *William Faulkner: The Cofield Collection* demonstrate that Estelle, or rather Cofield's art, gained the upper hand. Faulkner is represented in such a way that the shabbiness of his apparel is not shown. Moreover, the author appears in half-profile with a tight-lipped mouth, energetic chin, powerful nose, and, above all, a forcefully forward-looking eye which calls up positive associations for viewers. The frontal portrait, Jack Cofield's apt choice for opening his collection of studio portraits, is an even more effective promotion photo. The young artist, this time looking viewers directly in the eye, his right forearm and cigarette-holding hand completing a fortifying square of upper arms and shoulders, has become a powerful icon of creative will power and artistic independence. Apparently Faulkner, after Estelle and Cofield had impressed upon him the necessity of promotion photos, decided to cooperate and, talented actor that he was, entered into the part. Consequently, the photo shows nothing of the arrogance of a shy introvert, and certainly nothing of the cantankerous person telling Cofield that the photo session was "a waste of his valuable time" (3). The image viewers receive when looking at this portrait is that of an absolutely serious artist whose first major achievements had given him the confidence that he would do even better. Looking at this portrait of the artist as a mature man, viewers would never suspect that it could—as indeed it would—be replaced by that of the artist as bum or dandy. The unstated promotional message is, "Here is a writer from whom you can expect much."

The personal and authentic quality of this photo stands out even more strikingly when compared to a roughly contemporary one which presents an image of Faulkner as a movie star from Hollywood's great time (plate 3). This photograph illustrates the influence of period styles on photographic role-playing in regard to both the posture of the depicted person and the crafting of the photograph. Faulkner is well groomed and looks elegant, his knowing eyes gazing at viewers with slight condescension; there is no question that he acts the part of the movie star superbly. The photo, too, is a highly finished product, clever in format and lighting (observe, for instance, his eyes and the pipe stem), and very professional in the handling of focus and retouch. One would be hard put to find anything in Faulkner's literary role-playing to match the suave urbanity here attained by the "simple country boy." Not surprisingly, the result is one of the least authentic among Faulkner's photos, betraying too much finesse to be "true."

This example confirms that in studying photos or portraits in other visual arts, it is imperative to take their generic, stylistic, and thematic features as well as the nonliterary nature of their transfer or metaphoricity into account. The publication of *The Marble Faun* constitutes an interesting example of three simultaneous yet different self-fashionings of the author ("*The Marble Faun* preface [is] . . . an anticipation of the various literary poses that Faulkner self-consciously adopted during his apprenticeship" [Millgate, "Unreal Estate," 73]). The late romantic poems present a highly stylized image of the artist as a static faun dreaming in his pastoral setting of vitalistic movement. However, the preface, written by Phil Stone but obviously with Faulkner's approval, projects a picture of the author in the style of regionalist realism: "The author of these poems is a man steeped in the soil of his native land." Moreover, the case is further complicated by the publicity photographs taken in the late summer of 1924 for the promotion of *The Marble Faun*. These two photos, reproduced in Blotner's Faulkner biography (1984), are stylistically equally remote from the late romantic faun and from the regionalist poet of the preface. Yet the two poses, adopted in the photos and showing Faulkner's talent for acting, relate well to the texts. The contemplative pipe

Plate 2: A portrait of the resolutely independent artist (The Cofield Collection, Center for the Study of Southern Culture, University of Mississipi)

Plate 3: The movie star image (William Faulkner Collection, Special
Collections Department, University of Virginia Library; and Jill Faulkner
Summers)

Plate 4: Faulkner's faun drawing in *Mayday* (William Faulkner Collection, Special Collections Department, University of Virginia Library; and Jill Faulkner Summers)

smoker obviously impersonates the romantic poet, while the energetically upward-looking young man with an open shirt and intrepid eyes might well evoke the sense of a fresh start which is characteristic of the spirit of regionalism. The two photos, however, have a greater impact on us than their relation purely with Faulkner's volume of poems deserves, and, through the way Blotner has juxtaposed them, come to affect us as representative of two basic and consistent attitudes of Faulkner. In studying Faulkner's masks, it seems important to assess these metonymic side effects of our visual impressions and to relate them to our metaphorizing activity when accommodating verbal images.

Viewers get involved in this metaphorizing not only in the case of Faulkner's drawings of fauns (plate 4), a motif with a rich heritage of stylized representation and manifold iconographic connotations from antiquity, the Renaissance, and, closer to Faulkner's own art work, from the works of Aubrey Beardsley (plate 6). They also metaphorize, or transcend the actual when, looking more closely at the realistic photos taken in Paris, viewers discover affinities between the faun drawing (plate 4), the little self-portrait sketched in ink (plate 5), and the photo (plate 7). Furthermore, these photographs of Faulkner, because of the iconography of the frenchified "artiste," take spectators far beyond the merely documentary. In fact, photography here invades, as literary metaphor does, *"le domaine de l'impalpable et de l'imaginaire,"* which Baudelaire, in his notorious remark in the Salon of 1859, had denied it was capable of doing. Of interest here is that this particular impersonation of the Mississippian as "artiste" illustrates how a specific role helped him to focus on a specific sensibility such as that informing the grand conclusion of *Sanctuary*: "It had been a gray day, a gray summer, a gray year. On the street old men wore overcoats, and in the Luxembourg Gardens as Temple and her father passed the women sat knitting in shawls . . ." (221).

These Paris photos, if they are juxtaposed with a photo taken in New Orleans at the same time (plate 8), document Faulkner's amazing talent for self-transformation and role-playing. In the New Orleans photo, a fairly young man fixes a challenging stare on viewers, expressing greater self-confidence than his achievement so far warranted. In contrast, both Paris photos portray a much older, distinguished-looking man, an "internationalized Faulkner" with a frenchifying hat and beard. The difference between the Paris and the New Orleans photos is such that one might take the Faulkner in the Paris photos for an altogether different person. This is not simply the effect of his style of clothing and the newly grown beard, but the result of the facial expression and the poses he adopts. The full-length photo and the two photos of the half-figure photographed from the right and from the left in Cofield (70) convey the impression of a sensitive, lonely, distinguished gentleman engaged in profound if somewhat melancholy meditation.[2] The repetition of this pose and his insistence on being presented in profile show how purposefully, if instinctively, Faulkner created this image of himself.

This supposition is further supported by the small pen-and-ink self-portrait (plate 5), which, given the difference between the media (drawing and photography), is very close to the photos in expression and intention. However, this drawing takes on different implications when viewed within its literary context, his letter modifying the solemn and melancholic effect of this little icon by a self-ironic commentary to keep the tragic mask and the imposing beard unscathed by any vitriolic comment from Maud and the rest of his family. Finally, the fact that this little self-portrait resembles one of Faulkner's faun drawings confirms the marble faun of the poetry volume as a persona of the artist and the underlying intentions and strategies behind Faulkner's faun mask.

Many photographs of Faulkner impress viewers not only through their particular content but by encapsulating a whole performance. Such an example is the photo of ex-Royal Flying Corps Faulkner posing in an R. A. F. lieutenant's uniform in December 1918 (plate 9). With his officer's cap set at a rakish angle, a cigarette between lips which are set in a thin smile of superiority, his eyelids contracted and his glance ignoring the camera, and, above all, through the careful diagonal composition of the walking stick in his right hand and his left not fully inserted in the trouser pocket, a twenty-one-year-old Faulkner personifies to perfection a military dandy who is a much older and more impressive man. Surely, this cannot be an immature cadet but must be a proven combat pilot, handicapped but victorious, tough, arrogant, and elegant. Viewers appreciate Faulkner's histrionic achievement even more if they relate it to an ensemble of similar photos from the same period. These photos from the Cofield collec-

My beard is coming along fine. Makes me look sort of distinguished, like someone you'd care to know.

Billy

Plate 5: Pen-and-ink self-portrait (William Faulkner Collection, Special Collections Department, University of Virginia Library; and Jill Faulkner Summers)

Plate 6: Aubrey Beardsley "A Footnote" (*The Later Work of Aubrey Beardsley,* [New York: Dover, 1967] plate 115)

Plate 7: An American in Paris, 1925 (William Faulkner Collection, Special Collections Department, University of Virginia Library; and Jill Faulkner Summers)

Plate 8: A less-stylized Faulkner in New Orleans, 1925
(George W. Healy, Jr.)

tion (53), two in an officer's uniform (plate 9) and two in a cadet's, help us contextualize the well-known dandy photo.[3] Again, the existence of a whole photo series demonstrates that they were the outcome of a role-playing session or performance.

Through a comparison of the similarities and differences in the postures and iconographic details of the series, viewers come to appreciate the effort of the performer and his artistic achievement in the dandy photo (plate 9). For instance, the slight advancement of the right foot should be noted, as well as the transfer of the cigarette from the right hand to the mouth, and, above all, the energetic turn of the head parallel to the right shoulder, with the cigarette underlining this effect; viewers also become aware in this way of the awkwardness of the unbent arms, which, in the cadet photo, draw attention to the unattractive tunic. By the same token, the unbent arms and the parallel running seam of the tunic elongate the figure, an effect supported by the walking stick and legs and echoed by the two flanking pillars of the pseudobaroque balustrade on the backcloth. The determination marking the white face is enhanced by the white hands, particularly by the right one gripping the stick. The photo of the actual cadet Faulkner, albeit so much less attractive than that of the fictive lieutenant Faulkner, shows itself to be a powerful icon, particularly when the inner function of the elongated forms is realized in relation to the facial expression of determination.

In connection with *Soldiers' Pay*, the photographs of cadet and officer Faulkner illustrate particularly well how these histrionics function in the process of literary creation. Cadet Julian Lowe's juvenile envy of the rank and paraphernalia of the officer serves as departure point and foil for his horrifying realization of the officer's physical and mental mutilation (25–29). The fact that officer Donald Mahon wears the kind of insignia and wings and brass of a British officer that had attracted young Faulkner so very much is particularly revealing. Clearly, the encounter of cadet and officer, rehearsed and reflected in photographed—and literary—impersonations, suggests the uncanny confrontation of the young artist with a maimed counterself. In contrast to Quentin Compson, William Faulkner survived the meeting with his wraith by capturing it in his writing. Of particular interest in this respect is the double aspect of the wounded veteran mask: there is a hero, but he is wounded. Faulkner's pretence to the type of experiences that Hemingway actually went through is of less importance in relation to his mask than is his urge to share the specific contemporary ideological and emotional dispositions, to express, and then to *reenact* the experience suggested by this mask.

In this postmodernist age, which has seen Hemingway's best-sellers go out of fashion, readers can appreciate the irony of the peculiar war wounds and the obvious self-pity of these disturbed macho men. However, our privilege of distance also allows us to evaluate an interesting variant of the role of the wounded war hero in Faulkner's late phase. When he told Jean Stein "his usual World War I stories, including the one of crashing in a plane," he seemed to be trying to fend off his apocalyptic visions and "to say no to death" (Karl 886). Why Faulkner felt the urge "to say no to death" can be seen in his very complex reaction on hearing of Hemingway's suicide. After being disturbed by the news—about which his initial comment was "It wasn't an accident. He killed himself"—he then adopted the mask of the moralist in this matter: "I don't like a man that takes the short way home" (Blotner, *Faulkner* [1984] 690). Is this surprising in an author who had his most intimate persona commit suicide, and who initially "instructed Joan [Williams] to address her letters to 'Quentin Compson' " (Williamson 280)?

Through studying Faulkner's role-playing, the reader soon comes to realize that not only can one mask represent several different thematic aspects, but also that different roles can be representative of the same psychological trait or set of traits. Bayard Sartoris's character as foolhardy rider tallies with that of reckless driver, and, finally, with that of devil-may-care test pilot. These three episodes, like variants of a dream, have one psychoanalytic theme: Faulkner's concern with self-destructive violence and, ultimately, his suicidal urge. Apart from this similarity, the hero's three life-threatening pursuits each have different sociocultural connotations: in *Flags in the Dust* the riding belongs to the disappearing chivalrous world of the South, while the reckless driving and test flying reflect the impact of the modern emerging South and the postwar malaise.

During Faulkner's time, American, British, and even German combat pilots (Immelmann and von Richthofen) were surrounded with a glamour similar to that of the chivalrous champions of Sir Walter Scott's *Ivanhoe*. This fact explains why pilots figure in Faulkner's fic-

Plate 9: The dandy posing as an R. A. F. lieutenant (The Cofield Collection, Center for the Study of Southern Culture, University of Mississippi)

tion prominently, but not why they would be of such importance to him as impersonations and symbolic representatives of complex moral and emotional states. Obviously, for Faulkner flying was not only a hobby but, like acting as dandy or foxhunting squire, the basis for a new and elevated mode of imaginative existence.

The photo of a friendly and relaxed Faulkner in front of his Waco airplane (Blotner, *Faulkner* [1984] 332ff.) reveals no element of flying's tragic dimension, which Faulkner had already encapsulated in art—*Pylon* was published on March 25, 1935—before his brother Dean's death from a plane crash on November 10, 1935. The depth of his grief should not make us overlook the more specific and modifying effect which the uncanny anticipation of the personal tragedy in his writing must have had on Faulkner. Naturally, as readers, we have no means of accurately assessing his psychological situation, but he must have felt haunted by a sense of repetition, self-alienation, and lack of immediacy which tainted and aggravated his grief. This in addition to the more obvious cause—remorse at having been Dean's mentor and patron in the world of flying—might have been the reason for the lasting effect which the loss of his brother had on him. Obviously, this particular reenactment of art in life is an extreme case of role-playing, but, with its elements of repetition and self-distancing consciousness, it displays essential features of the thematic complex "mask and role."

When studying this phenomenon, readers must pay no less attention to shifts in content and thematic nuances than to structural patterns. The implications in *Flags in the Dust* of Bayard Sartoris's traumatic memories of his brother John's death in an air battle during World War I are very different from those of "All the Dead Pilots." Some of them rise again—in "Death Drag" and *Pylon*—as entertainers who, by demonstrating their willingness to risk their lives ("We will do all the jumping you want, if you pay enough" [CS 191]) are a cross between the gladiators of the Roman circus and modern stuntmen. Nevertheless, the description at the beginning of "All the Dead Pilots," aiming at a symbolist transformation—"an esoteric look; a look not exactly human, like that of some dim and threatful apotheosis of the race" (CS 511)—explains why these fliers should fascinate Faulkner: "they were outside the range of God, not only of respectability, of love, but of God too. That they had escaped the compulsion of accepting a past and a future, that they were—they had no past" (*FU* 36). Clearly, they are the antipodes of the characters in *Absalom, Absalom!*, who are products of history or obsessed with the past; like the clowns and the other circus people in the works of Picasso, Beckmann, and so many other early twentieth century painters and writers, the fliers represent the otherness of the modernist artists vis-à-vis their society ("No ties; no place" [*P* 805]).

The reporter in *Pylon* admires the fliers for qualities he himself lacks, because, unlike himself, they have the courage to accept the uprootedness and deadly freedom of their existence, while he goes through peculiar processes of splitting and reflecting ("that without knowing it you listen and see in one language and then do what you call writing in another" [(*P* 803]). These metaphoric experiences are suggestive of Faulkner's own switching between *Absalom, Absalom!*, "the novel merely written to get away from the great work" (*FU* 36), and *Pylon* and his wavering between a historically and socially overdetermined life in Oxford, Mississippi, and the nondescript utopian world of Hollywood, between regionalism and modernist rootlessness. That the reporter is close to the author and has a persona quality is not only evident from his incredible bouts of drinking and his manneristic metaphorics. It also emerges in his Don Quixote-like features ("with that air of worn and dreamy fury which Don Quixote must have had" [807]), and the idealistic worship of Laverne which follows the pattern shaping the Horace Benbow-Ruby Lamar, Byron Bunch-Lena Grove, and Gavin Stevens-Eula Varner Snopes configurations. Moreover, the persona aspect of the reporter is further confirmed by details such as the leitmotif of the skeleton with which he—like the poet of "Carcassonne"—leads a peculiar metaphoric coexistence ("while the reporter leaned above the desk like a dissolute and eager skeleton" [807]). Of interest to me and in connection with the main theme of Faulkner's masquerading is that in the cases of *Pylon* and *Absalom, Absalom!*, the author explores two diametrically opposed, though complementary, personae of the artist: the reporter is exposed to the modernist waste land ("no place, no past"), and Quentin is driven to mourn and recover southern history ("a barracks filled with stubborn backlooking ghosts" [*AA* 9]).

"and I got to talking to a funny man. A little kind of black man—"

"A nigger?"

"No. He was a white man, except he was awful sunburned and kind of shabby dressed—no necktie and hat. Say, he said some funny things to me . . . He said he was a liar by profession . . . I think he was crazy. Not dangerous: just crazy."

"I remembered [his name] because he was such a funny kind of man."

"Faulkner?" the niece pondered in turn.

"Never heard of him," she said at last with finality. (*MOS* 144–45)

It may be that I took up writing as—what do you call it?—a protest to being—against being small and insignificant, that I wanted to be big and brave and handsome and rich, it could be that, I dont know. (Gresset, "Faulkner's Voice" 184)

While thinking about the self-aggrandizing war hero and dashing air force officer, readers should not lose sight of the several instances of Faulkner's portrayal of himself as small and unattractive. How important his self-consciousness about his small stature was is clear from his statements in both fiction and nonfiction. Moreover, Faulkner's habit of playing a marginal role as observer, listener, and hanger-on, for instance, in the New Orleans circle, seems to complement his acting out of imaginary "impostor" roles. Spratling's 1925 caricature of Faulkner and himself, in which the writer appears dwarfed by the much larger head of his artist friend (Blotner, *Faulkner* [1984] 140 ff.)—whose superior talent finally convinced Faulkner that his own vocation was not the visual arts—may reflect Faulkner's tendency to stay aloof. The dwarfishness of Faulkner's appearance and the bottles under his easy chair are ironic emblems of the writer as Bohemian drunkard and clownish observer, the "funny little man" in *Mosquitoes*.

Apart from these literary and visual caricatures and self-caricatures, there are very few pictures of Faulkner in which his small stature is evident. Consequently, the image of him which most readers have is not that of a small man.[4] Nevertheless, it would be grotesquely reductive if undue importance were attached to Faulkner's diminutive size and to his efforts in masking and role-playing to disguise and compensate for this "handicap." Rather, we should see

Faulkner's smallness in the wider context of his sociopsychic problems: his suicidal alcoholism and his love problems (see the Talliaferro persona), his imprudent expenditures and financial worries, his painful waverings between political liberalism and emotional patriarchalism. Above all, Faulkner's ambiguous attitude towards his appearance should be seen in relation to his uncanny aesthetics, in which "the splendor of failure in trying to do the impossible" (*LiG* 238 and 122) was the ultimate test of the quality of art. There is little doubt that Faulkner's idealistic challenge of highest risk and most splendid failure reflects the precarious drama between his suicidal urge and his will to live.

Awareness of this tension can perhaps help us to understand better the central role of the "puny voice" in the Nobel Prize speech, which is more popular with pedagogues than with Faulkner scholars. They may perhaps feel less awkward about the sonorous phrases if they take the psychological implications of the apocalyptic imagery and the shrillness of the "puny voice" more into account: "that when the last ding-dong of doom has clanged and faded from the last worthless rock hanging tideless in the last red and dying evening, that even then there will still be one more sound: that of his puny inexhaustible voice, still talking" (Fant and Ashley 131). A closer observation of his rhetoric may help us to connect Faulkner's moralizing insistence (*"I decline* to accept the end of man . . . . *I refuse* . . . . *I believe* . . . . the *poet's voice* . . . . *pillars* to help him endure and prevail") with his overall penchant for the outré, the structural extremism and stylistic insistence that is the hallmark of his manneristic genius. Moreover, one of the suppressed passages from the tapes of Faulkner's class conferences at the University of Virginia which Michel Gresset has recovered suggests that the affirmation of the Nobel Prize moralist "writing . . . against being small and insignificant" (*Fascination* 270, 297 n. 8; "Faulkner's Self-Portraits" 2–13) might hide the fearful child in the dark cellar whistling to cheer himself on.

While several of the epithets in Faulkner's ironic self-portrait in *Mosquitoes*, "funny, shabby dress, liar by profession, crazy but not dangerous," are analogous to the traditional ("liar") and the contemporary iconography ("funny, crazy") of the asocial entertainer of society, as viewers encounter it in Picasso's circus paintings or Max Beckmann's "Self-portrait as Clown" (1921), the metaphoric cluster "little kind of black man . . . never heard of him," refers to Faulkner's specific predicament. In expressing not only his "smallness" but also his "darkness," Faulkner endows with a special importance features which might otherwise appear as indifferent biographical material. The two qualities "small" and "dark" carry different connotations of inferiority, but they have the same self-demeaning function. That the young author thus draws attention to his unattractive features seems to go beyond the relaxed humor of a self-confident person and to relate to the suicidal streak in his character. Furthermore, in view of the psychology of Faulkner's segregated society and of Joel Williamson's findings about the black branch of the Faulkner family, the clarification of the misunderstanding—"A little kind of black man," the phrase "A nigger?" "No. he was a white man, except he was awful sunburned"—assumes the quality of a psychoanalytic metaphor, particularly when one takes into account the "doubtful" racial features of Joe Christmas (*Light in August*) and Charles Bon (*Absalom, Absalom!*) and Ike McCaslin's confrontation with the black counterself ("The Bear," *Go Down, Moses*).

If one follows Judith Wittenberg and other psychoanalytic critics in regarding some of Faulkner's characters as reflections of ego fragments of the author, there is no difficulty in finding, in *Sanctuary*, a striking configuration of variants of the "little kind of black man." Not only Horace Benbow but also Popeye may be read as projections in which Faulkner castigated, objectified and distanced weaknesses of his own. Popeye's smallness, as well as his sexual problems, which link him with the more obvious Faulkner persona Horace Benbow, who seeks a divorce from Belle, come to mind. Furthermore, in chapter 23, Horace undergoes one of the feminizations which critics such as Frann Michel and Karen Sass have discerned in other Faulkner heroes. After the titillating vision of Little Belle—Horace shares Gavin Stevens's predilection for being attracted to young girls—he vomits, while metaphorically identifying with Temple's sexual experience ("She was bound naked on her back on a flat car moving at speed through a black tunnel . . ." [*Sanctuary* 223]). Another instance of Horace Benbow's smallness is his positive but slightly ridiculous role as Ruby Lamar's caretaker, as a result of which he shows particular concern over her baby's milk bottle. In this regard, Horace resembles Byron Bunch, in *Light in August*, who also appears as an inferior Joseph to Lena Grove's dominant part as a secular madonna. In addi-

24

tion to these more direct, thematic mirrorings of the experience of smallness, there are also more indirect repercussions among the stylistic devices of self-portrayal.

One of the iconographic echoes of this central protest against inferiority and insignificance seems to be the striking preoccupation with the vertical in Faulkner's drawings and photos. Interestingly, this remains a recurring feature from his Pierrot persona in the Beardsleyesque *Marionettes* illustrations to that late photo, in which one of the powerful columns of the University of Virginia helps elevate its writer-in-residence. Perhaps this projection of the appearance of a much bigger man can be related to a literary projection, the image of Father conveyed through the leitmotif "not big . . . big to us" that young Bayard Sartoris in *The Unvanquished* evokes: "He was not big; it was just the things he did, that we knew he was doing, had been doing in Virginia and Tennessee that made him big to us . . . He was not big, yet somehow he looked even smaller on the horse than off of him, because Jupiter was big and when you thought of Father you thought of him as big too and so when you thought of Father being on Jupiter it was as if you said: 'Together they will be too big; you won't believe it.' So you didn't believe it and so it wasn't" (*U* 10).[5] If this may be falsification of the actual, Faulknerians will appreciate it as the result of that stylization he called "sublimating the actual into the apocryphal" (*LiG* 255), one that also manifests intself in the letters and interviews.

The reason for dealing with specimens of letters and interviews in one section is that self-fashioning in both these genres occurs as a performance involving clearly recognizable partners. The interviews will receive greater attention for the simple reason that, from the evidence of *Selected Letters*, Faulkner was generally not a great letter writer. Apart from the letters to his mother, his epistolary style, as compared with the manneristic wealth of so much of his fictional prose, is strangely reticent, cramped, and uninspired. Apparently his shy and inhibited nature (cf. his privacy complex) made him shun the revelatory quality characterizing the genre of letter writing.

However, the three following examples of his masquerading in letters to his mother, to his nephew Jimmy, and to Joan Williams give us a rough idea of the assimilative and transformational processes preceding and concomitant with literary creation. In regard to the problem of role-playing, it is striking that Faulkner's closeness to his mother allowed and forced him to appear more natural than he usually let himself be. Still, his overly positive observations in this correspondence show that a calculated process of self-fashioning took place, too. However, compared with the cramped and cold rigidity of later roles, characterized by abrasive politeness in protecting his privacy or the pseudoaffability of a southern gentleman or grand old man of American literature (at the Virginia class conferences, for instance), the Faulkner revealed in his letters to his mother certainly appears to his advantage. Wearing only the thin disguise or mask of deprecatory humor which many of us wear in our role-playing with our relatives, he does not put on the same dense camouflage as in some of the other letters and interviews. This aspect of Faulkner's self-fashioning arises in part from the exceptional circumstances of his correspondence with his mother: he is abroad and for the first time exposed to the famous scenery and art treasures of Europe. She is not only intelligent, understanding, and fascinated by anything that her beloved artist-son might see (she was a sometime-painter herself), but is also curious due to her narrowly circumscribed provincial life. Furthermore, both son and mother are aware of the tradition of the grand tour and its importance in the education of American writers and painters, knowing that young artists write about these kinds of experiences. Faulkner's reply to Maud's suggestion supports this: "No, I am not keeping the diary. I'll write it all someday though" (*SL* 17).

It is stylizing factors such as these that make up the masks emerging from these letters. Faulkner clearly writes from a specific vantage point, one that remains fairly consistent throughout the entire period of his journey. The characteristics of his posture are positive, informative, and entertaining. His frank enthusiasm and his unfamiliarity with European art and culture ("the Winged Victory and the Venus de Milo, the real ones" [*SL* 13]) make him, at the age of twenty-eight, appear much younger than the far-travelled and world-weary seventeen-year-olds of our time. Faulkner's recent experiences and his fascination with the most diverse art forms help him to shape an attractively naive perspective which enhances the vividness of his descriptions: "The cathedral of Notre Dame is grand. Like the cathedral at Milan it is all covered with cardinals mitred like Assyrian kings, . . . and beautiful naked Greek figures that have no religious significance what ever, and gargoyles—. . . Also went to a very very modernist exhibition the other day—futurist and vorticist. I was talking to a painter, a real one" (*SL* 12–13).

Experienced Faulkner readers recognize how this perspective enabled the young artist to assimilate materials which the novelist would later utilize in a startling manner. Wary of appearing as a too-quickly-Europeanized snob to his family in Mississippi, the young traveler occasionally adopts a kind of Mark Twain mask, presenting a very American vision of French rococo: "I went to Meudon this week, where Madame de Pompadour had a castle, where *folks fought duels all over the place*. And I have seen the chapel where *James I* [sic!] of England was buried after both the French and the English threw him out. Those poor *Stewarts had an awful time*. Tomorrow I am going to Versailles—*Marie Antoinette's hang-out*,—and Fontainebleau" (16, my emphasis). The young man is using rather casual language and may have mixed the Stuarts up, but the glimpses of French rococo art which he caught while playing the American tourist surfaced later, when his versatile genius produced the stylized settings in *A Fable* in which the new absolute military power of the time incongruously presents itself: ". . . in its valanced alcoves and pilastered medaillonned ceiling and crystal chandeliers and sconces and mirrors and girandoles and buhl étagères and glazed cabinets of faience bibelots, and a white rug into which war-bleached boots sank ankle-deep as into the muck of trenches, . . ." (228). Of course the best-known example of material used from the European tour is the description of the Luxembourg gardens in *Sanctuary*. What Faulkner in the conclusion to this novel introduced as an aesthetic contrast to the bleak landscape of Mississippi was a scenery assimilated by the young artist as an American in Paris: "I have come to think of the Luxembourg as my garden now" (*SL* 17).

This letter to his mother is interesting, as it shows Faulkner's self-fashioning in the role of *son as artist*. The content of the letter, the pleasure over his most recent literary achievement, is confidential and the tone informal ("I have just written such a beautiful thing that I am about to bust" [*SL* 17]). It is the kind of communication an artist would exchange with a friendly fellow artist. Apparently, Faulkner's sense of his artistic vocation and his status as his mother's son are for him intimately related, and our study of Faulkner's role-playing in letters to his mother confirms the findings of feminist critics.[6] To his mother, the author who promulgates the ideal of impersonality confides his feeling of insufficient maturity to conclude *Mosquitoes* (*SL* 13–14), and to her he speaks of his arduous work process and his obsession with making the "2000 words about the Luxembourg gardens and death" perfect. In this phase, Faulkner's aesthetic goals are oriented towards the kind of painstaking craftsmanship which most modernists associated with Flaubert and which made them insist "that prose ought to be at least as well written as poetry": ". . . it is poetry though written in prose form. I have worked on it for two whole days and every word is perfect. I havent slept hardly for two nights, thinking about it, comparing words, accepting and rejecting them, then changing again. But now it is perfect—a jewel. I am going to put it away for a week, then show it to someone for an opinion. So tomorrow I will wake up feeling rotten, I expect. Reaction. But its worth it, to have done a thing like this" (*SL* 17). What he also reveals to his mother, though veiled in self-ironic phrasing and not yet fully developed, is a psychological pattern that was to mark his whole career: bursts of creative exuberance and artistic achievement giving way to bouts of depression (marked by suicidal drinking). To the fact that these periods were followed in turn by the emergence of his will to live, the world owes one of the great narrative oeuvres of all time.

A comic leitmotif of interest in connection with his early role-playing is the beard he grew at the time, which apparently was intended to make him look more impressive than he felt. This effort clearly was successful; a contemporary photo showing him with beard and hat does make him appear older and more mature than he seems in his letters (plate 7). "My beard is coming along fine. Makes me look sort of distinguished, like someone you'd care to know," he wrote, adding a little caricatural pen-and-ink self-portrait (plate 5). In the photo Faulkner does indeed look distinguished and like a mature artist, while in the letter to his mother he refers to his beard in humorous deprecation.

Clearly, the role of the letter writer made the young author register his observations and temper his sensibility with ironic distance. What begins as a chatty remark about his relatives, "Vannye looks quite

28

young—no gray at all," is expanded upon by the *artist as letter writer*, developing into a precise description laced with caricaturistic metaphors which points forward to Mrs. Marder, Frankie, and the scene at the Mitchells' in *Flags in the Dust*: "The daughter is a tall girl with a sort of sweet dull marcelled look and bold brown eyes and her nose is too short. They are very nice, of the purest Babbitt ray serene. They carry their guidebooks like you would a handkerchief. They make you think of two people in a picture show who are busy talking to each other all the time" (*SL* 22). Obviously developing the accuracy and pliability of a satiric prose was of no less importance to the young novelist than his flirtations with symbolist prose-poetry.

The letter Faulkner wrote on April 3, 1943, to his nephew Jimmy, who was then serving in the air force, is one of the instances where he told fabricated tales about his World War I exploits. Blotner only mentions the fact that Faulkner sent Jimmy "his goggles, his leather flying jacket, and one of the RAF pips as a good-luck piece" (*Faulkner* [1984] 449) and does not raise the issue of imposture. However, by pointing to an affinity between the emotion in the letter to Jimmy and the tone in the story "Two Soldiers" of 1942, he indicates a relationship between Faulkner's retelling of his untrue war stories in the letter and his literary work. Similarly, he hints at the reuse in a letter to his stepson, Malcolm Franklin, of the ideological goals dramatized in the war film scripts Faulkner worked on at that time. Moreover, Blotner presents the psychological dimension of these letters to the young men about to enter the army: "It was another letter to a surrogate son." Frederick Karl regards the letter to Jimmy as a kind of autobiographical projection, seeing a discrepancy between Faulkner's genuine worry about his nephew and the telling of lies about his own war exploits. However, these seemingly contradictory emotions disappear when the phenomenon is examined in the light of the mask theory. Faulkner the role-player reenacts his imaginary war stories under the impact of his sincere feelings for his nephew who is about to be exposed to air battles. Similarly, in his letter to his stepson, he reenacts the internalized ideology of his war film scripts. Professional and family pressures, personal psychological problems compounded by his frustrated attempts to contribute to the war effort, and the daily exposure to war news and defense measures (the hooded street-lamps in Hollywood, the barrage balloons and searchlights men-

29

tioned at the beginning of the letter to Malcolm) fuse together and lead to his compensatory role-playing.

The air force letter to his nephew contains two striking features, one artistic and the other psychological. It reveals, in the development of the details, Faulkner's rich novelistic imagination ("I would have liked for you to have had my dog-tag, R.A.F., but I lost it in Europe, in Germany. I think the Gestapo has it" [*SL* 170]) as well as his preoccupation with the foolhardiness of fear ("... The next milestone is fear" [71]). There is also a revealing reference to "Uncle Dean," whose death in an air crash had caused a profound crisis in Faulkner's life. The topic of fear and how to cope with it seems strange for a war veteran, an experienced pilot, and a rider of difficult hunting horses. Is he attempting, for Jimmy's or even his own sake, to normalize his fear, and thus render it acceptable? Might Jimmy have known that this was one of his uncle's often-told tall tales? Or did Faulkner enact roles demanding high courage in order to court suicidal danger and to exorcize it?

In contrast to the gloomy war ritual, the role-playing evidenced by Faulkner's letter to Joan Williams of September 29, 1950, belongs with the tragicomic side of his life. Assuming the mask of a literary mentor to the twenty-one-year-old college girl yearning to be a writer, the fifty-three-year-old Faulkner—a recent recipient of the American Academy's Howells Medal for Fiction and about to receive the 1949 Nobel Prize for Literature—suggests to her that she make their evolving affair the subject of a short story. "I have an idea for you ... A young woman, senior at school, a man of fifty, famous— could be artist, soldier, whatever seems best. He has come to spend the day with her. [But he appears strangely preoccupied.] She does not know why, until after he has gone. They talk, about everything, anything, whatever you like. She is more than just flattered that a man of fame has come up to see her; ...." (*SL* 307). One would like to regard this ludicrous invitation to self-fashioning and literary mirroring as parody, if it were not for his further suggestion of a "tragic turn of the plot": Joan's literary double is to learn from a telegram the day after the famous man's departure that the something "inconclusive" in his behavior arose from his anticipating his approaching end: "he is dead, heart" (*SL* 307). The master, masquerading as tutor in creative writing, cannot overcome the suspicion that his mask served more of an amorous than a literary purpose, although in concluding, he speaks soberly of brevity, "objectivity," and point of view (*SL* 307). As the blatant sentimentality of this charade confirms, Faulkner obviously had not yet reached the distance of irony that would later enable him, in *The Town*, to refashion his relationship with Joan into the humorous configuration of Gavin, the infatuated fool, and Linda, the bewildered teenager.

What aligns Faulkner's letters with his interviews as mask-creating opportunities is the fact that in contrast to the role-playing in other social contexts, specific audiences are involved. But while the recipients of his letters function as silent partners, influencing his self-projection only as inspiring images, the interviewers directly affect the process of his self-fashioning. The situation of the interviews—time and place, and, above all, the "chemistry" between interviewer and subject—affect their interaction. Readers should also take into account their own reaction; their experience of an image emerging from an interview is different from one they form while reading a letter.

In the following, I shall focus on the Faulkner image suggested to us rather than on the content of questions and answers. Interviews are performances during which a complex process of revelation and disguise takes place, consisting of separate, cooperative, and antagonistic mask-building. Interest in an extended study of the interviews arises not so much from the desire to create an epiphany of the "true" Faulkner as from the fascination in observing the rituals in which he and his interviewers offer and decline, modify and confirm, explode and replace the several masks. This dazzling show becomes even more bewildering when it is admitted that perceptions vary immensely from reader to reader. The image of Faulkner held by a European scholar doing historical research on the collected interviews in 1997 is naturally very different from that of an African American in the Mississippi of 1956 who hears on the evening news that the Nobel Prize winner William Faulkner has declared that "if it came to fighting I'd fight for Mississippi against the United States even if it meant going out into the street and shooting Negroes" (*LiG* 261).

Further, the Faulkner masks emerging in *Lion in the Garden* are given additional coloring from the number, date, and distribution of the interviews in the author's career. Most of them took place after his most creative period;[7] in other words, they do not coincide with his most important writing, but contain *post festum* declarations of a writer who had established fixed attitudes about his work and had designed a public persona for himself. Although there are numerous variants of this public persona, it is obvious that Faulkner found it convenient to cling to a certain core of views and value judgments. Since he clearly felt pushed out of his depth when challenged to engage in the kind of literary thinking at which T. S. Eliot or Thomas Mann excelled, he took refuge in the repetition of pithy sayings and handy formulae which nowadays nobody would look at if they had not been expressed by Faulkner. Nevertheless, these clichés reflect true features inasmuch as they are indicative of his predilection for certain behavior patterns or masks.

In view of the source material available, our examples are from two phases: the years 1931–1932, when Faulkner had clearly emerged as a major American author, and the 1950s, when he had received the Nobel Prize and had become America's leading writer. In studying the processes of stylization in this corpus of texts, one notes that both the interviewer and the subject of the interview are not afraid of repeating previously used images and clichés. Several interviewers flatter Faulkner by comparing him to Dostoevsky or by repeating Arnold Bennett's bon mot that he writes "like an angel." Faulkner, for his part, readily reproduced, particularly in the later interviews, variants of his stereotypical list of favorite authors or rankings of his contemporaries, as this absolved him from soul searching and subtle literary reflections. As literary and communicative devices, these lists give the respective Faulkner impression something mechanical and schematic. However, the interviewers jumped at these pronouncements because there was little else: no exciting or sophisticated comments on his writing, nothing revealing about his private life. This was one reason why several interviewers helped themselves by inventing a kind of "writer at home" atmosphere for their readers. The interviewers at the class conferences derived some enjoyment from Faulkner's lists of authors because they contained something definite and positive. After all, Faulkner's promulgation of his literary preferences, such as his admiration for *Moby-Dick* and Mark Twain and his disgust at "un-American" writers like Edgar Allan Poe and Henry James, do play an important role in his self-fashioning.

This also goes for his favorite self-characterization as somebody "writing about people." This explanation, dispensed in several interviews, may be masking the subtleties of literary processes, but it is revealing in regard to the goals of Faulkner's self-stylization: "I was just trying to write about people, which to me are the important thing. Just the human heart, it's not ideas. I don't know anything about ideas, don't have much confidence in them" (*FU* 10). The reference to the "human heart" and the frequent preference for people as opposed to ideas show that Faulkner is not just distinguishing his literary talent from that of a novelist of ideas like the Thomas Mann of *The Magic Mountain* or *Doctor Faustus*. Rather, the leitmotif "write about people" has a certain ideological slant, carrying naturalist, anti-intellectualist, and populist connotations implying that the author does not want to be regarded as one of the theorizing literati, or *hommes de lettres* in the European sense. In projecting this role, Faulkner shows himself embracing an ideal of the writer that is characteristic of the thirties, evolving at the time in connection with regionalist tendencies in several literatures (see chapter 7). The author writing about people is a major Faulkner persona that came to replace earlier and more rarified personae of the artist as a "marble faun," Beardsleyesque Pierrot, and Mississippian Verlaine.

The little vignette of 1926 in the New Orleans *Item* provides a fitting overture to our gallery of masks. Faulkner, the author of *Soldiers' Pay* and the prospective *Mosquitoes*, is portrayed as a tough manual laborer (Pascagoula schooner, lumber mill) and as *Naturbursche* à la Hemingway, not as the effete fin de siècle artiste and Europeanizing dabbler in Swinburnean and Verlainean verse who emerges from the playlet *The Marionettes* and the early prose and poetry. Clearly, the unknown journalist, and possibly the young writer feeding his cues, went for "Hemingwaves" (*If I Forget Thee, Jerusalem*) in the lines of this portrait.

The impact on readers is quite different once the contours of his mask evolve, as each of the two very different publications by Marshall J. Smith, based on the same 1931 interview, shows. The *Press Scimitar* article includes a dialogue between the author and interviewer, respectively from snippets of such a dialogue, interspersed with reported statements and descriptive touches. After the opening flourish, "A great voice crying in the . . . literary wilderness of Mississippi" (*LiG* 6), suggesting Faulkner's stature in terms of Mencken's characterization of the South, "the Sahara of the Bozart," Smith presents the author of *Sanctuary* against a sociopolitical backcloth: "Bilboland." This is appropriate in terms of the involvement of the Falkner family in the redneck politics of Bilbo, Vardaman, and Lee Russell (Blotner, *Faulkner* [1984] 47) if hardly correct in regard to Faulkner's own "dirt farming with a hoe and a plow" (*LiG* 6).

Faulkner does not appear as a sophisticated international littérateur but rather is presented within the context of regional politics. Smith seeks to catch the reader's attention by sketching contradictory features: the southern dirt farmer—"praised by the New Critics," the man who wrote of Memphis "hell holes"—"touched with a little sadness and a mild frustration, the writer who talks not of books but of men, of fishing, of the corn in the bottoms" (*LiG* 7). As a consequence of this strategy of seesawing, readers, looking for *the* Faulkner picture, get involved in a process of reconciling differences and contradictions, eventually to be left pondering admiringly on the paradoxes of genius.

At this point, Smith, the experienced feature writer, gives readers the privilege of meeting the great man at home. And what a home! Faulkner, the notoriously difficult recluse, appears as an affable host in a "characteristic" southern setting—complete with historical associations, dialect coloring, and magnolias: "But the man himself— there are no velvet curtains to be ripped aside, no secretaries or watchdogs set up as barriers. He is at home. Faulkner lives in a house that was showing its age when Gen. Bedford Forrest was 'skeerin' the Yankees in 1863. The Faulkner home on the outskirts of Oxford is a frame building. Simple wooden columns lend gentle dignity. It was built in 1830 [1840s] and surrounded with cedars. An architect from the Old World laid out a garden of magnolias and crepe myrtles. Today Faulkner sits beneath these cedars. With the sky for a canopy he talks, talks in the cool of the evening—. . ." (*LiG* 6–7). Never mind that the same Faulkner who a few paragraphs earlier was presented as "dirt farmer with hoe and plow" now appears as planter aristocrat in the moonlight and magnolia setting of the plantation novel. But the interviewer, in thus staging his author, is only making use of a scenery which Faulkner himself had designed in buying and restoring the Shegog house.

How important Faulkner's self-fashioning was in developing his novelistic vision is evidenced by such details as the "architect from the Old World who laid out a garden" of the Shegog house, who will resurface in *Absalom, Absalom!* as the creator of the formal gardens in which the upstart Sutpen seeks to achieve his gentrification. Conversely, the ruin of Sutpen's design and the advance of the Snopeses leave no doubt about Faulkner's awareness that his nostalgia for an aristocratic culture was futile. But then Faulkner had several southern masks available and enjoyed the mundane posture of the tall tale humorists as much as that of the decadent heir of the plantation tradition. "He is laughing to himself when he says quite seriously: 'I was born in 1826 of a negro slave and an alligator—both named Gladys Rock. I have two brothers. One is Dr. Walter E. Traprock and the other is Eaglerock—an airplane' " (*LiG* 7).

The different arrangement of the same material in the *Bookman* version shows both Smith's journalistic cleverness and his appreciation of this particular Faulkner mask. He thus retains, in both articles, Faulkner's comic "telegram-phrasing" that provides coherence and the "unity of effect" of the bank, war, and bookselling anecdotes: "Got job in grandfather's bank and learned medicinal value of his liquor. . . . Was still pilot. Crashed. Cost British Government 2000 pounds. Quit. Cost British Government $84.30. King said, 'Well done.' . . . Got married that summer. Needed $500. Wrote Smith . . ." (*LiG* 7–8). More important, he also employs the same strategy of contrasting two different Faulkners: "It was Faulkner, but not the man I expected. I was looking for an author whose interest was in idiocy, rape, suicide and a lost gentility. Instead I found another William Faulkner" (*LiG* 9). There is Faulkner the great writer, "a new luminary in the South, in the very darkest part of the South," whose image arises from his tragic books, and there is the other, "real," private, Faulkner. This "other Faulkner" is suggested by an image of the writer "bottling home-made beer with neighbor Sam," the implication being that the setting is nonliterary, realistic, regional, and relaxing.

The greater length of the *Bookman* article is accounted for by the increase in the descriptive elements and, above all, by the introduction of an analytic purpose that appeals to more sophisticated readers and in turn modifies Faulkner's tall tale mask: " 'Born?' He restated

35

the query to get set for his smart-crack. 'Yes. I was born male and single at an early age in Mississippi . . . I was born of a Negro slave and an alligator, both named Gladys Rock.' . . . This was Faulkner's barrier, the hazard he places about the sensitive part of him that can create such novels as *Soldiers' Pay*, *Mosquitoes*, *Sartoris*, and *As I Lay Dying*" (*LiG* 9). The introductory remark that sets the stage ("to get set for his smart-crack") announces the analytic attitude and emerges fully when the tall tale biography is interpreted as a defense strategy, a barrier. In other words, the interviewer, while helping Faulkner to fabricate his tall tale mask, alerts his readers to the masquerading, and thus connives with them in the creation of a further, more sophisticated mask.

The prominence and wide range of metaphors of masks and disguise in Smith's article confirm that, unlike many other interviewers, he was intensely aware of Faulkner's role-playing. ". . . I recalled the description of Bayard Sartoris who lived 'where the dusk was peopled with ghosts of glamorous and old things . . .' The phrase 'glamorous fatality' seems at times *to cloak Faulkner*. But Faulkner is not walking about *in a veil of heavy tragedy with the poison cup of Socrates in his hand*. While to the critics Faulkner is a figure to be *compared* with the Russians and is termed a 'genius' *and one who 'writes like an angel*,' he gives the *impression* that he is much more interested in where the catfish are biting and how to keep rabbits out of his field peas" (*LiG* 10, my emphasis). The oxymoronic character of "glamorous fatality," the theatricality of "glamorous" aligned with the existential "fatality," metaphorically suggests mask and role-playing which the phrase "seems at times to cloak Faulkner" then directly states. Smith expands this theme of acting by first introducing and then rejecting the metaphor of Faulkner as actor in a tragedy ("veil of heavy tragedy . . . Socrates") and then, in a second move, by dismissing the Faulkner projection of the critics, "compared with the Russians . . . writes like an angel," and by finally returning to the farmer-mask that he had earlier discarded as a mere surface image.

Despite Smith's promise, there is no epiphany of Faulkner the artist. True, he gets us closer to Faulkner than many other reporters by being allowed to ask a literary question. However, the question is rather basic (why was it so hard to understand portions of his books?) and, more important, the answer that he receives is evasive.

Clearly, emerging from behind the mask of a Mississippi gentleman is not *the* artist but a role-playing ironist offering a series of truisms; Faulkner is playing possum again: "Folks try too hard to understand. . . . Read a book and let it go at that . . . If you have something to say—you can write it—in fact, you have got to write it" (*LiG* 10).

Studying the modes of role-playing and the forms of verbal mask-making reveals a strange mixture of clear-cut purposes and unconscious drives on the parts of both the interviewer and the interviewed. The outcome of their cooperative and antagonistic endeavors are conflicting impressions which readers transform still further in their attempts to understand, clarify, and evaluate their impressions of the writer. Yet there are major tendencies in these transformations and metaphorics which emerge fairly clearly and which are striking, perhaps most of all because of their conflicting nature.

After the last of the several tall tales depicting Faulkner's comic mask as a "no-gooder" who gets fired as often as he gets a job (*LiG* 14), the interviewer hastens to justify "this dilemma" as a rejection of the American success myth and then, rather surprisingly, concludes his article with Faulkner's pronouncements in favor of a work ethic: "We are here to work. It is either sweat or die" (*LiG* 14). The two Faulkners—the somewhat irregular member of the labor force and the proponent of hard work—however, are not mutually exclusive; if the former is seen as a variant of the antiutilitarian artist of late romanticism, the latter can be recognized as a Puritan ("Where is there a law requiring we should be happy?" [*LiG* 14]), ignoring "the pursuit of happiness" that the Declaration of Independence stipulates. Both the bum and the advocate of hard work are self-projections that helped Faulkner define and create characters as diverse as Horace Benbow in *Flags in the Dust* and Simon McEachern in *Light in August*.

Marshall J. Smith's interview proved a source of inspiration for Henry Nash Smith's in the *Dallas Morning News* in 1932, thus illustrating the intertextual aspect of literary masks. Although Henry Nash Smith is better read in Faulkner and more sophisticated in his literary comments than Marshall J. Smith, both interviewers try to detach their subjects from "preposterous legends" (*LiG* 29), and both draw their strength from portraying Faulkner in a congenial southern atmosphere. That even goes for the way in which they deal with Faulkner's reticence: *"Like many writers*, Faulkner is disinclined to talk about his books, but he is *Mississippian enough to be polite about questions.* He showed me his work table—a small typewriter table with curving legs, on which rested a sort of metal rack holding a completed page of manuscript. There were also several sheets of typewriter paper ruled in pencil about two inches from the top and, vertically, two inches from the left side. He writes with a fountain pen in a beautiful and almost illegible hand, . . . 'I bind my own manuscripts,' he said . . ." (*LiG* 30, my emphasis). If Faulkner shows Smith his study, this indicates his southern politeness and his appreciation of his interviewer's calibre. Besides, it seems a good way out of the dilemma of not being able or willing to talk about his work yet giving some access to his professional life. There is something unprepossessing and modest, even spartan, rigid, and Puritan about Faulkner's arrangements, the most revelatory detail being Faulkner's "beautiful and almost illegible hand."

The qualification "beautiful" and "illegible" may appear contradictory, but it is really very much to the point, apart from being fittingly symbolic. There is indeed a strange and striking continuity between Faulkner's writing in the calligraphic and illuminated early manuscripts and the cramped print-like script of the manuscripts of the great novels. Tallying with this is the fact that Faulkner himself bound not only copies of his symbolist-art nouveau play *The Marionettes* but also, as he says, some of his later manuscripts. The neatness, smallness, and isolation of the letters together with the evenness of the lines and the relentless insistence of the columns of the great text produce one effect, characterized above all by the complete absence of large, round, continuously flowing forms. From this perspective, Faulkner's handwriting is the most telling mask of the man that the poet Donald Hall has described as "small, tidy, delicate, stern, stony, aloof" (qtd. in Blotner, *Faulkner* [1984] 629).[8]

Smith in the 1932 interview provides an interesting clue to the circumstances of the mask-creating process by hinting that in his effort to learn about Faulkner's sources, he "insisted perhaps a little too vigorously." Faulkner, denying any direct influence from Joyce and upholding his image as the original genius of the rural South, is on the alert and, at the interviewer's insistence ("But surely you had some idea of modern experimentation with the technique of the novel" [*LiG* 30]), enters the masquerade in superior style. He smiles and assumes the stance of an urbane philosopher for whom the co-presence of similar ideas in several minds at the same time is a given: "sometimes I think there must be a sort of pollen of ideas floating in the air, which fertilizes similarly minds here and there . . ." (*LiG* 30–31). To discard any suspicion of a direct Joyce influence ("I had heard of Joyce of course")—and in contrast to what specialists have found out about Faulkner's sophisticated method of narration—he represents the writing of *The Sound and the Fury* as a wholly uncertain process ("I had no idea of writing the book it finally became"), employing organicist metaphors ("It simply *grew* from day to day" [*LiG* 31, my emphasis]). Faulkner's naive desire to appear absolutely original, together with his jealous aversion to the "literariness" of better-educated writers—ultimately, the fear he shares with most artists that "consciousness" might kill the creative instinct—makes him insinuate to the interviewer the mask of an author who exclusively and simply "writes from life" (*LiG* 31) and who "has no theory of fiction" (*LiG* 32).

In regard to imposture, Smith's persistent questions about Faulkner's experiences with the British air forces in France, and the novelist's equally persistent refusal to answer them in a definite manner provide an interesting insight. Faulkner dons masks and enters into roles as part of psychoartistic assimilation processes, but retracts from the role-playing when questioned by serious correspondents like Cowley or interviewers like Smith. How cleverly he operates in his retraction efforts becomes clear in the way he seeks to detract the guileless Smith from his inquiry by displaying a pronounced interest in the trimotored cabin plane on which the interviewer had traveled from Dallas to Memphis. "I tried to get him to talk about his experiences with the British air forces in France. I had heard that during the war he had been pulled out, more dead than alive, from under a couple of wrecked planes. But he didn't have much to say about that. 'I just smashed them up,' he said. He was interested, however, in the fact that I had come from Dallas to Jackson in a trimotored cabin plane. 'I've never ridden in a cabin plane,' he said. 'I'd like to have a chance to fly one. I was looking at the inside of one' . . . But he still refused to say much about the war" (*LiG* 31–32). Obviously, Faulkner was fully aware that his creative role-playing would come to a humiliating end if his public confirmation of the legends provoked an attempted verification and the revelation of the trivial truth. In private contacts, under psychological pressures and inspired by artistic needs, he would continue to play the game, with remarkable artistic results as attested to by such great self-projective characters as Bayard Sartoris in *Flags in the Dust* and the runner in *A Fable*.

Evidently, the categories true and false and correct and distorted would prove reductive in this instance and fail to do justice to the creativity involved in both the collusion of the sympathetic or antagonistic interview partners and the imaginative cooperation they in turn elicit from readers. In contrast to the congenial presentations by Marshall J. Smith and Henry Nash Smith, the interview in the *New York Herald Tribune* (*LiG* 19–22) is of interest because Faulkner and the reporter lacked the necessary rapport. This led to a distortion of Faulkner's views (noted critically by editors Meriwether and Millgate), and, since all interviews are interactions to a special form of role-playing, the reporter and Faulkner cooperate in the creation of "Faulkner as the reactionary southerner": "William Faulkner, the Mississippi novelist, who has been called the Dostoievsky of the South, revealed himself yesterday in an interview as a curious mixture of the modern and the conservative, a Southern sage who reads scarcely at all, thinks the Negroes were better off under slavery, and votes Democratic to protect his property.... He believes that Negroes are like children ... Mr. Faulkner is interested in politics, but not national politics" (*LiG* 19–21).

There must have been, right from the outset, some friction between the interview partners, possibly caused by what Faulkner, with his sociocultural inferiority complex, took to be the cosmopolitan arrogance of the Yankee press. Eventually, the "provincial southerner" gets so irritated by the unfortunate questions of the reporter that he gives wilfully perverse answers, the bitter irony of which escapes the reporter because he in turn lets himself be provoked by Faulkner's answers. His very first sentence, quoted above, sets the tone, and the whole piece reads like a study in failed communication, with patterns of negation predominating: "He refused to take any stock ... He refused, ... to name ..."; "I never sold ... I never read [reviews] ... never read any of Hemingway's ... never been to a party where there were Negroes" (*LiG* 20, 21). And there are corresponding structural features: while most interviewers tended to depict conflicting features in Faulkner to emphasize the mysteriousness of genius and to stimulate the curiosity of their readers, the *New York Herald Tribune* interviewer introduces the author's heterogeneous traits to resolve them negatively and to "reveal" Faulkner's "true nature" which is—thus the gist of the article—"reactionary and racist." Although he follows other journalists in according to Faulkner the positive sobriquets "Dostoievsky of the South" and one who "writes like an angel," he eventually lets these be overwhelmed by negative features: "The Dostoievsky of the South, *revealed himself* . . . as a *curious mixture* . . . who *reads scarcely* at all, thinks the Negroes were *better off under slavery* . . . Arnold Bennett said of him, 'He writes like an angel.' *But* Mr. Faulkner *hates* interviews, *hates* being asked questions . . ." (*LiG* 19, my emphasis). In comparison to the romantic southernness in other Faulkner interviews, the southernness depicted here ("Ah don't care much about talkin'," "Southern drawl so low . . . difficult to understand" [*LiG* 19]) serves to call up connotations of backwardness that "enlightened" northerners would associate with the "racist bigotry" of the South.

In contrast to the *New York Herald Tribune* journalist who interviewed Faulkner in 1931, Betty Beale, the tactful society columnist who had an equally hard time with Faulkner when she interviewed him in June 1957, did not draw an equally negative picture. In both of her articles, from the 1954 interview which went very well and from the disastrous one of 1957, she portrays Faulkner as the great public figure whom readers—thanks to Betty Beale's contacts—have the privilege to observe at close quarters among the wealthy and eminent: "William Faulkner, the literary giant of the South . . . at the A. Burks Summers' party . . . buffet dinner for two or three hundred that included Senators Mundt, Welker . . . [etc.]" (*LiG* 77–78; 1954 interview). "William Faulkner, considered by many to be the greatest living American novelist . . . was the honored guest at the big outdoor supper given by Mr. and Mrs. Burks Summers . . ." (*LiG* 267–268; 1957 interview). In the 1954 interview, the McCarthy hearings form part of the background, and Beale creates the image of a politically courageous Faulkner who, as a committed Democrat in a Republican setting, wittily "spoke up" and controversially pondered "that in a world situation like we have today democracy simply cannot work."

The Faulkner mask emerging from Beale's interview of 1954 could not be more different from the image of the reactionary Faulkner in the 1931 *New York Herald Tribune* interview.

In Beale's ingenious article on the disastrous 1957 interview, the central device is a specific kind of friendly and understanding irony with which she cleverly cloaks her annoyance at Faulkner's ugly mood. This ironic perspective suggests to readers—and also to the influential Summers and Faulkner families—that if there was any unpleasantness in the interview, it only arose from the exhaustion and the excusable caprice of the great man: "William Faulkner, considered by many to be the greatest living American novelist" was not cruel and nasty to a female reporter doing her difficult job but—in Beale's parodic euphemism—"resumed his oft-held battle with the Fourth Estate last night" (*LiG* 267). She manages to keep the Nobel Prize winner on the pedestal by ironically subjecting his diatribe against the press to her elegant syntax and the viewpoint of reported speech ("The Nobel Prize winner said the press has no integrity, doesn't write the truth" [*LiG* 267]). She indicates by her humorous euphemism—"neither in a gay nor talkative mood"—that she does not resent the fact that Faulkner after standing for a long time in the reception line was less friendly than at the previous interview. Crowding Faulkner's negations in a rapid sequence of short sentences ("I never read criticisms . . . I don't read them . . . He bores me . . . but never finished them . . . he replied in a negative vein"), she makes her central point: that he is only wearing a negative mask, that he is not really as unpleasant as he appears but a great humorist who may be just assuming a negative role. "One had the feeling that it was not the real Faulkner talking, simply the mood he was in. Or perhaps deep down inside he was tickled, but his expression was too deadpan to tell" (*LiG* 268). Beale's own style, including the final bon mot, "To the best of these reportorial ears, all the above is true" (*LiG* 269), is likewise "too deadpan to tell." However, readers know from her letter to one of the editors of *Lion in the Garden* (*LiG* 267) of the gap between her real impression and the Faulkner mask which she created with so much verbal skill. Meanwhile, a much more negative Faulkner image had emerged from the interview with Russell Howe on February 21, 1956, of which two versions appeared, one in the *London Sunday Times* and the other in *The Reporter*.

The Russell Howe interview poses with particular intensity the question of the relationship between the factual and the intentional and the wider problem of Faulkner's masquerades. Moreover, it illustrates the conflict between political morals and sociocultural patterns as well as the impact of such a conflict on the formation of imagery in the process of communication. It became "the infamous interview" (Karl 932) largely because of the following sentences, which Faulkner maintained, albeit unconvincingly, that "no sane or sober man would have uttered": "If I have to choose between the United States government and Mississippi, then I'll choose Mississippi . . . As long as there's a middle road, all right, I'll be on it. But if it came to fighting I'd fight for Mississippi against the United States even if it meant going out into the street and shooting Negroes" (*LiG* 260–61).

Although much has been written to explain away Faulkner's strange pronouncement, the mask created in the Howe interview has startled and continues to shock every generation of readers and critics anew. As to the incident itself, Karl's assessment and evaluation is fairly representative of the view most Faulkner scholars hold: "If Faulkner did say this—Howe insisted that he did . . .—it is reprehensible beyond belief. But there may have been a context which, while it could not excuse the comment . . . We must conjecture that Faulkner was drunk, provoked, at the end of his tether, and Howe pushed him over the edge" (933). [9] In other words, Karl is inclined to acknowledge the fact and then attempts a sympathetic explanation of Faulkner's behavior. In addition to this plausible biographical account, I will offer a supplementary reading of the interview, appraising some strategic and stylistic aspects of the mask formation. Subconsciously, Faulkner may have been irritated by the cool superiority of the British journalist, but he was far too disturbed and torn between his sympathies toward civil rights and his loyalty to his home state to notice Howe's irony and to develop a grotesque mask as he did in other interviews. Indeed, the Faulkner persona arising from the Howe interview seems to be less influenced by the interaction of the partners than by sociocultural patterns informing the deep structure of his personality. As the rhetoric and metaphorics of the article show, the interview became an occasion for dramatically reenacting patterns of the southern Civil War myth which Faulkner had assimilated in his childhood and had then so successfully rehearsed in writing *Flags in the Dust*, *Absalom, Absalom!*, and *The Unvanquished*.

Faulkner's mistaken perception of the situation ("These white people will accept another Civil War knowing they're going to lose" [*LiG* 259]) resulted partly from his artistic exploration and reenactment of the southern past. Moreover, in this situation—clearly a radical departure from his previous stance on race—he seems to have lost the sense that role-playing in the sociopolitical sphere needs, besides empathy, as much tact, discrimination, and detachment as in the private cosmos of Yoknapatawpha. The role-playing necessary for many writers as part of their artistic assimilation of experience tends to become habitual, tempting them to practice it outside the novelistic sphere where they are not guided by the checks of their theme and their artistic judgement.

A study of the image clusters and leitmotifs in the text of the interview shows how Faulkner, apparently driven by personal anxieties (Blotner, Karl) and the social insecurity of a transition period, fell back on historical patterns informing southern culture and indulged in an inauthentic use of the Civil War motif and in a replay of the mythicized role of Robert E. Lee: "But it is bad that Americans should be fighting Americans. That is what will happen because the Southern whites are back in the spirit of 1860. There could easily be another Civil War and the South will be whipped again" (*LiG* 258). "I will go on saying that the Southerners are wrong and that their position is untenable, but if I have to make the same choice Robert E. Lee made then I'll make it. My grandfather had slaves and he must have known that it was wrong, but he fought in one of the first regiments raised by the Confederate Army, not in defense of his ethical position but to protect his native land from being invaded" (262). The persistent references to weapons and fighting are as striking as the attempts to point out the similarity between the present situation in the South and the one at the eve of the Civil War. Faulkner, who had so creatively exploded the lost cause mythology in his fiction, now nostalgically flirts with it in real life to exorcize his personal and sociopolitical difficulties.

In line with his construction of a Civil War situation with himself donning the attractive mask of the southern archtragedian Lee facing the historic choice is his patriachal imagery: "My people owned slaves

44

and the very obligation we have to take care of these people is morally bad . . . I have known Negroes all my life and Negroes work my land . . ." (258). "My Negro boys down on the plantation would fight against the North with me. If I say to them 'Go get your shotguns, boys,' they'll come" (262). The dilemma of Faulkner, the liberal with patriarchal instincts, who declares himself in favor of the Montgomery bus boycott (260) but maintains that "segregation doesn't have to imply inferiority" (259) and whose "go slow" strategy isolated him from reformists and reactionaries alike, symbolically surfaces in a peculiarly unsteady and shifting use of nouns and pronouns:

> But I would wish now that *the liberals* would stop—*they* should let *us* [Faulkner not as liberal but as Southerner] sweat in *our own* fears for a little while. If *we* are pushed by the government we shall become an underdog people fighting back because *we* can do nothing else. (258)

> It isn't just a solidarity of race—you get doctors and lawyers and preachers and newspaper editors and some Negroes too, all grouped against a few *liberals like me* [Faulkner as liberal] . . . But the *other liberals in my part* of the country carry guns all the time. (264)

> **Q:** How would you re-educate the Southern white to a different way of thinking?
> **Faulkner:** . . . Let him see . . . Give *him* time—don't force *us* . . . [emotional transition from *him* as white supremacist to *us* as Southerners]. (259)

> The government will send in its troops and *we* [the country, or we, Southerners] shall be back at 1860. They must stop pushing *these people* [the white supremacists]. (260, my emphasis)

Study of the context shows that the emotional outbreak that has made the Howe interview infamous and which Faulkner sought to retract does not constitute an isolated passage but is only the climax of a more encompassing masquerade. Looking at it from the perspective of masks and role-playing rather than treating it as Faulkner's political testament makes the text appear less embarrassing. However, one would prefer America's greatest novelist to have played a more politically correct role. As to his halfhearted and wavering attitude, which has been so disappointing to critics, it seems characteristic for a writer of his background and time. Along these lines, in "Faulkner and Racism," Arthur Kinney, after carefully reviewing the treatment of race as a theme in several of Faulkner's stories and novels, focuses on the startling difference between the prolynching *Commercial Appeal* letter and the antilynching short story "Dry September," as revealed by Neil R. McMillen and Noel Polk's publication.[10] By distinguishing between the racism of an individual and "his participation in a culture imbued with the racial myth," Kinney finds an interesting formula allowing us to relate the racist traits in the public letter and the Howe interview to the enlightened sociopolitical philosophy within such fiction as "Dry September," "That Evening Sun," and *Intruder in the Dust*.

On February 15, 1957, Faulkner began a series of class conferences at the University of Virginia from which features of a portrait emerge that are totally different from both the disastrous Russell Howe interview and the heavily retouched Betty Beale interview of 1957. Faulkner's partners were not individual reporters but groups of students and staff, and, although the groups differed, the communicative situation remained remarkably similar throughout. Instead of one interviewer intent on structuring the discourse, numerous questioners bombard Faulkner in a rapid exchange, often on heterogeneous matters. As a consequence, readers of *Faulkner in the University* are jolted from one impression to another and have difficulty deriving the kind of unified Faulkner image suggested by many interviews in *Lion in the Garden*.

In contrast to the intensity of the one on one interviews, a more casual atmosphere informs the University of Virginia meetings. Faulkner here seems always ready to talk, whereas in some interviews with reporters, he was on the defensive. Since he enjoyed his stay as writer-in-residence at the university and was dedicated to making a success of it, he never appears impatient or ill tempered as he did in the Beale interview. In contrast to the interviews, where he posed as an unliterary writer ("more interested in Mrs. Faulkner's new draperies and the hand-hammered locks on the doors than in anything he has written" [*LiG* 32]), he now answers readily and well inquiries about the specifics of his works, even occasionally volunteering autobiographical information. Despite silly questions and some that must have jarred his sense of privacy, he adheres throughout to the friendly, if somewhat aloof, persona of the affable great man.

This image is reinvigorated by the fact that the questions, coming from young people, tended to be of a basic or general cast, inviting him to generalize, simplify, and dispense wisdom:

> **Q:** The role of fate seems very strong in your work. Do you believe in free will for your characters?
> **Faulkner:** I would think I do, yes. But I think that man's free will functions against a Greek background of fate. (*FU* 38)

The Faulkner of the class conferences is a more philosophical, though never intellectual, artist than the one projected in the interviews of the thirties. Essential features of the new mask are affability and modesty, together with a relaxed sense of humor and an air of naturalness which differs greatly from the attitudinizing in the interviews where he uses deadpan irony and bouts of tall tale grotesque as strategies of evasion. In the class conferences, Faulkner hardly ever fails to give a direct, if often pat, answer to any question. He had obviously anticipated the situation in the classroom, and when he noticed that his response to it was very successful, he quickly felt comfortable and enjoyed himself, as is evident from the frontispiece. In contrast to the interviews by individual journalists with whom Faulkner, for all his airs of superiority, was ill at ease, the group meetings with the students were respectful and friendly and took a foreseeable course.

Moreover, they occurred after the Nobel Prize had forced Faulkner to accept a public role. In this respect the comparison between his attitude in the Mississippi class conferences of 1947 (*LiG* 52–58) and in the Virginia class conferences of 1957 and 1958 are of interest. In the 1947 meetings, which, of course, were not recorded but have been reconstructed from notes, the questions are almost all literary, and the answers tend to be brief, while in the 1957 and 1958 Virginia sessions, the range of topics is wide, and, more important, Faulkner allows them to take him further afield. There are brief glimpses of the clown jester ("I like Virginia, and I like Virginians. Because Virginians are all snobs, and I like snobs" [*FU* 12]), but on the whole, Faulkner in the university, apart from answering questions about his works, dons the cloak of a public teacher. Inspired by secularized southern Puritanism and a commitment to the civil rights spirit of the time, he enunciates a moderately antibourgeois morality of courage and tenaciousness ("Respectability is an artificial standard" [*FU*

35]; "man will prevail" [5]). However, the readers who relate this persona to his life and works sense that there are more personal motives behind his will to prevail, and that it derives peculiar urgency from a very personal battle against the death instinct rather than from the abstract existentialism of Camus's Sisyphus.

The comprehensiveness and precision of Faulkner's comments about his work and the seriousness and intellectual distinction of many of his remarks on topics ranging from political to cultural and moral criticism have established *Faulkner in the University* as a central source in Faulkner scholarship. This makes it tempting to ignore the fact that the role Faulkner played in *Faulkner in the University* is just one among many and to attribute undue weight to the pronouncements made by the late Faulkner in the role of public man. As students of Faulkner, we can appreciate so much his explanation of why he turned from working on *Absalom, Absalom!* to *Pylon* that we tend to pay little attention to the circumstances and the particular perspective of the author who states that the characters in *Pylon* "were outside the range of God, not only of respectability, of love, but of God too" and that "they had no past" (*FU* 36). Apparently, the students brought out in Faulkner qualities of critical reflection which, in the interviews at the peak of his creative career around 1930, he had shunned. Now, in 1957, when asked about the fyce "as representing the primitive," he shows his readiness and ability to generalize and to deal with more abstract propositions, insisting that in writing about the South, he "wasn't writing sociology at all. I was just trying to write about people" (*FU* 10).

The warning not to lose sight of the fact that Faulkner in the university is only another of his masks should be heeded as well in the case of the 1956 Jean Stein interview, named by critics the "most important and most influential of all Faulkner's interviews" (*LiG* 237) (Blotner, *Faulkner* [1984] 619; Karl 927). And who would quarrel with them? The interviews of his late phase show without a doubt that Faulkner had abandoned his former reticence, and since receiving the Nobel Prize was more used to presenting himself as a public persona. He talks about his work now as he did not dare to then when he was involved in the risky process of writing the majority of his most important works. But the eminent quotability of Faulkner's literary statements in *Faulkner in the University* and in the Stein interview should not persuade readers that they are encountering the "real Faulker" in these texts, or that the roles he played on these occasions are more relevant than the others.

What makes it so tempting to overrate such pronouncements as "A writer is trying to create believable people in credible moving situations in the most moving way he can" (*LiG* 248) is its rhetoric of summarizing and encapsulating essentials. Once more, Faulkner gives us his list of favorite authors, from which one could easily reconstruct a stylized literary self-portrait. The continuing fascination with the Old Testament or Dickens attests to Faulkner's narrative urge. Countervailing this is his invocation of Flaubert, the patron saint of novelistic craftsmanship. His mention of Conrad suggests Faulkner's preoccupation with point of view, respectively fine writing, and the penchant for *Don Quixote* coincides with his own parody of the failed idealists Horace Benbow and Gavin Stevens. His admiration of Balzac and the Russians (Dostoievsky, Tolstoy) characterizes the author as someone who himself has created a huge narrative cosmos. What seems to have recommended Melville and Mark Twain to him was the pronounced Americanness of their literary genius. Shakespeare and Marlowe are included not only because of their characters but also because of their poetic language.

This tallies with Faulkner's predilection for a wide range of poets: Campion, Jonson, and Herrick because of their songlike quality, Shelley because of his visionary dimension. He probably liked Donne for that manneristic quality which he had also encountered—without mentioning him—in the early T.S. Eliot. The absence of Eliot from this Faulkner mask constructed from his reading preferences is as revealing as the presence of the other authors. Did he not want to admit to Eliot's considerable influence on his work? Or did he leave him out because he simply no longer enjoyed reading him? As for his continuing love of Housman's rural setting and self-conscious fatalism, it seems biographically motivated, while his reference to Keats marks the center of his aesthetics. However, there is a subterranean link between his addiction to Housman—from whom his daughter, Jill, heard him quote when the drinking bouts would come on—and his fascination with Keats's "Ode on a Grecian Urn": "The aim of every artist is to arrest motion, which is life, by artificial means and hold it fixed so that 100 years later when a stranger looks at it, it moves again since it is life. Since man is mortal, the only immortality possible for him is to leave something behind him that is immortal since it will always move. This is the artist's way of scribbling 'Kilroy was here' on the wall of the final and irrevocable oblivion through which he must someday pass" (*LiG* 253). Reading Housman as a subtext to Keats makes one perceive, beneath the harmonized phrasing of the Stein interview, the dangerous dialectics of art as arrested life and the autobiographical tensions projected in the double portrait of the suicidal and the narrative Quentin of *The Sound and the Fury* and *Absalom, Absalom!*

The theory of masks acknowledges no finality. Instead, it suggests focussing on the strategies of mask shaping and on their possible effects on readers. In this respect, readers should realize that the Stein interview tends to canonize the author and to codify his literary opinions. By the same token, it should be admitted that, in dealing with this particular text in the concluding section of the chapter, readers are themselves also contributing to this dominating influence of the Stein interview. But consideration of the circumstances and scenario of the interview may serve as an antidote to the illusion that Stein lets them see the "real Faulkner."

While the content of his pronouncements in this interview has been frequently discussed, the communicative strategy in it, particularly the separate and cooperative role-playing of the partners, has not. For instance, the interview is noticeably less dramatic than those by journalists who, not having the privileged status of Stein as Faulkner's intimate friend, really had to try and find out about him.[11] In the case of the Stein interview, everything had been so well prepared by the partners that the role remaining for Stein in the actual text amounts to giving the cues. Critics, taking the Stein interview as a final document of Faulkner's aesthetics, overlook that it is also a carefully contrived performance designed to correct "wrong" views of Faulkner and to instigate the "right" image. The opening question, "Mr. Faulkner, you were saying a while ago that you don't like interviews," is a characteristic example of this.

The Stein interview, presenting a grand retrospective vista of America's great writer and pretending to an authoritative picture of him, must also be recognized as a work of love. One could argue that Faulkner himself choreographed the proceedings of the interview—an essay in an interview format—to present a summary of sorts of those questions he would have liked to have been asked. In regard to role-playing, the situation of Jean Stein, addressing her partner in the interview as "Mr. Faulkner," is comparable to that of Joan Williams collaborating with Faulkner on literary projects. This may be the reason why Stein as an interviewer is less in evidence than Marshall Smith or Betty Beale. However, she does not let Faulkner have it all his own way, and, by using her authority, insists on precise answers, checking, for instance, his affirmation "The artist is of no importance" with "Isn't the individuality of the writer important?" (*LiG* 238). As questioner, Stein appears intelligent, sophisticated, and sensitive but not detached, tough, and experienced like Russell Howe.

Furthermore, although privileged as interviewer, she was also handicapped by their relationship. Conversely, Faulkner, as paternal lover being exceptionally cooperative, was also unduly influential, creating, one suspects, a self-portrait. However, there is also evidence that Stein does not accept all of Faulkner's self-fashioning. It is amusing to observe, for instance, how she, as a young and serious literary person, fails to appreciate Faulkner's bouts of telling tall tales and keeps trying to return him quickly to "essential" questions. Ironically, the collaborative effort that was to produce an authenticated, "official" portrait renders an amazing collection of coexisting Faulkner features, some of which coagulate into diverse Faulkner masks. In his effort to project his idea of the artist, the great role-player drew on a whole arsenal of historical and contemporary prototypes and patterns.

The clever opening on his reluctance to be interviewed for introducing the impersonality ideal of the artist harkens back to "Tradition and the Individual Talent" (1917), Eliot's reaction against romantic individualism and its dominant category, sincerity: "The artist is of no importance. Only what he creates is important" (238). However, Faulkner promulgates his commitment to the impersonality ideal with a fervor which suggests further psychological reasons for his embracement of this widespread modernist concept. In addition to the confession at the beginning of the interview, "I seem to react violently to personal questions" (*LiG* 237), his essay "On Privacy: The American Dream and What Happened to It" (1955) should be noted, as should the wide range of similar statements, notably the respective passages in the Cowley letters. "I will protest to the last: no photographs, no recorded documents. It is my ambition to be, as a private individual, abolished and voided from history, leaving it markless, no refuse save the printed books" (*SL* 285).

Although explaining his ardent wish for anonymity by referring to the precedent of the Elizabethans, who "had not signed their books," through the vehemence of his phrasing ("abolished and voided from history, leaving it markless") and his description of his books as "refuse," he betrays a profound feeling of psychological insecurity which contrasts with his sure sense of his artistic achievement. For all his attitudinizing, when Faulkner threatens that questions about his personality may provoke evasiveness or lead to his assuming a mask ("I may answer or I may not, but even if I do, if the same question is asked tomorrow, the answer may be different" [237]), it is not superficial caprice. If he shared the longing for the impersonality of masks for sociological, historical, and aesthetic reasons with his contemporaries (e.g., Yeats, Gordon Craig, and Eugene O'Neill), he had his own very personal motives as well. His artistic role-playing is a drama enacted against the lure of suicidal self-effacement.

No wonder that *The Sound and the Fury*, with its theme of the decaying Compson family and the story of Quentin's suicide, was the book closest to him (*LiG* 146–47; *FU* 6, 61, 77); it is, in his own words, the "one which caused me the most grief and anguish" (*LiG* 244). From a psychoanalytic perspective, it is not surprising that he should avoid referring to his persona, Quentin, choosing instead to focus on the source of his suffering, "the tragedy of two lost women: Caddy and her daughter," and to point out the embodiment of his maternalistic salvation, saying, "Dilsey is one of my own favorite characters because she is brave, courageous, generous, gentle and honest" (*LiG* 245). His added personal remark on Dilsey ("She's much more brave and honest and generous than me") is revealing. John Irwin's unifying, and, in this, problematic view of the two Quentins in *The Sound and the Fury* and *Absalom, Absalom!* also opens up a new perspective on the interrelationship between the threat of suicidal self-effacement and salvation through narration. This allows us to relate the variants of Faulkner's Quentin persona to a tradition of the self-portrait, running from Oscar Wilde's *De Profundis* to the Nietzsche-Leverkühn figure in Thomas Mann's *Doctor Faustus*, of the artist as "man of sorrow."

Linked to this mask of the artist seems to be that of the failed idealist, which in a strange way dominates Faulkner's aesthetics: "All of us failed to match our dream of perfection. So I rate us on the basis of our splendid failure to do the impossible" (*LiG* 238). Both the psychoanalytic and aesthetic aspects of this mask of the artist as frustrated idealist emerge when the dark undercurrent of his poetological discourse is discerned within his burlesque metaphorics: "Once he [the artist] did it, once he matched the work to the image, the *dream*, nothing would remain but to *cut his throat*, jump off the other side of that pinnacle of cut *perfection into suicide*" (*LiG* 238, my emphasis). In the case of the image of artist as driven by demons, Faulkner is not creating any new mask but turning to that time-honored role model evolved by the romantics (Goethe's Faust, Byron, Shelley). His originality in donning this well-known mask lies in his grotesque phrasing, in the kind of tall tale swagger with which he wears the traditional costume of the romantic/late romantic artist ("If a writer has to rob his mother, he will not hesitate; the *Ode on a Grecian Urn* is worth any number of old ladies" [*LiG* 239]).

But this dimension escapes his young and serious-minded interviewer, who primly and persistently ignores Faulkner's attempts to play the role of the clown, a favorite persona with so many modernist painters and writers. She evidently does not quite know how to proceed with the interview when Faulkner, in answering her question about the best environment for a writer, draws a burlesque picture of the writer as landlord of a brothel (239). There is a perceptible pause after the author, whom she obviously wants to portray as "the great and therefore profoundly serious writer," has given a grotesque account of his experience as script writer in Hollywood, and she rather humorlessly tries to put him back on track: "You say that the writer must compromise in working for the motion pictures. How about his writing?" (243). It is amusing to observe that Faulkner makes an honest effort to oblige her with a serious answer—speaking about the subjectivity of the writer's standards—but then he is carried away again by his urge for grotesque role-playing in the southwestern tall tale tradition: "if I were reincarnated, I'd want to come back a buzzard" (243). This Sut Lovingood mask ("And then I like Sut Lovingood" [251]) was, of course, an aspect of his personality which Jean Stein's elegant cosmopolitan intelligence could not easily accommodate. However, this is clearly recognizable for readers, if not for the interviewer.

The Stein interview must appear as a difficult text if one were to try to reconcile the several coexisting features and to arrive at a unified concept of the writer: on the one hand, he projects the image of the restless and ruthless experimenter ("Sometimes technique charges and takes command of the dream before the writer himself" [244]), and, on the other, he says that the writer is unconscious, as the metaphor suggests, "at the behest of his characters." However, there are different psychological and sociological, individual and historical factors that make Faulkner articulate and emphasize particular features. His insistence that "the writer doesn't need economic freedom . . . The good writer never applies to a foundation" (*LiG* 240), for instance, is derived from his antipathy toward the WPA and the spirit of other New Deal measures, which he saw as a threat to the independence of the individual. His often-quoted reference to the discovery of his "own little postage stamp of native soil" (*LiG* 255) bespeaks his affinities with the aesthetics of regionalism which modern Faulkner critics tend to suppress in favor of his modernist features (see chapters 7 and 8). His image of the writer as a "tough guy" ("People are afraid to find out how tough they are" [*LiG* 240]) has an American pioneer coloring which to Europeans smacks of social Darwinism.

Some of the contradictory features in Faulkner's self-fashioning are easily reconciled when the particular context from which they evolved is noted. That the same man who flirts with being the prototype of the plantation aristocrat also says of himself "By temperament I'm a vagabond and a tramp" (*LiG* 249) ceases to be contradictory when one remembers instances such as the conclusion of *Flags in the Dust*, in which the plantation heir, Bayard Sartoris, unable to recover from his war trauma, leaves home and starts an odyssey leading him to his suicidal death as test pilot. The "immorality" of the artist is stressed in the Stein interview when the point is the rejection of narrow didactic and moral claims (*LiG* 247), while the morality of art is propagated in the attempt to define the new Faulknerian gospel of moral courage, for example, in the comparisons among the young

Jewish pilot, the French quartermaster general, and the English battalion runner in *A Fable*. Fortunately for his fiction, Faulkner did not assume this mask of outspoken moralist very often, and readers must guard against the glib finality of the pronouncements in the class conferences and the Stein interview which hide the openness of his work.

In an attempt to conclude their official Faulkner portrait with a final flourish, Stein provides Faulkner with a clue for a major and comprehensive statement about his aesthetic goals: "What happened to you between *Soldiers' Pay* and *Sartoris*—what caused you to begin the Yoknapatawpha saga?" Faulkner takes up the cue, putting on the most sublime mask of the writer, the creator of his cosmos, complete with self-conscious rhetorical thunder and the farewell pose of Prospero: "My last book will be the Doomsday Book, the Golden Book, of Yoknapatawpha County. Then I shall break the pencil and I'll have to stop" (*LiG* 255). New historicism and the old tradition of critical irony make us distrust the grand pose of an ultimate Faulkner. In this respect, the exposure of the crafting of the portraits and of the communicative strategies of the interviews may help us to new readings of his work.

Ishmael is the witness in *Moby Dick* as I am Quentin in *The Sound and the Fury*.

—William Faulkner

Authors are actors, books are theaters.

—Wallace Stevens

Every complex spirit needs a mask: even more, around every complex spirit a mask continually grows.

—Friedrich Nietzsche

T W O

Masks and Metaphors
On Theory

The examination of samples of Faulkner masks and role-play in the previous chapter allows us to attempt a preliminary survey of some recurrent features and suggests a study of theoretical underpinnings. So far the few critics who have dealt with Faulkner's masks have tended to focus on the thematic aspects and on a small number of masks, often conceived of as complementary pairs, such as rustic and aesthete or dandy and bum (Grimwood 287; Blotner "Metafiction"; Lombardo). While one need not quarrel with these models per se, neither should they be relied on exclusively. A commendable alternative to both—the treatment only of single masks or of complementary pairs—seems to be a method of observing the variants of particular masks as they occur in shifting configurations and constellations in the writer's life and in his works.

Thus Josh, in *Mosquitoes*, appears as a specialization and further development of one aspect of the title hero of *Elmer*, and the sterile immobility of Hightower in *Light in August* can be regarded as a fuller realization of character problems anticipated in the paralysis of the marble faun. The most telling examples of recurring personae in changing constellations are, of course, the Quentins and Gavins, who were to be rewritten in several novels and stories. The characters we can read as masks of the artist—Pierrot or Darl, marble faun or Horace Benbow—are neither representations of "right" or "wrong" attitudes nor mimetic, self-congratulatory autobiography, but are exploratory impersonations of certain aesthetic and psychological problems, solutions, and failings, arising with the changes in the author's outer and inner life story. They appear as sketches of an intensely stylized, albeit unflattering, self-portrait which remained unfinished, ultimately, because in Faulkner's tragic life the anticipations of death and love cancelled each other out.

To speak of the development of Faulkner's persona—to employ evolutionary diction and metaphorics—would suggest a clearness of direction and singleness of purpose alien to his perspectivist philosophy and narration. However, there are noticeable currents in Faulkner's role-playing, like the fascination in his early work with the radically different and frequently changing personae of the artist (the late romantic marble faun, the symbolist Pierrot of Paris, the Sherwood Anderson type of a young man in *The Hill*, and the glassblowing lawyer in the first Yoknapatawpha novel). This tendency, culminating in a kind of artists' convention of different artist personae (*Mosquitoes*), becomes, not surprisingly, less pronounced after Faulkner's emergence as major writer. There are also characteristic preoccupations, such as the contrast between the several painfully reflecting personae (Horace, Darl, Quentin) and their active counterparts (Bayard, Jewel, Sutpen). Finally, there are repetitions, like the use of the Cyrano de Bergerac and Don Quixote metaphors in the fictionalizing of both the early Helen Baird encounter and the late Joan Williams affair, and continuities, like the interest in the foxhunting country gentleman and the motif of the war veteran. Given the many different and similar masks overlaying each other, the metaphor of the palimpsest should perhaps be employed, or one of an endless all-over painting, to define Faulkner's biographical and literary self-fashionings.

One of the striking features of recent literary criticism is the re-emergence of biography. This renewal of interest in biographical information for the purpose of practical criticism coincides with the arrival of neopsychoanalytical, new historicist, and, above all, feminist and multiculturalist criticism. However, the author in the positivistic sense of the nineteenth century has not returned. What has resurfaced is the author's narrative voice participating in the discursive practice of his time; in other words, nowadays the author appears to be tied to the conditions of discourse criticism and new historicism. The Faulkner epigraph to this chapter, "Ishmael is the witness in *Moby Dick* as I am Quentin in *The Sound and the Fury*," alerts us to the new discursive status of the "biographical I" which I shall illustrate later by engaging the concept of the mask. Furthermore, this epigraph draws attention to the narrative role-playing by the author, respectively, to the metaphoric dimension of a detached, volatile narrative figure, and finally, to the intimate relationship ("Ishmael . . . as I am Quentin") between the seemingly unrelated critical aspects of mask and metaphor.

Despite increased critical awareness of the present, the new biographical criticism is affected by unadmitted presuppositions and metaphors informing the organization of the biographical material. My goal in pointing out some of these metaphoric schemata in recent criticism is not to discredit them but to indicate how they influence our Faulkner image. The dramatic pattern with which Michael Grimwood presents Faulkner's struggles with his vocation initially announces itself in the title of his book, *Heart in Conflict*. This dramatization helps the author push his point across but also, unavoidably, distorts it. The same can be said of Karl F. Zender's *The Crossing of the Ways*, which links the affective image of the crossing of the ways to a combination of a binary and a triangular schema, and presents a vague and contradictory matter as clear-cut: "the opposition between the creative self and the South on the one hand and the modern world on the other" (66).

Both Martin Kreiswirth and Judith Sensibar arrange their material in accordance with a developmental or evolutionary schemata, but each uses a different variant of this linear model. The titles of both books, *William Faulkner: The Making of a Novelist* and *The Origins of Faulkner's Art*, guide readers metaphorically but in different directions. Kreiswirth's image of "the making" suggests a forward development of something that at the beginning (in the juvenalia) is not yet made, but ultimately is "gloriously accomplished" in Faulkner's great works; moreover, it indicates that he will describe the ingredients and the formative processes that made Faulkner a great novelist. *Origins* implies that, if we follow Sensibar, she will tell us where it all derived from, namely, the Conrad Aiken influence in Faulkner's poetry cycle *Vision in Spring*, which she published in the same year. Both books present interesting new material and teach us much about the early Faulkner; however, they were published, as their governing metaphors show, before the assumptions of traditional biographical criticism were seriously challenged. "The making of" and "the origins of" suggest that there is *one artistic identity* about which the critic has a clear idea, and, although focusing on the *development* towards it, he or she prefers to keep readers in suspense. This given artistic identity develops according to a master plan which the biographical critic reveals to us in a continuous argument. In regard to elements which do not fit the given or assumed image of the artist, the critic feels obliged to show how Faulkner, in becoming his true southern self, outgrew these alien influences.

Faulkner's "un-American" flirtation with European aestheticism is a case in point. Ironically, both Cleanth Brooks, one of the leading critics of the previous generation, and Wesley Morris, one of the most astute contemporary critics of Faulkner, let their hero *outgrow*—note the value-charged organicism of this metaphor—the influence of European aestheticism because it would have jarred their respective images of Faulkner. While Brooks (*William Faulkner: Toward Yoknapatawpha and Beyond*) obviously felt that traits of European decadence were unbecoming in a great writer of an "essentially healthy" southern heritage, Morris makes Faulkner discard these aestheticist elements because he regards them as incongruous with Faulkner's participation in the sociopolitical discourse of the contemporary South. Apparently, the critical tradition of seeking homogeneity is so strong that even a critic well versed in Derrida will not accept the "incongruous aestheticist features" in Faulkner as *traces* in the deconstructivist sense, but assumes a "career decision that moved Faulkner away from aestheticism to representationalism, away from art to life" (Morris 63). However, as Morris's own subtle reading of Mr. Compson's Sutpen story illustrates (85), fin de siècle elements appear side by side with modernist and regionalist features as part of the very

59

diverse contemporary discourse in which the mature Faulkner participates.

The image of the "true" Faulkner as opposed to his "false" appearances presupposes an organicist model with a holistic identity that
evolves in orderly stages towards maturity. In view of Faulkner's role-
playing and his many "false" stories, particularly those about military
honors he had not earned and war wounds he never sustained, critics
like Sensibar and Grimwood have had recourse to psychological imposture theories, or have approached Faulkner's career in terms of
"the psychopathology of vocation" (Grimwood 35–84). Drawing on
Greenacre's and Finkelstein's psychological work, Sensibar (41–50)
supplements the psychoanalytical biography of Judith Bryant Wittenberg's *The Transfiguration of Biography* in that particular respect. The
same goes for Grimwood's study of "the psychogenesis of Faulkner's
various impostures"; his interpretation, for instance, of *The Marble
Faun*—after a paragraph on "Maud's corset" (79, 35–39)—provides
an additional dimension to the literary exegesis of the faun's paralysis. The drawback of this approach is that the very complex phenomenon of Faulkner's role-playing, comprising sociological, psychological, historical, and aesthetic aspects, appears reduced to a scientific
determinism and a moral perspective. It tends to become an individual case of psychopathology or moral failure: "Faulkner's literary vocation was fatally rooted in deception and fraudulence" (35–39). Of
equal importance, the wearing of masks and role-playing is perceived
not as a matter of discourse but as an ontological issue.

The imposture theory presupposes philosophical realism and ontological or causal oppositions such as being/seeming, original/copy,
character/mask, underlying causes/surface appearances. "Imposture"
implies a dichotomy of true and false and normal and pathological
with moralistic and clinical implications that are closer to the tradition of Cesare Lombroso's *Genio e follia* (1864) than to our present-
day conviction that role-playing functions as a decisive factor in all
human behavior and, particularly, in any artistic transformation of
life. Indeed we can do better justice to Faulkner if we regard his many
masks as so many shifting responses to contemporary social, psychological, and literary contexts and, above all, if we see him as participating in a discursive practice in which role-playing is understood as
a communicative act and an artistic strategy.

International modernism is rich in pertinent specimens of masks and role-playing. The very phrasing of Joyce's title *Portrait of the Artist as a Young Man* points beyond the mere fact that we are presented with a young artist by alluding to the tradition of stylized self-portrayal well known in art history. The self-stylization of the American-born T. S. Eliot as Anglican Royalist—and in "Prufrock" as a nondescript bank clerk and "Clown" ("Suite Clownesque")—reflects this same tendency. The masquerading of the modernists had been prepared for by the decadence movement's previous fascination with masks; Oscar Wilde's *The Decay of Lying* (1889), Max Beerbohm's *A Defence of Cosmetics* (1894), and Aubrey Beardsley's cycle *The Comedy Ballet of Marionettes* (1894) are characteristic documents. Faulkner's playlet *The Marionettes*—like the early work of F. Scott Fitzgerald, Wallace Stevens, Ezra Pound, and several other American modernists—clearly shows the impact of this tradition.[1] Literary historians tend to be less aware of this latter type of self-fashioning because self-portrayal is not so firmly established as a genre in literature as it is in painting and art history. However, examples like the numerous masks and self-portraits of Rembrandt or of the German expressionist and United States emigrant, Max Beckmann, illustrate the wide range and relevance of the phenomenon. Rembrandt and Beckmann, whose self-portraits further document the importance of costumes and poses as part of an adopted role, are only two outstanding examples in a long tradition of elevating and distorting self-portrayal. This tradition is of interest in relation to the mask motif because self-portraits always involve a certain degree of masquerade, whether we think of Rembrandt as a biblical figure or of Faulkner as a war hero.

In assessing the role of masks within modernism, we also have to consider the intimate relationship between the biographical aspect of role-playing and the use of masks as a motif in modernist art and as a central device in contemporary theatre. In their fascination with masks, modernists drew not only on the venerable genre of Greek drama, but also on the shamanistic tradition that had been explored by ethnologists such as Franz Boas.[2] The inspiration which artists like Picasso and Braque derived from African masks and which W. B. Yeats found in Noh-plays (*Certain Noble Plays of Japan*, 1916) also allowed Eugene O'Neill (*The Great God Brown*) and Luigi Pirandello (*La favola del figlio cambiato*), as well as the actor, director, and designer

Gordon Craig and the Bauhaus artist Oskar Schlemmer, to employ masks in the theatre. Yeats was first introduced to the Japanese Noh-plays through Ezra Pound, whose 1908 volume of poems bears the characteristic title *Personae*, while Wallace Stevens's pronouncement "Authors are actors, books are theaters" (*Opus Posthumous* 157) epito-mizes the phenomenon of masquerading and thus appears as an apt epigraph for our study of William Faulkner's self-portrayal.

This understanding of role-playing as the transformation of the ac-tual into art and as a means to achieve a richer experience in the encounter with the nonself would also be in line with the aesthetics of Keats, the archsaint both of the late romantics and of the form-conscious modernists. In "Ode on a Grecian Urn," Keats provided Faulkner with the central formula for his theme of stasis and motion; moreover, in his famous letter of October 27, 1818, to Woodhouse, he anticipated Faulkner's view on the impersonality of the artist and his many masks. Keats's assessment of the predicament of the artist goes a long way toward explaining the inner relationship between Faulk-ner's cult of anonymity, impersonality, and privacy and the comple-mentary phenomena of role-playing and narrative perspectivism:

> As to the poetical Character itself . . . it is not itself—it has no self—it is every thing and nothing—It has no character—. . . . It has as much delight in conceiving an Iago as an Imogen. What shocks the virtuous philosopher delights the *camelion Poet . . . A Poet is the most unpoetical of any thing in existence; because he has no Identity—he is continually . . . filling some other Body*—The Sun, the Moon, the Sea and Men and Women who are creatures of impulse are poetical and have about them an unchangeable attribute—the poet has none; . . . *not one word I ever utter can be taken for granted as an opinion growing out of my identical nature—how can it, when I have no nature?* When I am in a room with People if I ever am free from speculating on creations of my own brain, then not myself goes home to myself: but the identity of every one in the room begins to press upon me that I am in a very little time annihilated—not only among Men; it would be the same in a Nursery of children. (*Letters* 386–87, my emphasis)

Quentin had grown up with that; the mere names were interchangeable and almost myriad. His childhood was full of them; *his very body was an empty hall echoing with sonorous defeated names; he was not a being, an entity, he was a commonwealth. He was a barracks filled with stubborn back-looking ghosts* still recovering, even forty-three years afterward, from the *fever* which had cured the *disease*, waking from the *fever* without even knowing that it had been the *fever* itself which they had fought against and not the *sickness*, looking with stubborn recalcitrance backward beyond the *fever* and into the *disease* with actual regret, weak from the *fever* yet free of the *disease* and not even aware that the *freedom was that of impotence*. (*AA* 9, my emphasis)

Both Keats and Faulkner stress the absence of a firmly established identity and fixed character, "no self . . . no Identity," "not a being, an entity . . . an empty hall," which is then taken over or filled by the other. The difference between the two writers lies in the way they envisage the empty vessel or space being filled. For the English romantic poet, the filling of the "receptacle" appears as a positive and enriching experience, resulting from the romantic openness toward natural phenomena and creative human beings ("The Sun, the Moon, the Sea and Men and Women who are creatures of impulse are poetical").

In contrast, the imagery in Faulkner's *Absalom, Absalom!*, both a historical novel and a novel of the depressed South of the thirties, has negative connotations. The spatial metaphor "empty hall echoing" and its transmutation into "barracks filled with stubborn back-looking ghosts" are reminders of the military defeat of the South and of reactionary veterans animating the lost cause mystique. The Faulkner persona Quentin, listener and narrator, heir and witness to the southern debacle, experiences the past as "back-looking ghosts" who invade his undefined and undefinable self which he describes in a daring modernist metaphor: "his very body was an empty hall." However, Faulkner's own complex relation with southern history is not fully defined by the metaphor of the ghostly invasion of Quentin's empty self.[3] In fact, the ensuing metaphoric passage structured by the repetition of the leitmotif cluster "fever, sickness, disease" *revises* the preceding image of the history-ridden nonentity and supplements it with that of the disillusioned southerners. Through their "fever" of fighting the Civil War, they have been "freed" in a dialectical process from the fever but not from the disease itself, their will to secede (of which the fighting was only a concomitant). With the lost war and the fever gone, they are free of the secessionist disease, but are left without their own regionalist values and consequently without a sense of direction.

Southerners after the Civil War—ranging from the redeemers and the patriarchal new southerners of company towns and plantation commissaries to President Wilson and other enthusiastic viewers of Dixon/Griffith's *Birth of a Nation*—showed few symptoms of having recuperated from either the fever or disease. Therefore, it is safe to say that Faulkner, rewriting the South from the point of view of the thirties, is projecting his disillusionment with the southern myth onto his southern heroes. However, before turning to the fascinating diversity of masks which Faulkner assumed in confronting his own southern dilemma, we should realize that this preoccupation with role-play emerges as part of a wider philosophical context before and after the turn of the century.

Masks and metaphors are intimately related, historically and systematically, to the philosophy of perspectivism of which Nietzsche is the most important representative. Corresponding to his *On Truth and Falsity in Their Ultramoral Sense* are Oscar Wilde's *Decay of Lying* and Walter Pater's "relative spirit."[4] These parallels illustrate an international intellectual tradition manifesting itself in three major aesthetic themes which link the fin de siècle and modernism and which are central to the understanding of Faulkner's art: the problem of narrative perspectivism or point of view, the fascination with mask and role-playing, and the emphasis on metaphor as a literary form and a form of knowledge. However, in drawing on Nietzsche, we do not propose to regard him in any positivist sense as a Faulkner source. Instead, we follow the example of deconstructionists and new historicists who, in developing their approaches to literature, have rediscovered Nietzsche as methodological inspiration.[5] Moreover, certain parallels do exist between Nietzsche and Faulkner, whose fascination with masks and metaphorics was sparked as much by social and philosophical factors as by psychological ones. Both suffered under "the great and continually increasing weight of the past," "the dark invisible burden of history," and in their respective societies from the alienation experienced by an artist ("Art is not part of Southern life").[6] From these parallels, an analogy emerges which relates Nietzsche's view of the burden of history to Quentin's metaphorization of "a barracks filled with stubborn back-looking ghosts." Finally, the following quotation from Nietzsche's *Beyond Good and Evil* concerning alienation and role-playing constitutes a helpful subtext for the reading of

Faulkner's *On Privacy. The American Dream: What Happened to It?* Faulkner doubtless would have appreciated Nietzsche's view that disguises and masks—including the role of the fool—are a means of "proud and sensitive natures to protect themselves from importunate curiosity" and that "to respect the masks of others is a sign of true humanity": "Forms of disguise . . . There are free aggressive insolent spirits, who would like to conceal and deny that they are broken, proud, incurable hearts . . . and sometimes folly itself that is the mask for an unhappy all too certain knowledge. From which it follows that it is part of more refined humanity to have reverence 'for the mask' and not to practice psychology and inquisitiveness in the wrong place" (209).

Regarding the current interest in Nietzsche, it is revealing that both deconstructionists and new historicists have rediscovered the master of philosophical aphorism, and that Derrida and Hayden White (347)—who explore Nietzsche in key works—focus on the complex "perspectivism-mask-metaphor." The following passage from Nietzsche's *On Truth and Falsity in Their Ultramoral Sense* (1873) occupies a central position in "White Mythology" (1971), Derrida's seminal essay on the functioning of metaphor in the text of philosophy: "What then is *truth*? A *mobile* army of *metaphors, metonymics, and anthromorphism*: in short a sum of human relations which became poetically and rhetorically intensified, metamorphosed, adorned, and after long usage, seem to a nation fixed, canonic and binding; *truths are illusions of which one has forgotten that they are illusions; worn-out metaphors* which have become powerless to affect the senses (*die abgenutzt und sinnlich kraftlos geworden sind*), *coins* which have their obverse (Bild) *effaced* and now are no longer of account as coins but merely as metal" (5–33, 14, my emphasis). The substitution of truth by metaphor and other forms of imagery—the whole array being not fixed but in motion ("a mobile army")—implies a radical departure from the philosophical tradition since Plato. One can see why Nietzsche's cynical tone ("truths are illusions of which one has forgotten that they are illusions") appealed to the deconstructionist predilection for reversal, and why the image of coins with their obverse effaced invited them to some playful deconstructionist allegorizing.

The following quotation from the Nietzsche chapter in Hayden White's *Metahistory* concerns itself primarily with "perspective seeing," the complex mode of perceiving, feeling, and thinking that, on the one hand, corresponds to the concept of role-playing and, on the other, to the totality of the metaphor: "All seeing is essentially perspective, and so is all knowing. The more emotions we allow to speak in a given matter, the more different spectacles we can put on in order to view a given spectacle, the more complete will be our conception of it the greater our objectivity" (369). Nietzsche's perspectivism includes both an emphasis on multiple points of view and a fusion of the intellectual with the emotional, and thus constitutes a congenial method of approaching Faulkner. In turn, such a reading of Faulkner which stresses his heterogeneity and multiplicity—and, one could say, Bakhtinian openness[7]—seems more congenial to the contemporary sensibility than the harmonized Yoknapatawpha picture presented by Cleanth Brooks. This new way of appreciating Faulkner shows itself in the tendency among critics to shift the focus from *The Sound and the Fury*, a favorite of the formalists, to *The Hamlet*, emphasizing its "noncenteredness" (Matthews, *Play* 165) and its "anarchy, indeed a madness built into the structure" (Kartiganer 114).

Apart from the conceptual framework of perspectivism-mask-metaphor, which is an essential inspiration of my new reading of Faulkner, there are some aspects of Nietzsche's mask concept that are of special interest, such as, for instance, his emphasis on the freedom from moral qualms and the joyful recreational use of masks in popular culture since ancient times: "What is and remains to be popular is the *mask* . . . And as for ancient life! What can we understand of that as long as we do not understand the *delight in masks* and *the good conscience in using any kind of mask*! Here is the bath and the recreation of the antique spirit . . ." (*The Gay Science* 132, my emphasis). For Nietzsche, the mask is not so much a means of hiding sinister intent as it is a concomitant or consequence of profundity: "Everything profound loves the mask; the profoundest things of all hate even image and parable . . . Shame is inventive. It is not the worst things of which one is most ashamed: there is not only deceit behind a mask . . . Every profound spirit needs a mask: more, around every profound spirit a mask is continually growing, thanks to the constantly false, that is to say shallow interpretation of every word he says [N. is thinking about himself!], every step he takes, every sign of life he gives" (*Beyond Good and Evil* 69–70). Here, Nietzsche supplements his view of the mask in several ways that are relevant to Faulkner. First, masks may originate from the reticence of a profound thinker to reveal himself to an uncongenial public and thus serve as a protective device unavoidably accompanying his attempts to communicate. Second, there is also the possibility that masks are produced not by the author but by the "misinterpreting" audience. Acknowledging Nietzsche's implicit suggestion, our concern should be not only with the masks of Faulkner's creation, but also with those of our own devising.

In view of Nietzsche's fascination with the phenomena of the mask, it is not surprising that he also deals with the problem of the actor in *The Gay Science*, where he speaks of the actor's "falseness" as practiced with "a good conscience," presenting the actor, because of "his delight in dissimulation and disguise, as a prototype of the artist." Nietzsche's depth of involvement in the problem of the actor is illustrated in the phrase "it has worried me longest, I was uncertain about it." As a consequence of his philosophical perspectivism, which changes truth "into a mobile army of metaphors," "character," traditionally a fixed entity in criticism, also evaporates into "so-called character." Character as a clear identity is overwhelmed and dislocated by the "powerful urge to dissimulate": "The problem of the actor has troubled me for the longest time. I felt unsure (and sometimes still do) whether it is not only from this angle that one can get at the dangerous concept of the 'artist'—a concept that has so far been treated with unpardonable generosity—. Falseness with good conscience; the delight in simulating exploding as a power that pushes aside one's so-called 'character,' flooding it and at times extinguishing it; the inner craving for a role and mask, for *appearance* . . ." (*The Gay Science* 316, my emphasis). In view of Faulkner's enjoyment of tall tale poses in his fiction as well as in his interviews, it is of interest that Nietzsche in his aphorism on the actor should name the braggarts, tall tale narrators, and clowns of the folk theater as precursors of the modern artist.

The role-playing of impostors and actors may serve as threshold for some brief methodological reflections on the psychological and sociological aspects of the phenomenon and on the necessity to integrate these several views in a new approach, the aesthetics of role-playing. Jeremy Hawthorn's study, *Multiple Personality and the Disinte-*

gration of Literary Character: From Oliver Goldsmith to Sylvia Plath, drawing on Ernest Hilgard's clinical study, *Divided Consciousness: Multiple Controls in Human Thought and Action* (1977), is a fairly representative example of the psychological approach. Hawthorn's approach resembles Sensibar's and Grimwood's in positing a homogeneous personality, the difference being the scientific connotations of his term "dissociation" in lieu of their moralizing implications. However, scepticism of the indiscriminate application of psychiatric models does not speak against their modified use. In fact, such phenomena as "doubling" have been effectively studied by psychoanalytic critics including Masao Myoshi (*The Divided Self*) and, in the Faulkner field, John Irwin (*Doubling and Incest/Repetition and Revenge*).

The advantage of anthropological and sociological over psychological concepts in the project of an aesthetics of role-playing is that they accept multiple modes of existence as positive or at least as neutral. Thus, they help us avoid the imposture theory that has hampered the scholarly debate on the role-playing of artists. If instead of a psychiatric approach, we accept the tenets of Hellmuth Plessner's philosophical anthropology,[8] we shall find the metaphorics of actor, role-playing, and mask offering a more promising vantage point for the discussion of the problem of the writer's persona than the negative imagery of "dis-sociation" and "im-posture." Moreover, the metaphorics of actor and theatre constitute an important semblance point between Nietzsche's *The Gay Science* ("the inner desire to slip into a role and mask") and Plessner's seminal essay, "On the Anthropology of the Actor," where the actor appears as paradigmatic of the human condition. In view of this emphasis on the actor and role-playing, it comes as no surprise that Plessner, like Nietzsche, rejects the dichotomies of true and false, real and seeming, essence and mask. In contrast to a psychoanalytic understanding of roles and its inherent ontological implications emerging in the metaphorics of surface and depth, a sociological interpretation of roles tends to be functionalist and communication-oriented.

With Plessner the human ability to establish distance from oneself and assume the role of the other in an act of play appears as a liberating and enriching confirmation of a special human talent, not, as in Marx's view of alienation, as a loss of identity or an impairment. According to Plessner, the idea of the temporary relinquishment of selfhood, as stipulated by the concept of role-playing, offers individuals the opportunity to be themselves even under the sophisticated conditions of the division of labor in the modern industrial society. From this anthropological concept of *Homo sapiens* as mask wearer, role-player, and actor, Plessner and, following him, Ralph Dahrendorf, derive their view of role-playing as a central sociological fact, occurring at the demarcation line between the individual and society.

However, to derive one's inspiration for an aesthetics of role-playing exclusively from sociological models has several drawbacks. First, sociological role models are designed for assessing the rules of "normal" behavior. Therefore, their application will only lead to registering highly individual strategies and motives of the role-playing artists and their fictionalizing experiences as "deviant." In other words, the application of sociological role models could produce the same unfortunate results as the psychological model which criminalizes the "lying artist" as an impostor. Nevertheless, the modified or indirect use of sociological models has proved very helpful in studying Faulkner's role-playing in the interviews. Above all, these schemata alert one to the specific strategies and devices of the masquerading artists. However, the more important question—namely, how these impersonations function in the artistic process—can only be dealt with (see this book's part 2) by supplementing the sociological approach with specific literary studies of metaphors and other devices of artistic self-stylization, as the next chapter will show.

Nietzsche's view of language as a mask and of philosophy as a hiding place explains Derrida's fascination with the notorious German and helps us focus on the inner relationship between masks and metaphors. Nietzsche regards language as: "Writings of a hermit . . . Echo of the desert . . . Every philosophy also conceals a philosophy; every opinion is also a hiding-place, every word also a mask" (*Beyond Good and Evil* 216). After the initial metaphor of the hermit, which encapsulates the alienated status of the thinker and artist, Nietzsche proceeds to identify mask and metaphor by referring to an element of concealment involved in all philosophical statements ("every word also a mask"). If we take this image seriously, we realize that Nietzsche here goes considerably beyond the romantic definition of language as being essentially metaphoric. "Every word also a mask" suggests an unorthodox dynamism in the metaphorization process, whereby masquerading complicates and deflects straightforward communication.

Nietzsche's idea that the expression of something always implies or refers to something unexpressed, and thus hidden, is the kind of thought that must have appealed to Derrida because it prepares for his own concept of *"différance*, deferral, *Verweis"* (Culler 95). This element of deferral is of interest here because it is one of the characteristic features inherent in both masks and metaphors. But in our time, the site in which this deferral occurs is no longer a place ordered by theories of correspondence or by a platonic dichotomy of ideas and appearances. Instead, our contemporary concept of reality and mimesis is characterized by the "serial representation" of Andy Warhol and other pop artists. "An *original* is an outmoded idea in a society where mass production obscures the model and repetition of *the same* has displaced the quest for the unique"[9] as Walter Benjamin in *The Work of Art in the Age of Mechanical Representation* had anticipated in 1936. Naturally, such a view of reality and representation strongly affects the concept of mask and metaphor.

On the basis of these aesthetics of serial representation, a model of shifting masks and role-playing comes to replace traditional concepts of the artist's identity and the sincerity of his expression. Similarly, in the discussion of metaphor, the focus shifts from the former preoccupation with the distinction between tenor and vehicle to the study of metaphorization as a syntactical event. The sentence and the larger textual units are viewed as "open situations" in which the metaphoric "deferral" unrolls as a multifaceted and complex process. Alan Singer, in his fine book *A Metaphorics of Fiction*, quotes a passage from Derrida that is relevant to this aspect of metaphor: "The signified concept is never present in itself, in an adequate presence that would refer only to itself. Every concept is necessarily and eventually described in a chain or a system, within which it refers to another and to other concepts, by the systematic play of difference. Such a play, then—the difference—is no longer simply a concept, but the possibility of conceptuality" (51).

Derrida's philosophical model with its strong Saussurean echoes is one to which many critics would subscribe today. It certainly has left its mark on the present study, in which both masks and metaphors will appear as multiple, reflexive, and, above all, as characterized by a specific imaginative dynamism. Singer's book is germane to my argument because the postmodern literature and poststructuralist criticism which he outlines in his introductory chapters "The Fictions of Metaphor" and "The Metaphors of Fiction" also condition our present-day reading of Faulkner. My approach to the imagery in Faulkner's novels and stories inevitably reflects the deconstruction or evaporation of the border between fiction and fact which Singer traces in contemporary theory and in such fiction as Jorge Luis Borges's programmatic short story "Pierre Menard's Don Quixote."

Jorge Luis Borges's parodic masterpiece on rewriting reminds us of a further aspect of the new Bakhtinian openness, characterizing our contemporary experience of literature: the impact of reception aesthetics on the concepts of masks and metaphors. Current critical theory/practice regards literature not as existing per se but as being re-created by the reader. In reading Faulkner's biography and books, for example, we actively engage in the transfer involved in masquerades and in the transfer of metaphors between separate areas of meaning. As Faulkner's masks and metaphors are intimately related to his narrative perspectivism, it should also be pointed out that this novelistic strategy enhances the role of readers who take on the weight, if not the authority, of the omniscient narrator fragmented in polyvocalism.

What distinguishes recent critical writing from that of the past is a new awareness of the importance of images and eidola. Approaches based on Gérard Genette's *Translinguistics*, such as those of James A. Snead (*Figures of Division*, "Litotes and Chiasm"), who relates the "hidden Figures of Longinus" to Freud's "slips," and the psychohistorical studies of Michael Paul Rogin (*Fathers and Children*) and Annette Kolodny (*The Lay of the Land*) mark the width of the spectrum. Here, the cognitive aspect of metaphor is emphasized, and masks are regarded as devices which hide and reveal, as a means of offering different viewpoints and of assimilating new experiences. The change is, therefore, from a view of metaphor as a rhetorical figure to a concept of metaphoricity as an aesthetic principle. This sense of the radicality or totality of metaphor characterizes present-day writing both in the liberal arts and in the social sciences, linking such diverse critical texts as Michel Foucault's *The Archeology of Knowledge* (1969) and Jacques Derrida's *The Retrait of Metaphor* (1978).

Preludes

One possible reason for the preoccupation with metaphors in this tradition—as with masks and role-playing—seems to be the heightened contemporary consciousness that "being" is only accessible in its state of withdrawal or "deferral." Proceeding from this experience is the recent shift in our thinking on expression and representation, from positions of ontological realism or aesthetic formalism to the problem of discursivity and the process or structure of signification. Furthermore, this change of focus has been instrumental in overcoming the separation of positivistic biography and formalist criticism and explains the renewal of interest in biographical criticism. In turn, the reconciliation of biographical and formalist criticism on the new basis of discourse analysis has given us our new sense of the contiguity of masks and metaphors. What should be stressed, however, is that concomitant with the pervasiveness of metaphoricity in all thinking, there also emerges an eerie new feeling that the traditional distinction and opposition between the referential and the metaphorical has collapsed. But despite the tendency to regard all so-called referentiality as metaphorical and to read *Absalom, Absalom!* as a postmodernist novel, we should not lose sight of the respective differences between Faulkner's modernist and our postmodernist metaphors of reality.[10]

My study proceeds from the assumption that Faulkner's imagery *together* with his narrative gift constitutes the core of his literary genius. In contrast to previous investigations, in which metaphor has usually appeared as a merely stylistic device, I will consider metaphors in relationship with masks and as constituting an aesthetic principle. The contemporary awareness of the universality of metaphor and its profound impact on philosophical, historical and even scientific thinking (Derrida, White, Foucault) also affects our practical criticism. Above all, it sensitizes us to the open and hidden sociopolitical and psychological dimensions of metaphor which traditional rhetoric and formalist criticism largely ignored. Since, in recent times, readers have become more aware of the openness of literary works, I will now study concrete examples from major Faulkner novels that reveal how, through their metaphors, the texts point beyond themselves, and how the reader is made to move between several contexts (see chapters 5, 6, and 8).

The terms "masquerade"—the creating and wearing of masks (as

Nietzsche writes, "Every opinion is also a hiding place, every word also a mask" [*Beyond Good and Evil* 216])—and "metaphorizing"—the "transcendence" or transference of meaning across categorical boundaries ("Metaphor is a transaction between two contexts," according to Paul Ricoeur [139])—help us focus simultaneously on the social and on the formal aspects, on the element of movement in Faulkner's role-playing as well as in his metaphoric thinking. In using "role" and "mask" side by side I am trying to differentiate between two related aspects of the same phenomenon: while "mask" focusses on the expression of otherness, implying its momentary and static quality, the term "role," like the more parodic image of "masquerade," refers to processes, the elements of acting, and thus to a more comprehensive attitude.

As the study of Faulkner's photos, letters and interviews has shown, his masks are of many kinds in terms of both content and appearance, expressing in stylized form individual desires and responses to social codes, to unconscious drives and political intentions, and, above all, to the discursive practice of their time. What makes the mask such an important aesthetic concept is that it functions as a prime model for resolving the tension between the urge for self-expression and the distancing of form. Masks can convey equally well timeless mythic patterns and the alienation of modern mass culture. In both cases, these masks show the individual as transformed by the collective will of the group. Furthermore, in the context of the cognitive sciences as in art, masks and metaphors appear as instruments and strategies of the elusive "I" attempting to assimilate and transform the "not-I." The respective masquerades and metaphorizing processes are *performances*, communicating experiences which traditional theory used to address as "expression" and "re-presentation."

Naturally, the experience of thinking as entangled in metaphorics is reflected in the rise of a new kind of poetological imagery. I envision phenomena such as masks and metaphors no longer in terms of fixed dichotomies (truth-mask, essence-appearance, thing-image, tenor-vehicle) but as processes, and in defining the processes of masquerading and metaphorizing, the focus of concentration is more on the modes of transfer than on the presumed poles between which the metamorphosis takes place.

Moreover, I intend to focus not so much on the theoretical aspects

73

of this "transcendence" as on its realization in concrete Faulkner texts and contexts, proposing to make Paul Ricoeur's eclectic and fairly representative *La métaphore vive* (1975) a departure and reference point. While the models of tenor-vehicle (I. A. Richards), metonymy-metaphor (Jakobson), and focus-frame (Max Black) still remain useful, Paul Ricoeur's view that "metaphor proceeds from the tension between predication and denomination" and that "metaphor is a transaction between two contexts" (117, 139) provides the underpinning for this new approach to Faulkner.

In this study, the term "metaphor" takes precedence over "image," partly for the reasons spelled out by Lorna Sage in her criticism of the latter term: "The effect of over-reliance on the word image is to encourage a focus on literature which makes syntax, argument, plot, temporal and relational structures recede into invisibility, while description and figurative language become foregrounded to a distorted degree. The whole thus isolated becomes a static 'spatial' experience, imagined as 'cluster' of 'images' " (Fowler 120). However, the main reasons for choosing the term "metaphor" are the ones apparent from the preceding outline: the emphasis on the cognitive and transformative dynamics of metaphor, and the philosophical, structural, and intertextual implications which the venerable Aristotelian concept has acquired in recent theory. But this distinction should not keep us from employing the term "image" for particular kinds of metaphor such as psychoanalytic images or for defining specific aspects such as the sensuous, material quality of iconic or nonreferential images for which the term "metaphor" is unsuitable.

Throughout the textual analyses, I will focus equally on metaphor as experienced by the reader and as created by the narrator. In contrast to previous criticism, which has mainly dealt with metaphor as an uncontextualized stylistic device, the emphasis in the present study will rest on the interplay of metaphor and narration, on the experience of metaphor in reading, and on the function of the metaphorizing processes in the psychological and sociopolitical discourse of *The Sound and the Fury*, *Light in August*, *A Fable*, and above all, in *Absalom, Absalom!* and *The Hamlet*. To prepare us for the investigation in part 3 ("Metaphorizing and Role-Play in Narration and Reading"), part 2 starts with the interaction of masquerade and metaphorization in various masks of the artist. The relating of lesser-known short stories such as "Black Music" and "Artist at Home" to "Carcassone" may help this much-discussed text appear in a new light and, in turn, these masks of the artist may enlarge our understanding of Faulkner's aesthetics.

Masks and Metaphors
of the Artist

Perhaps it is the very lack of moral severity, of any high and heroic ingredient in the character of the Faun, that makes it so delightful an object to the human eye and to the frailty of the human heart. The being here represented is endowed with no principle of virtue, and would be incapable of comprehending such; but he would be true and honest by dint of his simplicity. We would expect from him no sacrifice of effort for an abstract cause . . .

—Nathaniel Hawthorne, on *The Marble Faun*

THREE

The Artist as Visionary and as "Craftsman"

"Black Music," "Carcassonne," "Artist at Home," *Elmer*, and *Mosquitoes*

The yearning for pagan sensuality shyly announcing itself in the context of Hawthorne's Puritan culture emerges with Walter Pater and young Faulkner's literary idol, Swinburne, as a dominant cultural force. Sensuous fauns and naked Pans side by side with attractive female and male bodies in emancipatory bathing scenes are among the chief inspirations of the international art nouveau movement.[1] It is, therefore, not surprising that fauns constitute a major motif in Aubrey Beardsley's art nouveau drawings, whose impact is visible in Faulkner's *Marionettes* illustrations as well as by his references to Beardsley not only in *Soldiers' Pay* but also in major novels such as *Light in August* and *Absalom, Absalom!* Beardsley's drawings ("Pagan Papers" and "Design for Cover of the 'The Dancing Faun' "), in which the fauns capture the full attention of the ladies obviously enjoying their company, make us realize by contrast the peculiar positioning of Faulkner's fauns and nymphs. In all three of his drawings, the woman, a scantily dressed flapper, appears as the dominant figure and is obviously meant to display hauteur or disdain as opposed to the sexual inferiority of the faun, who is ignored by the nymph, and, in a subordinate position, continues piping his homage. This configuration in the early faun drawings anticipates the George-Cecily constellation in *Soldiers' Pay* (89), and, above all, the worshipful attitude of Gavin Stevens, the devotee of Cyrano de Bergerac and Don Quixote, towards Eula and Linda in *The Town*. As the features of the faun in the *Mayday* illustration bear some resemblance to those of Faulkner in his little pencil self-portrait of 1925 (plate 5), the lack of a relationship, the inferiority of the faun and the superiority of the nymph may have psychological implications, an assumption that is confirmed by *The Marble Faun*.

Since critics have exhaustively dealt with the content of this poetry cycle, the tension between the faun's paralysis ("My marble bonds" [*TMF* 12]) and his vitalistic urge to follow "Pan's piping and frolic with the nymphs,"[2] I shall confine myself to the aspects of literary role-playing. Here, two additional points are relevant. First, in embracing the faun mask, Faulkner was reusing a fashionable late romantic/early modernist variant of an ancient motif, with Beardsley and Mallarmé representing the poles of its thematic and stylistic range. Second, in doing so, he modified the usual vitalistic implications of the motif considerably, deploying, in the faun drawings as in *The Marble Faun* poems, the faun persona to convey erotic inhibitions and frustrations and projecting, if not achieving, their transubstantiation in art.[3]

Among Beardsley's drawings for Oscar Wilde's *Salome* is a design for the title page in which a marble faun figures prominently. Even more pertinent, as illustrating the context of Faulkner's use of the faun persona, seems to be a Beardsley drawing with the ironic title "A Footnote" (plate 6). What this "footnote" annotates is the self-reflective posture of the artist vis-à-vis the faun image and its sexual implications: Beardsley, ironically playing with phallic connotations, depicts a neorococo youth resembling Beardsley himself with a long pointer tucked under his left arm, mimicking the stele of a faun in the background to which the artist ironically appears fastened by a cord in elegant art nouveau curves. Unfortunately, the self-reflectiveness in Faulkner's faun poems was not of the ironic but of the sentimental kind.

However, this difference should not let us overlook the important similarity between Faulkner and Beardsley. Their faun personae are both sculptures and artworks of an idealized cast. Further, to be marble bound, even with young Faulkner, is not, as previous criticism has made out, an entirely painful experience, implying only inhibition and lack of erotic freedom. Marble as a valuable and beautiful material used for a sculpture also suggests the elevated status of the Keatsian notion of art to which one of Faulkner's personae of the artist remains indebted. Accordingly, in *Mosquitoes*, the face of Gordon, the sculptor and prototype of the form-conscious and aloof modernist artist, appears "like a silver faun's face" (152).

Concerning the motifs and modes of artistic self-fashioning, it is of interest that in *Soldiers' Pay*, Faulkner no longer employs the faun as neorococo garden sculpture, embodying art as arrested life. Rather, postwar and personal malaise make him express the inhibitions and frustrations, as conveyed in the poem cycle by the marble-bound character, through Donald Mahon's wound and his status as an invalid war veteran. However, he also reemploys the faun motif but in a modified form. Besides Januarius, the dilettante, impersonating the lecherous faun of mythological tradition, Faulkner retains the faun as expressing twentieth century vitalism. But this faun is metaphoric, occurring in Mrs. Powers's melancholic reflection on a photo of Donald before the war had mutilated him: "She [Mrs. Powers] took it [the photo]: thin faced, with the serenity of a wild thing, the passionate serene alertness of a faun; . . ." (*SP* 83).

The short story "Black Music" (1925–26), stemming from the same period as *Soldiers' Pay*, bears a resemblance to the scene of Donald's "faun photo" in that the narrator meets the faun long after his "apotheosis" (*CS* 799): "At one time in my life I was a farn" (805). Wilfred Midgleston, the faun, is not only quite ordinary in his original setting of a New York architectural bureau but also later in his exile in an unremarkable Latin American port city with a Conradian atmosphere of shabby exotism. By this readers better understand that the only important event in his life is the Pan episode, his temporary ecstasy through divine choice.

What fascinated Faulkner in "Black Music"—the intrusion of the *meta*-physical as disconcerting tremendum into reality—is an interest he shared with E. M. Forster ("The Story of a Panic") and other writers and artists of the early twentieth century. Most used the Pan and faun motif to communicate their vitalistic-spiritualistic protest against complacent middle-class pragmatism and its scientistic reduction of nature. Forster's story is close to Faulkner's in its urge to return to nature, to explore instincts and uncontrollable subconscious drives.

However, at the center of "Black Music" is not only the psychospiritual theme—the metamorphosis of the mediocre Midgleston into a faun—but also the sociocultural theme—his disturbing effect on the plutocratic Mrs. Van Dyming and her grotesque plans of a Disneyland country seat with "Acropolises and Coliseums" (810) in the Virginia mountains. The parodic picture of the cultural aspirations of Babbitt's America (the community garage made to look like it was an Acropolis) as monuments of Veblen's "conspicuous consumption" (*The Theory of the Leisure Class*, 1899) corresponds with the pronouncement of Forster's Mr. Sandbach: "Pan is dead." Undoubtedly, the faun as an artist persona came to express the author's satiric distance from his society and to communicate his hopes of a new vitalistic transcendence.

Furthermore, the title "Black Music," with its occult implications, and the position of the story in the section entitled "Beyond" of *Collected Stories* suggest that as a persona of the artist, the faun is to make readers transcend the borderline between banal modernity and the visionary. For that purpose, Faulkner emphasizes—as Hawthorne had done in his description of the faun quoted above—the faun's mythic innocence: "like the face of a child" (*CS* 803). The faun persona confirms that Faulkner shared the interest in the rediscovery of myth so widespread among the modernists, whether we think of T. S. Eliot's *The Waste Land*, Igor Stravinsky's ritualistic ballet, *The Rite of Spring*, or the use of "the mythic method"—Eliot's term—by James Joyce and W. B. Yeats. How fruitful Faulkner's participation in this tradition was will become evident in the examination of his use of "the mythic method" in the Eula plot and the Ike Snopes and cow episode of *The Hamlet*.

The relevance of "Black Music" in connection with the theme of the artist and the affinity of the faun story with the prose poem "Carcassonne," in regards to both the scenery and the artist persona, have been noted by Noel Polk and other critics.[4] However, in assessing the role of "Carcassonne" in Faulkner's mask-building creativity, some initial inspiration can also be drawn from the author's own commentary. There are two unrelated passages in *Faulkner in the University* touching on "Carcassonne" which, when they are compared, reflect on the young writer's attempt to cast a persona for himself and to define through this self-fashioning his aesthetic and personal goals.

> **Q.:** From what viewpoint did you write . . . "Carcassonne"?
> **Faulkner:** I was still writing about a young man in conflict with his environment. I—it seemed to me that fantasy was the best way to tell that story. To have told it in terms of simple realism would have lost something, in my opinion. To use fantasy was the best, and that's a piece that I've always liked because there was the poet again. . . . failed poet, not a novelist at all. (*FU* 22)

> I myself am inclined to think it was because of the bareness of the Southerner's life, that he [the Southerner] had to resort to his own imagination, to create his own Carcassonne. (*FU* 136)

That Faulkner remembered so well this early text, which he had also used as a concluding piece to *These 13* and the carefully composed *Collected Stories*, indicates its privileged position among his stylized self-portraits. It seems significant that both passages focus on the tension between the artist and his world ("in conflict with his environment"—"bareness of Southern life . . . resort to his own imagination, to create his own Carcassonne") and on the fantastic as a response to an uncongenial social context. In both passages, the place name "Carcassonne" symbolizes an imaginative redemption from personal tensions and from the southern desert of the "bozart." The references to a poetic style as preferable to a realistic one and to the cultural bareness of southern life document the intimate relationship between the aesthetic and the sociopolitical.

What readers experience in the personae of both "Black Music" and "Carcassonne"—as in Faulkner's very early prose poem "The Hill"—is, above all, ecstasis, the quality which religionists seek to suggest through the metaphors of transfiguration or ascension or the symbolists through elevation: "Then his apotheosis soared glaring, and to him at least not brief, across the unfathomed sky above his lost earth like that of Elijah of old" (*CS*, "Black Music" 799). As in "Black Music" the movement of the Pegasus rider in "Carcassonne" is upwards, "galloping up the hill and right off into the high heaven of the world" (895) with the "dark and tragic figure of the Earth, his mother," left behind.

In both stories the lowly state of the elevated or chosen—a stereotypical feature of most comparable religious situations—is emphasized (the garret, rats, the tar paper bedclothing [895]). Both heroes are alienated, exiled from their societies ("Black Music") or, like anchorites, remote from ordinary life ("Carcassonne"). However, there is a difference in the quality of the two experiences of transcendence or epiphany to which the two heroes are exposed. While in "Black Music" the faun's epiphany, exploding Mrs. Van Dyming's pseudoculture, is characterized by pagan sensuality, closeness to nature, and vitalistic implications, the ascension of the rider in "Carcassonne" is the idealistic one of the romantic imagination and of a visionary kind.

However, for all the differences between the realistic commercial story "Black Music" and the symbolist prose poem "Carcassonne," both portray society as being represented by domineering women (Mrs. Van Dyming and Mrs. Widdrington) and being a place from which "farn" and Pegasus rider appear alienated. In "Carcassonne" in particular, the identification of the artist's patroness with Standard Oil, the notorious object of Ida Tarbell's muckraking journalism, strikingly illustrates the fusion of economic and psychological power. Grimwood has characterized the lady patrons of both "Black Music" and "Carcassonne" as belonging to the "repressive mother" type, whose several representatives in Faulkner's works he traces back to Maud Falkner. His findings, which are the results of a more traditional psychoanalytic approach, have recently been confirmed by the more avant-garde methods of feminist critics such as Karen R. Sass (127–38) and Doreen Fowler ("Matricide" 113–25). His patrons of the arts and would-be manipulators of artists, Mrs. Van Dyming and Mrs. Widdrington—like Mrs. Maurier in *Mosquitoes*—are sociologically no less relevant than psychologically. "But the Standard Oil Company, who *owned* the garret and the roofing paper, *owned* the *darkness too*; it was Mrs Widdrington's, the *Standard Oil Company's wife's*, *darkness he was using to sleep in*. She'd *make a poet of you* too, if you did *not work* anywhere" (*CS* 897–88, my emphasis). Of interest in this passage are both the psychological resentment against the patron as an overbearing mother figure and the sociocultural opposition of the puritan work ethic with the dearth of the southern cultural context. Moreover, the bitter tone of complaint and the modulating repetition of the metaphors "owned" and "darkness," with their fusion of socioeconomic and psychoanalytic implications, offer readers insights beyond the rational surface of the text. Does the Pegasus rider feel and resent that the innermost experience of his literary vocation is tainted by incestuous eroticism, or at least overshadowed by maternalist influence and power?

From this perspective, "the dark and tragic figure of the Earth, his mother," at the conclusion of "Carcassonne" cannot be dismissed as just another of the several earthy referencces in Faulkner's work attesting to his regionalist sympathies. The dominance of the "earth mother" ("the Earth, his mother" [900]) in Faulkner's work, from the regressive wishes of the marble faun ("And in the earth I shall sleep/ To never wake, to never weep/ For things I know, yet cannot know" [*TMF*]) to Mink's embrace of mother earth at the end of *The Mansion*, unavoidably affects also the reading of the conclusion of "Carcassonne," where the element of male dynamism and poetic idealism seem distanced by the final dominance of the vitalistic female principle. The fact that Pegasus and rider, for all their thunder, appear as "punily diminishing: a dying star,"[5] while the complex mother figure ("steadfast, fading, deepbreasted and grave of flank, muses the dark and tragic figure of the Earth, his mother" [900]) remains the readers' last impression of "Carcassonne," of the "Beyond" section and thus of *Collected Stories*, seems psychoanalytically important.[6]

"Carcassonne" is not all vision. There are indeed strong elements of scenic realism; however, the text is held together not by a continuous storyline but by metaphoric clusters and a closely knit web of leitmotifs. To their repetition and modulations readers have to respond as they would to a poem, preferably one as intertextually charged as T. S. Eliot's *The Waste Land*. That the prose poem "Carcassonne," despite its lack of a regular form, is highly structured is evident from such linkages as the motion conveyed by the protagonist's buckskin pony and that of the riderless Norman horse from the first crusade. As the upward movement of the buckskin pony suggests the elevation of the

Pegasus, the horse from the first crusade, which continues to gallop after it has been severed in two halves by the Saracen Emir (*CS* 896), becomes a grotesque embodiment of death in life, stasis in motion. As such, it ironically contributes to the central theme in the artist's dual role as galloping rider and motionless, prostrate skeleton. The main theme of motion emerges from Christ's central statement "for I am the Resurrection and the Life," blasphemously supplemented by the vitalistic reference to male and female genitals ("Of a man, the worm should be lusty, lean, haired over. Of women . . . it should be suavely shaped" [897]). The counterpointed theme of stasis is conveyed, realistically, by the protagonist's sleep beneath the tarred roofing paper and, symbolistically, by the deep sea image fusing with the skeleton motif: "bones knocking together to the spent motion of falling tides in the caverns and the grottoes of the sea" (897).

Performing as the central impulse of the artist persona ("I want to *perform* something bold and tragic and austere" [899]) is characteristic of the author as role-player and the vacillating subject of a multitude of masks. But no less relevant, psychoanalytically and sociologically, is the experience of extreme stillness ("He lay still beneath the wall paper, his body lay on the rippled floor" [899]). Characteristically, the Pegasus rider adopts the first-person perspective ("And me on a buckskin pony" [895]; "I want to perform" [899]), while the skeleton appears as a third-person narrator. In accounting for this strategy, it seems more to the point to see the two narrators as embodying the vitalistic and the suicidal principles than as representing an external and internal view. In "Artist at Home," Faulkner will offer a parodic variant of a comparable double portrait of the artist, juxtaposing the mundane fiction writer and the fake poet. What makes the coexistence or double existence of performer and skeleton uncanny metaphors is that this doubling seems to draw together in one reflection Faulkner's aesthetic theme of motion and stasis and his personal drama of creativity and self-destruction. The splitting or doubling of Pegasus rider and skeleton appears as a variant of the motifs of siblings (Horace/Narcissa, Quentin/Caddy) and dark twins (Bayard/John Sartoris, Charles Bon/Henry Sutpen) on which John T. Irwin (*Doubling and Incest/Repetition and Revenge*) and Michael Grimwood (*Heart in Conflict*) have written.

However, what seems even more significant than this psychoanalytic dimension is the fact that in the two complementary voices of this artist persona, Faulkner achieved a new language, whose character the text itself defines as "body consciousness, assuming the office of vision" (896). His new sensuospiritual prose poetry would allow him later in *The Sound and the Fury* and *Absalom, Absalom!* to communicate wholly new areas of experience. In "Carcassonne" this central experience of the coincidence of opposites as a specific form of transcendence has challenged Faulkner's genius for manneristic metaphors. The imagery of the prose poem suggests that the art associated with the Pegasus rider galloping "toward the blue precipice never gained" (895) can only be one of "splendid failures," an art at the rim of the abyss. Although critics have been puzzled by "Carcassonne,"[7] the prose is not really so unusual when other early pieces such as "Nympholepsis" are considered and, above all, when one takes into account the style of major works such as *The Sound and the Fury* and *Absalom, Absalom!* or the scene of Joe Christmas's castration and ascension in *Light in August* or of Ike's tryst with the cow in *The Hamlet*.

The narratological configuration of Pegasus rider and skeleton, in some respects, anticipates in miniature the split or dialogical narrative of *Absalom, Absalom!*, and, like Quentin and Shreve, the two narrators of "Carcassonne" make the production of their ambiguous text vacillating between prose poem and short story their theme. In this process, the skeleton narrator, for instance, ironically helps the Pegasus rider when he is looking for the right Norman equestrian term: "chamfron." Our reading experience of "Carcassonne" is conditioned as much by this element of metafiction as by the symbolist leitmotif technique, the one interrupting narrative continuity and the other creating cohesion of a poetic order. It is further affected by the realistic rendering of the manneristic or visionary details ("against the taut roundness of its belly" [896]). Finally, our sensibility in the reading process is modified by the clash between a trivial reality (Rincon, Standard Oil, Mrs. Widdrington's garret, tar paper) and the rich intertextuality of quotations and pseudoquotations. As readers we have to negotiate between archaic phrases like the Homeric "where I was King of Kings but the woman with the dog's eyes . . ." and medievalizing metaphors such as "the ranks of the Lamb's foes opened in the sacred dust." Readers are startled by the richly connotative place name Carcassonne and by quaint words like "mail: armor" or "chamfron." The exotic thrill of the Saracen Emir and the legendary appeal of Bouillon and Tancred are also felt. Above all, the artist as visionary carries the reader away with the metaphoric dualism of cosmic elevation (up the long blue hill of heaven) and the descent into the symbolist deep sea with its "opaline corridors" and "swaying caverns and grottoes."

As the texture of "Carcassonne" will frustrate any attempt to project a discursive argument into the story, readers, combining sensitivity and intelligence with some historical knowledge, are to mediate and establish relations between several outside contexts and the various layers of the text which Faulkner makes us experience. In doing so readers engage in an activity for which the term "metaphorizing" does not seem inappropriate. As a result of this metaphorizing, the double portrait of the artist as performer and skeleton becomes also that of the ironic narratologist and collage artist.

The importance of "Carcassonne" in Faulkner's literary role-playing lies in the fusion of narrative doubling with manneristic metaphorics. This combination, in turn, resulted in a new state of of perceptiveness, a "body consciousness, assuming the office of vision" (896), enabling the author to communicate whole new areas of experience: the subtle narrative modulations of Quentin in *The Sound and the Fury* and the verbal music of the balloon motif reflecting the semiconscious growth of young Sutpen's racist design in *Absalom, Absalom!*

While "Carcassonne" has been a challenge and therefore a favorite of sophisticated critics, "Artist at Home," for the same reason, has received little attention. What has led Faulkner readers for a long time to underrate and neglect this commercial story on artists and artistic role-playing are its drabness, farcical plotting, and cynical tone. These supposed faults on the author's part have made it difficult for readers to establish an immediate relation to the text and to realize that such unattractive features as stereotypes (the poet as lover) and trivialization (the parodic references to Shelley and Joyce) are really the adequate means of conveying the story's specific theme. One of the achievements of the story with the satiric title "Artist at Home" is the range and flexibility of its parodic language, reaching from rural metaphors for the writing process ("like forty hens in a sheet-iron corn-crib . . ." [*CS* 638]) to the manneristic comparison between Shelley's romantic death at sea and Blair's miserable death from the rain and flu (644).

Characteristic of the peculiar humor of "Artist at Home" and its self-ironic portrayal of the artist is the fiction writer's reaction when the poet confesses to him his love for the other's wife:

> "Listen," he says. "Tonight I kissed your wife. I'm going to again, if I can."
>
> "Ah," Roger says. He is too busy filling the pipe right to look at the poet, it seems. "Sit down."
>
> "No," the poet says.
>
> Roger lights the pipe. "Well," he says, "I'm afraid I can't advise you about that. I have written a little poetry, but I never could seduce women." (*CS* 637)

As this parodic association of poetry and seduction suggests, "Artist at Home" is very much a farcical story about art and artists, and, like Henry James's "The Real Thing," concerns the adaptability of life to literature, or rather, the attitudinizing and role-playing through which fiction writers and poets alike seek to transform life into literature.

How close the story was to being an ironic portrait of the fashionable contemporary writer is evidenced by the fraternization of the white avant-garde poet with the Howes' black maid, reminding one of the white fascination with the Harlem Renaissance and Carl Van Vechten's *Nigger Heaven* (1926). Roger's racist remark about the "wooden church full of sweating niggers," and John Blair's interest in black culture are conscious references to a subject that Faulkner himself had so impressively rendered at the end of *Soldiers' Pay* and in *The Sound and the Fury*.

Faulkner's participation in the *Zeitgeist* is attested to as much by "Artist at Home" as by *Mosquitoes*, not least by his caricaturing of parasitical would-be artists whom, in his New Orleans period, he had observed—and learned to shun: "The painters, the writers, that hadn't sold a book or a picture—men with beards sometimes in place of collars, who came and wore his shirts and socks and left them under the bureau when they departed, and women in smocks but sometimes not: those gaunt and eager and carnivorous tymbesteres of Art" (*CS* 627). The double portrait of novelist and poet in the story belongs with other artist portraits by Faulkner, such as the sculptor Gordon (in *Mosquitoes*), but also with those of the painter Elmer (in *Elmer* and "Portrait of Elmer") and the sketches of artists in *New Orleans Sketches*: "Wealthy Jew," "The Artist," and "Out of Nazareth." Apparently, Faulkner used the caricatures of fellow artists in *Mosquitoes* and the latter sketches as he would the portraits of dilettantes like Horace Benbow and Gavin Stevens or of commercial artists, such as Charlotte Rittenmeyer and Harry Wilbourne, to define his own status as a writer and to exorcize vocational uncertainties, doubts, and temptations.

Moreover, "Artist at Home" transforms and fictionalizes aspects of Faulkner's married and professional life as well as reminiscences of the Faulkner-Sherwood Anderson-Elizabeth Prall triangle. The poet and the commercial writer represent a castigating double self-portrait of Faulkner as a caricature of the absolute artist and idealistic lover and as cynical literary hack, turning his wife, his friend, and himself into copy. Above all, the story's leitmotifs reflect in humorous distortion the author's conflict between the challenges of art, caricatured in the would-be Shelley, John Blair, and the demands of the commercial writer, satirized in Roger Howes: "the bald husband, the rural plute, and this dashing blade, this home-wrecking poet. Both gentlemen, being artists: the one doesn't want the other to get wet: the other whose conscience won't let him wreck the house from inside" (642).

Roger Howes, like John Marcher in "The Beast in the Jungle," does not respond to his wife's need for attention and love, and when she turns in despair to John Blair, he makes this affair the subject of a commercial story. In fact, the beginning of the ludicrous liason between the poet and the writer's wife also marks the latter's return to writing.[8] The combination in the dominant leitmotif of the typewriter with market imagery ("the typewriting market picked up again" [640]) impresses on readers the venal and exploitive nature of Roger's writing.

John Blair, the poet, is no less a caricature of the artist, as indicated by the leitmotifs of the "sky-blue coat" ("sky-blue coat . . . like a short horse-blanket" [628, 631, 635]) and of the "old rooster" ("You take a rooster, an old rooster" [635]). Arrogant towards the literary hack whose protégé he is (632), he appears as a would-be Shelley ("So Young Shelley has not crashed through yet" [634]). In line with his Shelley-like features, he talks a lot about freedom and equality, but he dies as the poet of one poem, which Faulkner, in his satire of bohemian posturing, has Blair write on the back of a menu card from the Elite Café: "It seems that this was the shot" (643). There is little doubt that Faulkner caricatured and castigated himself in this story not only as a commercial writer but also as a failed poet.

But John Blair as a Faulkner persona is also of interest because of his peculiarly romantic and southern lady worship. Despite his sudden and unsolicited kisses (635), he clearly belongs, together with Horace Benbow and Gavin Stevens, to the type of worshipping would-be lover, "kneeling outside her door (in the rain)" (638). In making the romantic poet-lover catch a fatal cold in the rain and having the Howes worry about his health (642), Faulkner parodically rewrote the triangular configuration of Joyce's "The Dead," treating his own romantic posturings with irony. In regard to the psychological underpinnings of Faulkner's masks, it is revealing that he has John Blair, idealistic lover and failed poet, worship Anne because he can project his juvenile mother complex (leitmotif "narcissus smell") onto her:

> "When I was a little boy, we would have sherbet on Sunday," he says. "Just a breath of lemon in it. Like narcissus smells, I remember . . . Mother died and we moved to a city. Boarding-house. A brick wall. There was a one-eyed man with sore eyes. And a dead cat. But before that we had lots of trees, like you have." (636)

> He's had nothing, nothing. The only thing he remembers of his mother is the taste of sherbet on Sunday afternoon. He says my mouth tastes like that. He says my mouth is his mother. (640)

More revealing still, he uses Anne's sympathetic account of the scene as a means of brutally satirizing the juvenile sentimentality of the poetic lover, anticipating the bitter humor that made him invent the Gavin Stevens character in *The Town*. Finally, "Artist at Home," besides ironically exploding the poet's posturing and the fiction writer's voyeuristic detachment, reveals the victimization of the female.

In offering such a double portrait, "Artist at Home" resembles "Carcassonne." Obviously, Faulkner's predilection for these double portraits of the artist is connected with his urge for assuming complementary masks and his fascination with the motif of siblings or twins. The social and psychoanalytic factors embodied in the theme of doubling and splitting of personality have made "Artist at Home" an ironic, metafictionist text on writing and the masks of the writer.

The exotic vision of Henry Sutpen's initiation in New Orleans, contrasted in *Absalom, Absalom!* with the Anglo-Saxonism and puritan rigor of the writer's and his hero's north Mississippi upbringing provides us with a vivid picture of what the city must have meant to Faulkner: "I can imagine him, with his puritan heritage—that heritage peculiarly Anglo-Saxon—of fierce proud mysticism and that ability to be ashamed of ignorance and inexperience, in that city foreign and paradoxical, with its atmosphere at once fatal and languorous, at once feminine and steel-hard—this grim humorless yokel out of a granite heritage where even the houses, let alone clothing and conduct, are built in the image of a jealous and sadistic Jehovah, put suddenly down in a place whose denizens had created their All-Powerful and His supporting hierarch-chorus of beautiful saints and handsome angels in the image of their houses and personal ornaments and voluptuous lives" (*AA* 90). The rich cultural diversity and artistic milieu of this city helped the fledgling artist to his breakthrough; from here the shy and cramped countrytown boy ventured forth and undertook his European tour. Thanks to the enormous assimilative power of his genius, this relatively short encounter with the rich world beyond Jefferson enabled him to establish sufficient sociocultural and artistic distance to give his own region the universality of aesthetic shape.

The multiformity of Faulkner's early novels (*Elmer*, *Soldiers' Pay*, and *Mosquitoes*) and the *New Orleans Sketches* demonstrates that the New Orleans period, which appears—in the words of *Elmer*—as "an aimless hiatus of activity" (*ELM* 383), was in fact a time of intensive experimenting with poetic roles and literary styles. Moreover, New Orleans, with the sure sense of its long-established culture, helped the fidgety young modernist establish his artistic calm and ironic distance. What the city did for Faulkner becomes apparent from the first two pieces in *New Orleans Sketches* in which he juxtaposes the cosmopolitan "wealthy Jew" and the catholic priest as representatives of cultures strikingly different from that in which the author himself had grown up. His interest in foreign lifestyles and forms of culture indicates his sense of the relativity of his own culture, which throughout his work he showed as being in transition. It is no wonder then that this sociocultural aspect also figures prominently in Faulkner's artistic role-play. This becomes evident, for instance, when he associates the "wealthy Jew"[9] not only with exotic richness ("Phoenician ancestors . . . Ahenobarbus' gardens . . . What soil is foreign to me?" [NOS 3–4]) but more precisely with Théophile Gautier's parnassien ideals ("I love three things: gold; marble and purple; splendor, solidity, color" [3]) which had such a strong impact on modernist theory. In a similar manner, the catholic culture of the priest is a welcome excuse for the kind of aestheticist mannerism ("How like birds with golden wings the measured bell notes fly" [5]) which Faulkner would eventually functionalize in linguistically establishing the mythic dimension of the Eula and the Ike and the cow episodes in The Hamlet.

The portrait entitled "The Artist" in New Orleans Sketches is still dominated by the traditional poetological images of "dream" and "fire," suggesting the artist's visionary power and his divine "afflatus" ("A dream and a fire which I cannot control" [NOS 12]). But there emerges already in this early text, as background to "the joy to create," that specific Faulknerean fatalism ("driving me . . . decreed for man . . . inherited . . . the original and eternal dust") later popularized through the eschatological pathos surrounding creativity in the Nobel Prize speech. Characteristic of this early fictive self-portrait of the artist is the association of the artistic gift ("fire") with the fear of suppression and inhibition (12).

The distinctive feature in this portrait of the artist is the notion that creation is not experienced as an effortless pagan delight but as an existential battle against shapelessness. The drama between form and amorphousness provides the emotional and spiritual context from which the motives arose that drove Faulkner to embrace, in Elmer and Mosquitoes, the modernist masks of the writer as painter and as sculptor: ". . . what hand holds that blood to shape this dream within me in marble or sound, on canvas or paper, and live?" (NOS 12). What Elmer and Mosquitoes have in common is the preoccupation of the young writer with his craft[10] and—this has been less studied—with artistic personae and role models from the arts and the several branches of literature. However, there are also antimasks, such as Faulkner's Prufrock persona, Talliaferro, Josh, Frost, and the Wiseman siblings, who, set in opposition to the congenial personae Gordon and Fairchild, articulate, demarcate, and exorcize Faulkner's psychological and artistic worries, temptations, and failings. In fact, Faulkner's urge to castigate cruelly in artistic personae aspects of his own predicament did not diminish over time, and Horace Benbow's glassblowing ("with the outcome of only one almost perfect vase") in *Flags in the Dust* seems a merciless caricature of the dilettantism of Faulkner's juvenilia. Further, in *If I Forget Thee, Jerusalem*, Harry Wilbourne's confessional magazine stories ("the anesthesia of his monotonous inventing" [578]) and Charlotte Rittenmeyer's spurious puppets and marionettes satirically reflect their pseudoromance[11] and mirror the author's depressions about his own Hollywood hackwork and the clashes between his affairs and his effort to observe the southern family code.[12]

The several personae of the artist in their various configurations in *Elmer* and *Mosquitoes* embody a threefold donnée. First is the preoccupation of modernist writers with the arts and their ambition to use the sensuousness of painting and the plasticity of sculpture to redeem the verbal art from its abstractness and discursiveness. Second is their interest in the darker self and the unconscious and semiconscious motives of the soul which Freudianism had brought to the fore. Third, there is a continuing if modified fascination with the aesthetic ideal of romanticism: "I want never to be completely satisfied . . . so that I shall always paint again" (qtd. in McHaney, "Elmer Papers" 37–69).

The following text illustrates the conflation of the three impulses—and Faulkner's use of the color red—as much for poetically structuring his prose as for revealing the origins of the artist's anxiety. The color pattern, synaesthetically combined with sounds as a means of impressing on readers the central psychoanalytic fact "He had always hated to be seen unclothed," helps us to understand not only the obsession of Faulkner's heroes with virginity but also such seemingly unrelated features in his own character as his romantic insistence on never-achievable ideals of artistic perfection, his predilection for the sister motif, and his privacy complex. "*Red* said the label and *red* the rectangular border. When he was young *red* had troubled him. When he was five years old the house in which they were temporarily living had burned. . . . Never would he forget the *red horror of that night. He had always hated to be seen unclothed* . . . His sister with whom he slept, with whom he didn't mind being naked. She *stood fiercely erect* as ever, watching the fire in a dark proud defiance. . . . This *unearthly crimson* seemed to have lent her *black scrawniness a bitter beauty* like that of a salamander, something immortal and fleeting and unforgettable" (*ELM* 345–46, my emphasis).

The readers' sensuous experience of the psychoanalytic theme will make them appreciate more intensely the sister's elevated status suggested by the symbolist imagery. Moreover, it induces them also to register subconsciously the close ties of Elmer's vision of his sister ("stands fiercely erect") with his phallic obsession and the Diana-hermaphrodite leitmotif complex.[13] "Elmer hovered over them with a brooding *maternity*, taking up one at a time those fat portentous tubes in which was yet *wombed* his heart's desire, the world itself—thick-bodied and female and at the same time *phallic: hermaphroditic*" (*ELM* 345, my emphasis).

There is an ironic and at the same time serious scene in *Mosquitoes*, in which Mrs. Maurier's niece, Patricia, and Gordon, the sculptor, assisted by poor Mr. Talliaferro, develop the hermaphrodite motif and the aesthetic and psychological implications of its formalism and narcissism against a utilitarian background (26): " 'It's like me' . . . Her brown hand flashed slimly across the high unemphasis of the marble's breast. . . . Gordon examined with growing interest her flat breast and belly, her boy's body which the poise of it and the thinness of her arms belied. Sexless, yet somehow vaguely troubling" (*MOS* 24).

As in the iconographic tradition of the hermaphrodite,[14] there are implications of unfulfillment and tragic deferral of love and life in Faulkner's handling of the motif, becoming dominant in such maimed and frustrated personae as the paralyzed faun, the melancholy Pierrot, the wounded veteran Donald Mahon, and the incestuous and suicidal Quentin. But the positive connotations of the hermaphrodite motif are equally prominent. They emerge above all in Elmer's hermaphroditic vision of his adored sister Jo-Addie, his "fine sexless passion" (365) for his spinsterish teacher, and his homosexual worship of "an older boy, tall and beautiful as a young god," later echoed in the Angelo episodes (365–66).

What is important in Elmer's hermaphroditic vision of his sister is, first, that she clearly serves as a substitute for the tabooed erotic relation with the mother[15] and, second, that she is connected, on the one hand, with his nascent sense of form ("strange passion for form") and, on the other, with his virginity obsession ("pure blank"). This fusion of the aesthetic and psychological, of form and inhibition, manifests itself throughout in the combination of aesthetic and moralistic vocabulary ("as though he were on the verge of something *beautiful and clean and fine*" [348, my emphasis]).

Elmer's dichotomy of women as young girls "with troubling virginal bodies" like Myrtle ("like a star, clean and young and unattainable" [359]) and as crudely sexually attractive women such as Myrtle's father's mistress, Gloria ("her large unsubtle behind" [360]), anticipates the antagonism between Horace Benbow's sister, Narcissa (*nomen est omen*), and his mistress, Belle. While much has been written about the aesthetic aspect of Faulkner's *coincidentia oppositorum* (stasis in motion), its close relationship to the "troubling sexuality of virginal bodies" and the underlying psychological tensions of maternalism and juvenile phallism have been ignored.

The autobiographical roots of the idealistic features in major Faulkner personae and of the thematic complex shock/escapism/self-hatred (e.g., the motif of the "young man in the glass coffin" [*ELM* 421]) are revealed in the description of Elmer's "sex education": "Things that Elmer had heretofore accepted without question now had a soiled significance . . . his mother and father, his own body all become sinister, dirty" (370). In a contrapuntal development against this traumatic experience of sex emerges the leitmotif complex, "keen bitter *blue* . . . heard geese *lonely and high* . . . *clean again*" (370, my emphasis). The hero's decision, "he was through with women . . . He'd just be Elmer and paint pictures" (370), indicates the psychological origin of the narcissist persona of the artist, throwing light on Faulkner's heroes from the marble faun through the Quentins to the "celibate" Gavin Stevens. The continuity of this theme is impressively documented by the example of *The Town*, in which recurs even the association of erotic idealism with the color pattern "blue" which is so striking in *Elmer* (367–74). Characteristic of blue as metaphor is its dynamic, ambiguous, and all-embracing quality. Like James Joyce, Virginia Woolf, and other modernists, the young Mississippi writer posing as painter was finding out that color symbolism and the musically structured leitmotifs answer particularly well the purpose of transmitting psychoanalytic themes in a multivalent poetic prose.

No less important than the young artist's color sense is his ability to draw symbolic shapes. Again the aesthetic is made expressive of the psychological, for the shapes haunting young Elmer's imagination are phallic. Interestingly, Faulkner has Elmer stylize them in a way recalling the faun on his marble pedestal ("people armless and sweeping upward in two simple lines from a pedestal-like base" [378]). Incidentally, while the boy does his drawings, his mother and his father are oppressively present, reminding one very much of the unfortunate psychological constellation in Faulkner's home (378). In *Mosquitoes*, the Faulkner novel illustrating most vividly the range and the specific nature of both his intellectuality and literary culture, Gordon, a tragically inhibited, idealistic artist and a particularly important Faulkner-mask, speaks of his female torso with the bitterness of frustration:

> This is my feminine ideal: a virgin with no legs to leave me, no arms to hold me, no head to talk to me. (*MOS* 26)

> . . . motionless and passionately eternal—the virginal breastless torso of a girl, headless, armless, legless, in marble temporarily caught and hushed yet passionate still for escape, passionate and simple and eternal in the equivocal derisive darkness of the world. (11)

Gordon's torso of a girl embodies art as "deferral" of life.

In the same novel, Patricia's twin brother, Josh, is a comic counter-mask (to Gordon's serious portrayal), and in his preoccupation as modernist objet trouvé artist with phallic objects constitutes a parodic development of Elmer's juvenile obsession. The Josh narrative and the theme of form and utility (*MOS* 26, 47) reach their witty climax in what amounts to a parody of Marcel Duchamp's "ready-mades": the absence of the pipe, which the would-be artist Josh has removed from the ship's engine and turned into a *nonfunctional and ready-made* art work, causes engine trouble and has to be refunctionalized. The other major motif, in addition to the phallic shape and the torso of a virginal woman as chief emblem of art contributing to the thematic complex conveyed through the hermaphrodite motif, is that of the siblings. The interconnectedness of the motifs becomes apparent from the crossing over of gender traits in Patricia and Josh: "They were twins: just as there was something masculine about her jaw, so was there something feminine about his" (*MOS* 46). In the context of this and other Faulkner novels, the male and female twins, in their combination of male and female features and their sterile-because-taboo sexual relationship, carry thematic implications similar to the hermaphrodite's. Apart from *Elmer* and *Mosquitoes*, the sibling motif plays a key role in *Flags in the Dust, The Sound and the Fury, Absalom, Absalom!*, and *The Town*.

Underlying the motif of the hermaphrodite and the sterile relationship of the siblings is the central thematic complex life-art-virginity-pure form in their aesthetic and psychological aspects. In a key scene in *Mosquitoes*, in which the virginal torso is the departure point, the Semitic man ironically negotiates between the positions of nonfunctional, "pure" art (Gordon) and art as representing life, "love, youth, sorrow and hope and despair . . . a particular reaction to put in the mouth of some character" (Fairchild). Fairchild admits that he himself has felt the contemporary fascination of nonfunctional art, which in the nonreferential medium of sculpture is easier to realize than in writing, and the Semitic man echoes that by referring to Fairchild's unshakable faith in words: "It's like morphine, language is" (319). The metaphor "language . . . morphine" calls up the dangers of self-sufficient, nonreferential language, in particular the temptations of Faulkner's genius of manneristic metaphor as well as his tireless experimenting with the styles of his predecessors—the Bible and Shakespeare, Byron and Keats, Swinburne and Housman, Wilde and Aiken, Eliot and Joyce.

In contrast to the Semitic man, who, in the debate on biological and artistic creation sees art as a re-created life ("[artists are] not satisfied with the world as it stands and so must try to rebuild the very floor you are standing on" [320]), Fairchild emphasizes that art implies not just a mimesis of life but participation in its power: "It's getting into life, getting into it and wrapping it around you, becoming part of it" (320). In the traditional sexist way, he contrasts the biological creativity of women and the artistic creativity of men. The point here is not the reductiveness of this view of gender roles, which is obvious enough, but the identification of art and artist as male and *nonnatural*, "a perversion." "Women can do it without art—old biology takes care of that. But men, men . . . A woman conceives: does she care afterward whose seed it was? Not she. And bears, and all the rest of her life . . . is filled . . . But in art, a man can create without any assistance at all: what he does is his. A perversion, I grant you, but a perversion that builds Chartres and invents Lear is a pretty good thing" (320).

The passage, stressing the "basic rightness and naturalness of female creativity" in contrast to the "perverse male-ness of art," reminds us of mother figures such as Lena and other regionalist madonnas. Moreover, it calls to mind the superiority of earth women like Emmy over Cecily's "slim epicenity" (*SP* 143), or of heroic and womanly Ruby Lamar over the effete aristocratic flapper Temple Drake. Faulkner's fascination with and aversion to "epicene" women such as Cecily and Temple Drake[16] may derive from his ambivalent relationship with Estelle, and also—in the case of Temple Drake— from the contemporary context of his social criticism. But above all, his attitude seems to reflect his obsession with the psychological tensions embodied in the hermaphrodite motif.

> Lips that of thy weary all seem weariest,
> Seem wearier for the curled and pallid sly
> Still riddle of thy secret face, and thy
> Sick despair of its own ill obsessed. (252)

However, neither the epigonic fin de siècle sonnet on a Swinburnean hermaphrodite nor Fairchild's moralizing ramble against this icon of contemporary perversion does justice to the importance which this motif had for Faulkner, psychologically and aesthetically, in projecting his artistic personae. " 'Hermaphroditus,' he read. 'That's what it's about. It's a kind of dark perversion. Like a fire that don't need any fuel, that lives on its own heat. I mean, all modern verse is a kind of perversion. Like the day for healthy poetry is over and done with, that modern people were not born to write poetry any more . . . A kind of sterile race: women too masculine to conceive, men too feminine to beget . . .' " (252).

The study of the thematic complex hermaphrodite and siblings, juvenile phallocentrism (Elmer, Josh) and the dichotomy of woman into femme fatale or madonna, has established a context which helps us to understand Quentin's fictionalizing of his sister Caddy no less than the author's "making himself" "a beautiful and tragic girl":

"One day I seemed to shut a door between me and all publishers' addresses and book lists. I said to myself, Now I can write. Now I can make myself a vase like that of the old Roman kept at his bedside and wore the rim slowly away with kissing it. So I, who had never had a sister and was fated to lose my daughter in infancy, set out to make myself a beautiful and tragic girl" (220). In view of the isolation and aloofness of artist personae such as the marble faun, the Pegasus rider, and the sculptor ("Sufficient unto himself in the city of his arrogance, in the marble tower of his loneliness and pride" [153]), it is not surprising that Faulkner attributes his early masterpiece *The Sound and the Fury* to his break with the world of publishers and his separation from the public.[17] As regards the artist persona of *The Sound and the Fury*, respectively, the one created in the two 1933 versions of the introduction (Minter 220), both the affinity and the difference between the suicidal hero and the survival artist Faulkner are relevant to the problem of stylized self-portrayal.

Faulkner obviously shares with Quentin a major psychological disposition epitomized in their peculiar fascination with an imaginary sister.[18] As a projected art figure and variant of the Jungian anima archetype, the imaginary sister resembles both Gordon's hermaphroditic virgin and Dante's Beatrice associated in the same context, as well as the little Italian girl in *The Sound and the Fury* and the little sister Death in *Mayday*. Faulkner speaks of her in the introduction to *The Sound and the Fury* in the same terms ("making myself") which he uses in *Mosquitoes* in regard to Dante's projection of Beatrice. In both cases, the emphasis is as much on "making" in the sense of artistic crafting as on the psychological function of character projecting. Significantly, the reference in the text to Dante's anima figure follows the evocation of Gordon's virginal torso and an allusion to the leitmotif of parnassian art (gold, marble, purple): "*Then voices and sounds, shadows and echoes*, shadows and echoes change form swirling, becoming *the headless, armless, legless torso of a girl, motionless and virginal and passionately eternal before the shadows and echoes whirl away* . . . I love three things [gold, marble, purple] . . . Dante invented Beatrice, creating himself a maid that life had not had time to create, and laid upon her frail and unbowed shoulders the whole burden of man's history of his impossible heart's desire" (*MOS* 339, my emphasis). In view of the range of possible embodiments, the specific content of

100

Faulkner's anima figure as "virginal torso" and "maid" as well as their status as "artistic inventions" is psychologically and aesthetically revealing. The metaphorics and the syntax, from which Gordon's torso of the girl emerges, are characterized by the tension between motion ("swirling" impressions, "whirl away") and stasis ("motionless and virginal and passionately eternal").

That Faulkner, in projecting the suppressed opposite sex, should evoke the images of the sculpture and, in the introductions to *The Sound and the Fury*, the vase is of interest both in connection with his personae as painter and sculptor and with his efforts as artist who handcrafted the illuminated manuscripts of *The Marionettes*. No less relevant are the links between the artist persona, the vase image and the role of Keats's "Ode on a Grecian Urn" in Faulkner's aesthetics. In addition to the vase as psychological-poetological emblem in the introduction to *The Sound and the Fury*, Faulkner uses the vase as a dominant novelistic motif in the Horace Benbow narrative of *Flags in the Dust*, where the glassblowing brother associates his sister, whose telling name is Narcissa, with his vase and with Keats's "unravished bride of quietness." Only when these two instances of the vase are related, respectively of the anima figure to the counterimage of the urns in *Light in August*, suggesting sexual anxiety and disgust, do the full dialectics of the motif vase, urn/woman and the complexity of its psychoanalytical and aesthetic context emerge.

> There is a story somewhere about an old Roman who kept at his bedside a Tyrrhenian vase which he loved and the rim of which he wore slowly away with kissing it. I had made myself a vase, but I suppose I knew all the time that I could not live forever inside of it, . . . It's fine to think that you will leave something behind you when you die, but it's better to have made something you can die with. Much better the muddy bottom of a little doomed girl climbing a blooming pear tree in April to look in the window at the funeral. (*FD* 224)

> In the notseeing and the hardknowing as though in a cave he seemed to see a diminishing row of suavely shaped urns in moonlight, blanched. And not one was perfect. Each one was cracked and from each crack there issued something liquid, deathcolored, and foul. He touched a tree, leaning his propped arms against it, seeing the ranked and moonlit urns. He vomited. (*LA* 538)

The model of the "polarity of gender, originating from the rejection of maternity" (Sass 127–38) enables us to interrelate the positive and the negative connotation of the vase/urn metaphor proceeding from man's mythicizing of woman. Moreover, the metaphor of the artist, who "has made himself a vase" (aesthetic aspect) but who realizes that he "cannot forever live inside of it" (psychoanalytic aspect) makes us recognize Faulkner's predicament of being engaged in both the psychological "regress to the womb" and in the process of aesthetic shaping. The "suavely shaped urns," whose perfect shapes are cracked and leak the "deathcolored" liquid, suggest that in the case of the beautiful Tyrrhenian vase, too, form for Faulkner was a means of exorcizing sexual anxieties.

While Elmer as artist persona allowed Faulkner to introduce color patterns as a means to provide his poetic prose with nondiscursive structures, the persona of the sculptor suggested firmness of contour and the controlling force of form. Since the author's interest in Gordon obviously is in his "pure sense of form," the "sterile art of the hermaphroditic female torso" appears in the center of the novel and also of its criticism. But there is also the very important scene in which Faulkner's sculptor persona shifts his interest from the epicene icon inspired by Mrs. Maurier's niece to a possible sculpture of herself: " 'I'm not going to hurt you,' he said harshly, staring at her face as a surgeon might . . . Mr. Gordon! she implored through her dry lips, without making a sound. His hand moved over her face, learning the bones of her forehead and eyesockets and nose through her flesh" (*MOS* 154).

Assessed by the sculptor as possible subject of an art work, the patroness, who had been merely a caricature, emerges as a woman and as a scarred and mutilated victim of the aristocratic system of the New South: "The story is, that her people forced her to marry old Maurier. He had been overseer on a big plantation before the Civil War" (323). The projected artistic image of Mrs. Maurier, in pointing beyond the sterility of the hermaphroditic torso of her niece, marks the new humane sensibility and maturity of Gordon, the sculptor, and of Faulkner, the writer.

Among the several artists whom Mrs. Maurier has invited to a cruise aboard her yacht, the *Nausikaa*, Gordon and Fairchild play prominent roles. Since these two chief artists represent aesthetic positions that helped Faulkner to articulate his own aesthetics, I will pay special attention to them later. But there are also, among the minor artists and literati, dilettantes and connoisseurs in his New Orleans novel, some figures who are not only brilliant satiric portraits of contemporaries but to some extent ironic reflections and refractions of certain Faulknerian features. Clearly, in this novel Faulkner is experimenting with several artistic roles and is trying on several masks and countermasks.

If we no longer confine our attention to the content of the aesthetic pronouncements of characters in *Mosquitoes* but also take their style and tonality into account, we will soon become aware of that. Moreover, close observation of the nuances of phrasing, for instance in Fairchild's parodic reference to Freudian readings of Swinburne ("reduced to his mother and his old standby, the ocean" [116]), will help us today, when the problem of the Faulkner image is no longer the simplistic opposition sophisticated internationalist vs. country boy, to gauge for the first time the specific kind and exact degree of Faulkner's intellectuality, literary knowledge, and aesthetic awareness.

Since these qualities were underrated by the first generation of Faulkner critics, we, in reaction, have tended to overestimate them, or, rather, to assess them too crudely. That the country boy from north Mississippi was clearly very impressed by but also resentful of the artistic sophistication and cultural superiority displayed by the *Double-Dealer* crowd and the other New Orleans avant-gardist literati is obvious throughout the novel. It can be seen in his apparently verbatim transcription of their fashionable Freudianisms ("this park of dark and rootless trees which Dr. Ellis and your Germans have recently thrown open to the public" [251]), of their flirtations with belated fin de siècle moods (in the Hermaphroditus motif [252]), and of their modernist ideals (cf. "the discussion of color symphonies" [182]). But Faulkner's participation in the parodic time spirit and the aesthetic philosophy of the twenties makes him neither a "poeta doctus" of the Pound or Eliot kind nor an intellectual novelist like the author of *The Magic Mountain* or *Doctor Faustus*. However, if the heaviness of *A Fable* demonstrates that Faulkner was no Thomas Mann, the sophistication of *Absalom, Absalom!* shows no less clearly that the exposure to the aesthetic talk of the New Orleans group modified his sensibility.

103

Among the dilettante artists in *Mosquitoes* sharing features with Faulkner are Pat's twin brother, Josh (a variant of Elmer), illustrating psychological and aesthetic phallocentrism, and Mrs. Wiseman with her epigonic fin de siècle and early modernist poetry. Even Mark Frost's empty smartness[19] ("Katharsis by peristalsis") and the Semitic man's cynicism are characteristic period features of the twenties, which Faulkner had at one point found congenial and flirted with, as his ironic and worldly-wise attitudinizing in his early reviews and essays attests: "It is a time-honored custom to read Omar[20] to one's mistress as an accompaniment to consummation—a sort of stringed obligato among the sighs. I found that verse could be employed not only to temporarily blind the spirit to the ungraceful posturings of the flesh, but also to speed onward the whole affair. Ah, women, with their hungry snatching little souls! With a man it is— quite often—art for art's sake; with a woman it is always art for the artist's sake" (*EPP* 115). However, a closer look at this irritating macho mannerism reveals that it was a cover-up for a psychological dilemma later surfacing in Quentin's suicidal love for his sister and in Gavin Stevens's ludicrous love affairs with Eula and Linda.

By the same token, the posture of the ironic man of the world and disillusioned cynic in the early essays and in *Mosquitoes* helped the young author establish personae and ideolects that would later allow him to articulate Addie Bundren's disillusion with words in *As I Lay Dying* or the bleak view of *Homo politicus* in *A Fable*. The emergence of this ironic stance is evident in the following cleverly staged conversation between the Semitic man and the writer Fairchild. In view of the grotesque dance of Jenny and poor Talliaferro—Faulkner's variant of Eliot's Prufrock persona—the Semitic man displays his cynical view of words as a means of sexual as well as political seduction.

"The illusion that you can seduce women. Which you can't. They just elect you." . . . "And with words, at that," . . . "And you are a funny sort to disparage words; you, a member of that species all of whose actions are controlled by words. It's the word that overturns thrones and political parties and instigates vice crusades, not things: the Thing is merely the symbol for the Word." (130)

"Man is not only nourished by convictions, he is nourished by any conviction." "Do you know who is the happiest man in the world today? Mussolini, of course. And do you know who are next? The poor devils he will get killed with his Caesar illusion. Don't pity them, however: were it not Mussolini and his illusion it would be some one else and his cause . . . And it could be so much worse," he added. "Who knows? They might all migrate to America and fall into the hands of Henry Ford." (131)

The passage, with its cynical reference to Mussolini, which, in hindsight, particularly to an Italian or German, reads like political clairvoyance, was obviously only meant to be an example of the kind of twenties smart talk going on among Julius Kauffman, Sherwood Anderson, Faulkner, and the other members of the group. Nevertheless, the way in which the alienation of language and reality is conveyed by the speakers' flippant association of verbal seduction with the Word of St. John's gospel, and, in turn, of Mussolini's temptations with Henry Ford's, constitutes a brilliant achievement in realistic character portrayal as well as in parodic rendering of the *Zeitgeist*.

If *Mosquitoes* is too theoretical ever to become one of Faulkner's popular novels, for the same reason the book is attractive to critics, because here the reticent writer tells us, albeit in parodic indirectness, what he likes and dislikes in art and artists. As a consequence, readers have begun to realize the depth of Faulkner's involvement with aesthetics, be it the international tradition of bohemianism, the dandy, and the torso or the very new world problem of the great American novel.

While it is true that Fairchild displays essential features of Sherwood Anderson's aesthetics as well as quite a few of his characteristic weaknesses, he should not be regarded exclusively as a portrait of Faulkner's literary mentor. After all, Fairchild, like the other artists in the novel, is a fictional character, also allowing the author to embody certain artistic dispositions and aesthetic tenets of his own. He must be seen in the context of the fictional constellations within this novel, which Faulkner obviously wrote to clarify his vocational and aesthetic goals as well as his artistic potential and the perils of his particular talent. In this respect, Fairchild/Anderson appears, beside the sculptor Gordon, as one of Faulkner's own artistic personae. Many of the issues emerging in the dialogues, such as, for instance, those between the Semitic man and Mrs. Wiseman, his sister, and Fairchild, also concern Faulkner's own position as a young writer. If the criticism that Fairchild's "writing seems fumbling . . . because of his innate humorless belief that . . . life at bottom is sound and admirable and fine" (242) seems a remarkably clear and penetrating analysis of Sherwood Anderson's affirmativeness, one should not overlook that there was also a strong element of affirmativeness in Faulkner, which manifested itself not only in the Nobel Prize speech. However, the essential difference is that Faulkner rarely allowed this personal yearning for "the old verities and truths of the heart" to interfere with and impair his vision as a tragic or ironic novelist.

In several instances, Faulkner makes the Fairchild/Anderson figure the subject of discussions that closely concerned his own aesthetic premises, as, for instance, the debate on the Eurocentric international standards of Emerson and Lowell and the new "Americanness" of American literature (242). Mrs. Wiseman's characterization of Fairchild as "a man of undoubted talent, despite his fumbling bewilderment in the presence of sophisticated emotions" and as "provincial midwestern lower middle class," overestimating education, applies exclusively to Anderson. However, the suggestion that Fairchild should "[get] himself and his own bewilderment and inhibitions out of the way [and describe] American life as American life is" (243) was not only in line with Sherwood Anderson's treatment of his western theme but also with Faulkner's discovery of his "postage stamp of native soil."

At first sight, Gordon, the austere and remote formalist, and Fairchild, the chatty and flabby writer, the character of the one encapsulated in the image of the hawk ("Gordon's hawk's face brooded above them, remote and insufferable with arrogance" [27]) and the other "resembling a benevolent walrus" (33) may seem poles apart, but that should not keep us from regarding them both as Faulkner personae and masks. In fact, a closer look reveals that the sculptor and the novelist appear together in key scenes and constitute a complementary pair representing central features of Faulkner's "dialogic aesthetics." As such, they should be seen in the context of the other twin artists, the skeleton and the Pegasus rider in "Carcassonne" or the commercial artist and the poet in "Artist at Home." Compared with Gordon, the absolute artist, Fairchild, the novelist, is only an artist "when . . . telling about people" (51), as the Semitic man superciliously puts it. In other words, the novelist can never create abstract art as the sculptor or painter can. Faulkner had found that out in experimenting with color patterns in his abortive novel *Elmer*. As the novelist cannot achieve an aesthetic structure apart from content, he, unlike the sculptor, "is not always an artist," the implication being that the superiority of sculpture lies in form in this particular art being realizable independent of thematics.

Seen together, the nonidentical twins Gordon and Fairchild reflect Faulkner's attempt to reconcile the tension between formalism and the "stenographing of human content," the concern emerging as the center of his responses to the various aesthetic concepts of the New Orleans circle. He is fascinated with Gordon, the artist as "shaper," and his work: "forgotten form shapes cunningly sweated cunning to simplicity shapes out of chaos" (47). Yet, at the same time, he and the Semitic man in their dialogue recognize and define Gordon's limitations, the neglect of content and the human dimension: "He ought to get out of himself more," and "It's very difficult for a man like that to establish workable relations with people" (51).

Fairchild, who keeps returning to Gordon's sculpture, remains—like Faulkner—fascinated by the absoluteness of formalist art, but he has learned also, as had Faulkner in creating this persona, that it implies absence of life. Moreover, he knows that the timelessness and immaculate perfection of an aestheticist sculpture is not possible in the modern novel: "I see . . . that you too have been caught by this modern day fetish of virginity. But you have this advantage over us: yours will remain inviolate without your having to shut your eyes to its goings-on" (318). As Gordon is associated with the ideal of art, he appears in the guise of the romantic artist ("o israfel winged with loneliness . . . pride" [187]; "sufficient unto himself in the city of his arrogance . . ." [153]), but that does not make Fairchild, the fumbling, burly, talkative, drunk, and vomiting apostle of life and reality, a less important partner in Faulkner's role-playing and dialogic aesthetics.

In fact, it is not the sculptor but the novelist who is granted the most profound aesthetic vision, one that reaches beyond formalism: "listening to the dark and measured beating of the heart of things" (339), "hearing the dark and simple heart of things" (340). Fairchild, the novelist, enunciates the famous definition of genius as the gift of the visionary who experiences the "Passion Week of the heart" (339):

"It is that Passion Week of the heart, that instant of timeless beatitude . . . in which the hackneyed accidents which make up this world—love and life and death and sex and sorrow—brought together by chance in perfect proportions, take on a kind of splendid and timeless beauty" (339).

Moreover, in the face of a trivialized understanding of art as picture or mimesis ("art: . . . it means a picture" [183]), Fairchild proclaims a universal ideal of craftsmanship: "Art means anything consciously done well, to my notion. Living, or building a good lawn mower, or playing poker"; never mind that, in Fairchild's ludicrous phrasing, Faulkner parodies the faddish adherence of the New Orleans circle to the holistic aesthetics of Ruskin and the arts and crafts movement.

There is no doubt that Fairchild, whether we read him more as a Faulkner persona or more as homage to his mentor Sherwood Anderson, has tended to embarrass proponents of the new, essentially internationalist and modernist Faulkner of the post-Cleanth Brooks era. However, the fact that the subtle discourse-*cum*-Lacanian psychoanalysis narratologists of our time do not much appreciate Fairchild's (the name is indeed telling) naive aesthetics and his peculiar gift of "hearing the dark and simple heart of things" (340) does not exclude the possibility that Faulkner did and that, to some extent, he even identified with it. Moreover, in terms of our overall Faulkner image, it seems worth noting that the affirmativeness in Fairchild's aesthetics of 1927 anticipates the affirmativeness of "the old verities and truths of the heart," in the Nobel Prize speech of 1950, which critics have perhaps too readily put down as a symptom of the drying up of Faulkner's creativeness. That Faulkner in his major novels is a radical questioner and quester should not make us overlook that he is, in many different ways, also a great affirmer, whether we think of Dilsey or Lena, of Aunt Jenny or Miss Habersham. However, the background of the affirmation of old and simple values is a profound sense of insecurity and malaise.

This dilemma, the terms of its diagnosis and the metaphors of its antidote, are relevant in connection with the Fairchild persona. Fairchild's disapproval of Mrs. Wiseman's fin de siècle sonnet and her modernist verse as a "kind of perversion" links its aesthetic "unhealthiness" to a general decay in a manner that makes a German intellectual wince and straightaway think of the Nazi identification of modernist art as "degenerate art." Clearly, the following context is intensely value-charged: "I mean, all modern verse is a kind of perversion. Like the day for healthy poetry is over . . . A kind of sterile race: women too masculine to conceive, men too feminine to beget" (*MOS* 252). Fairchild develops the organicist implications of "healthy poetry" more fully in supplementing the Semitic man's vitriolic critique of Mark Frost's spurious smartness. Again he states the aesthetic problem in sexual terms, and again he invokes organicist metaphors against the shallowness and glibness, inauthenticity and superficial cleverness of the age: " 'Well, it is a kind of sterility—Words,' Fairchild admitted. 'You begin to substitute words for things and deeds, . . . But words brought into a happy conjunction produce something that lives, just as soil and climate and an acorn in proper conjunction will produce a tree' " (*MOS* 210).

In regard to the association of these organicist metaphors with the poetic process and with the particular self-fashioning of the artist, it is of interest that Phil Stone, in his introduction of Faulkner as the poet of *The Marble Faun* ("a man steeped in his native land"), and Faulkner himself,[21] in the roughly contemporary essay "Verse Old and Nascent: A Pilgrimage" (1925), use the same kind of root/soil imagery as the Fairchild/Anderson figure in the novel. The following passage on the South illustrates both the intimate relationship between organicism and regionalism and Faulkner's identification with the Fairchild persona: "The beauty—spiritual and physical—of the *South* lies in the fact that God has done so much for it and man so little. I have this for which to thank whatever gods may be: that having *fixed my roots in this soil all contact, saving by the printed word, with contemporary poets is impossible*" (*EPP* 116, my emphasis).

Given this background and our renewed sense of the historicity of sociocultural contexts, Faulkner's portrait of "Sherwood Anderson" takes on a meaning extending far beyond traditional influence studies and revealing in what sense the Fairchild/Sherwood Anderson figure also functions as Faulkner's persona. "Men grow from the soil, like corn and trees: I prefer to think of Mr. Anderson as a lusty corn field in his native Ohio. As he tells his own story, his father not only seeded him physically, but planted also in him that belief, necessary to a writer, that his own emotions are important, and also planted in him the desire to tell them to someone. Here are the green shoots, battling with earth for sustenance, threatened by the crows of starvation; . . ." (*NOS* 132–33). The humorous, slightly parodic tone does not put in doubt Faulkner's sympathies with Anderson's regionalism. Indeed, the extension of the organicist metaphor shows how unsatisfactory it would be if one were to limit Faulkner's artistic role-playing to modernist personae, such as the late romantic sculptor, Gordon, or the modernist painter, Elmer.

The evidence of his regionalist preoccupation is considerably enhanced by the interview-story "Out of Nazareth," also of 1925, whose hero combines features of Sherwood Anderson and of Faulkner, having a midwestern accent and sharing Faulkner's enthusiasm for the British regionalist poet A. E. Housman: " 'So you are a writer?' he asked me shyly. 'Do you write like this book?' From his sorry jacket he drew a battered 'Shropshire Lad' . . ." (*NOS* 48). That the narrator is a thinly disguised I persona of Faulkner and that his New Orleans *intimus* and travel companion to Europe, Spratling, is also present at the encounter with David ("one could imagine [the biblical] young David looking like that") indicate the projective quality of this portrait of the artist as young middle westerner.

In view of the rich cosmopolitan heritage of Jewish culture, celebrated in "Wealthy Jew," it is not surprising that, in *Mosquitoes*, Fairchild's nationalist-regionalist aesthetics should be attacked *by* Mrs. Wiseman and her brother, the Semitic man. What emerges from the conversation of the Kauffman siblings with Dawson Fairchild (*MOS* 183) is the antagonistic but also complementary relationship between the internationalist-elitist-formalist aspirations and the regionalist/nationalist-populist-organicist tendencies of the twenties. Close attention to the Fairchild persona confirms that he is Sherwood Anderson's rather than Faulkner's spokesman, but it also shows that the author used this figure in dialogically evolving his own modernist version of contemporary regionalism (see chapters 7 and 8).

FOUR

The Artist as "Human Failure"

Mosquitoes, *Flags in the Dust*, *The Town*, and *As I Lay Dying*

Neither Fairchild, the "bewildered stenographer with a gift for people" (51), nor Gordon, the forbidding sculptor of the ideal, has the final word in *Mosquitoes*. The novel concludes with Talliaferro, Faulkner's recasting of T. S. Eliot's Prufrock: "Old, old, an old man before I have lived at all . . . His hair was getting thin . . ." (347). Why should this modernist antihero, miserably impotent in love and art alike, have exercised such a fascination for Faulkner that we find features and traces of him not only in full-fledged poems such as "Love Song" in *Vision in Spring* and "We sit drinking tea" ("The Lilacs") in *A Green Bough* but also in many fragments of the Phil Stone papers?

Clearly Talliaferro/Prufrock embodies the modernist malaise of the artist in the international Waste Land more than he does Faulkner's experience of being different from and inferior to the surrounding southern society.[1] But above all, he serves as a persona projecting individual anxieties about erotic and artistic failings, which one would not expect of a man who engaged in love affairs and made self-confident pronouncements about his writing. His masks and metaphors, however, tell a very different story. Talliaferro is a dilettante who can only talk about art and love. Elmer has as much trouble becoming a painter as he had growing up. The projection of the artist in "Artist at Home" is split between that of a money-making cynic and that of an idealistic fool. Further, Faulkner's preoccupation with dilettantes such as Horace Benbow or with the talkative would-be artists in *Mosquitoes* reflects the artistic anxieties of a beginner with an urge to delimit himself from the amateurish or spurious and define himself as a serious writer. His second-rate drawings and epigonic poems[2] cannot have been very reassuring to the young genius whose untiring copying, dogged stylistic études and remorseless criticism demonstrate that he knew that one day he would do better. Moreover, there are the erotic inhibitions he apparently experienced and which manifested themselves in the grotesque portrait of Talliaferro ("Love was so simple for cats" [*MOS* 345]; "The trouble is, I haven't been bold enough with them" [348]). Faulkner's erotic frustrations and idealistic fantasies, about which we have in recent years learned so much from psychoanalytic feminist criticism,[3] characterize his most important tragic and tragicomic personae, Quentin and Gavin. Along these lines, Talliaferro and Horace Benbow appear as avatars of Faulkner's relentness self-criticism—or, should we say, of his masochistic self-castigation—caused ultimately by his extraordinary desire for motherly attention and approval: "They bear geniuses. But do you think they care anything about the pictures and music their children produce? That they have any other emotion than a fierce tolerance of the vagaries of the child? Do you think Shakespeare's mother was any prouder of him than, say, Tom o'Bedlam's?" (*MOS* 248).

An equally plausible source for his cruel self-caricatures is his sense of an inability to fulfill real and imaginary motherly expectations. Examples of this can be found not only in *Mosquitoes* in Talliaferro's dependence on Mrs. Maurier, and in the relation of mother and son in "The Brooch," but also in Narcissa's and Margaret's sanctions against their brother-sons Horace and Gavin in *Flags in the Dust*, *Sanctuary*, and *The Town*. Characteristically, these pressures and sanctions are in all three cases sexually related and spring from the projected jealousy of the mother-figure. Arising from a different configuration but resulting in a similar dilemma are the instances of the neglected and failing sons Quentin Compson (Polk, *Children*) and Darl Bundren. These are hardly surprising projections by an author whose artistic performance, suicidal suffering and alcoholism show him continuously operating at the brink of overachievement or self-annihilation.

It seems characteristic, in view of Faulkner's preoccupation with the impotent Prufrock/Talliaferro persona, that his own unflattering self-portrait in *Mosquitoes* emerges from a conversation between two young women, Jenny and Pat, who, attractive themselves, are not impressed by any male charms or marks of artistic genius in Faulkner: "Funny man . . ."; "Faulkner? . . . Never heard of him" (*MOS* 144-45). Obviously, this self-portrait belongs with the many examples of artists putting themselves humorously into the picture, or, more particularly, is informed by the prototype of the modernist artist as clown and entertainer. The latter motif, reflecting the alienation of the artist from society in the late nineteenth and early twentieth century, is for this reason fairly common in both the arts and the literature of that period (Hönnighausen, *William Faulkner* 128–53). As tragicomic icon, this model of self-portrait suggests the same remoteness of the artist from society which Faulkner also conveyed through the romantic metaphors of the suffering Christ and of Poe's aloof angel Israfel ("stars in my hair in my hair and beard i am crowned with stars christ by his own hand an autogethsemane carved darkly out of pure space . . . then israfel revolted" [*MOS* 47]). In less metaphoric but equally strong terms, the fifty-five-year-old Faulkner sought to express this gap between art and the middle class in a letter to Joan Williams: "And being an artist is going to be hard on you as a member of the human race. You must expect scorn and horror and misunderstanding from the rest of the world who are not cursed with the necessity to make things new and passionate; no artist escapes it" (*SL* 343). There is no doubt that the role which initially the romanticists had created for themselves for specific historical reasons appeared to Faulkner as the situation of artists of all times and, in a specific sense, his own: the tragedy of the exceptional being who as creator of new and passionate things is isolated from and despised by "the world."

Verbal echoes of Faulkner's early assimilation of the Prufrock persona, not only in *Mosquitoes* and *Flags in the Dust* ("whose hair is thin" [212]; "with a dying fall" [184]) but also in the late novel *The Town* ("space to discard a thousand frantic indecisions" [205]; "filled with a thousand indecisions" [206]), show the author faithfully reproducing identical features of the unflattering Prufrock mask when psychological and sociological reasons, erotic failure and social pressure made him engage in ironic self-portraiture.

As both mask and metaphor are characterized by the outreaching of the identical to the other, closer attention to the indirect and half-conscious modes of metaphoric expression may teach us more about the repetition of psychological patterns and the relations between art and eros, dilettantism, and unrealized love. Attention to the subtle structures and complex contents of the metaphors will show that it will not do to regard Horace and Gavin simply as caricatures of Faulkner's dilettantish friend Phil Stone, whose mentorship the author had quickly outgrown. One may wonder whether Faulkner's distorted embodiments of his vocation, in Horace and Gavin, evolved more from the writer's exposure to the uncongenial southern milieu (Grimwood 77–83) or in line with the international situation which made many artists of the time choose the clown as their favorite persona. In any case, the portrayal of these "weak artistic types" as clowns, as self-castigating masks, did help him to exorcize psychological problems and artistic uncertainties of his own.

In contrast to these psychological aspects of Faulkner's poetics, the related social satire in the poetological metaphor in *Flags in the Dust* has so far received little attention. But the caricatural features in the appearance of Mrs. Marder suggest that her defense of Horace as a poet really indicates the social irrelevance of the artist. This impression is confirmed by Horace's ensuing self-deprecatory commentary and the withering comparison of the poet with Caesar as the great man of action:

> "Horace is a poet," the other woman said in an admonitory tone. Her flesh draped loosely from her cheek-bones like rich, slightly soiled velvet; her eyes were like the eyes of an old turkey, mucous and predatory and unwinking. "Poets must be excused for what they do."

> "The law, like poetry, is the final resort of the lame, the halt, the imbecile and the blind. I dare say Caesar invented the law business to protect himself against poets." (*FD* 199)

The modes of Horace's characterization indicate that we must conceive of Faulkner's several masks not so much as rigidly independent round characters but as multiform, shifting, and interrelated verbal patterns, demanding of readers a flexible response. In this day and age, which has exchanged the holistic ideals of New Criticism for those of "marginality" (Derrida) and "dialogic imagination" (Bakhtin), readers will come to accept side by side the several masks of Horace both as lover of the narcissistic ideal and as degraded husband resembling Joyce's Leopold Bloom. Similarly, attention to the imagery will make them experience Gavin both as artist subject to "the chewed anguish of the poet's bitter thumbs" and as God-like creator ("yourself detached as God himself" [*T* 316]) of Yoknapatawpha. In this respect, it is hardly surprising that, in the conception of both the Horace and the Gavin figures, the author seems to have relied on several other prototypes besides Prufrock. Horace is a superb caricature of a literary poseur ("The meaning of peace, he said to himself again, releasing the grave words one by one . . ." [*FD* 184]) and has a blasé quality which Faulkner, like many other writers of the twenties, saw embodied in the dandies and artistic dabblers of the late romantic era. Gavin Stevens displays the predilection of the Eliot generation for John Donne, but, in his amatory dealings ("playing the fool because of her to notice, buffoon for her" [*T* 89]), he resembles the self-deprecatory lover of Edmond Rostand's romantic play *Cyrano de Bergerac*. Rostand's comedy, like the *Don Quixote* of Cervantes, characteristically another favorite book of Faulkner's, is a parody of chivalrous love worship. Faulkner, who, for all his affairs, hardly strikes one as being the paragon of a successful lover, shows a peculiar fascination with a type of idealistic hero whose goal is not consummation but continued worship (Roberts).

What Horace and Gavin have in common, and what they in turn share with both Don Quixote and Cyrano, is that they are not only failed lovers but also failed poets. The nature of Horace's pseudopoetic outburst ("still borne aloft on his flaming verbal wings . . . touched her face again with his hands after that fashion of a child" [*FD* 180]) is effectively brought home to readers by its being registered from Narcissa's detached viewpoint: "His voice became unintelligible, soaring into phrases which she did not herself recognise, but from the pitch of his voice she knew were Milton's archangels in their sonorous plunging ruin" (*FD* 180). Faulkner was all too aware of the dangerous proximity between the *furor poeticus* and the empty poetic gesturings of the dilettante, and we may see in Hightower's fatal imaginative outbursts psychological and artistic anxieties which the author tried to hide from himself and his critics by the defiant gesture of the genius always sure of himself. The following passage from Horace's "musing in metaphors" (*FD* 339) demonstrates how conscious this Faulkner persona was of the ironic posture of the *poet as liar* (Baudelaire, Nietzsche, Oscar Wilde, and William Carlos Williams) and, more important, of the problematics of autobiographical projection: "The pen ceased, and still poised, he sought the words that so rarely eluded him, realizing as he did so that, though one can lie about others with ready and extemporaneous promptitude, to lie about oneself requires deliberation and a careful choice of expression" (*FD* 399).

The tensions between personal pressures and the pains of the artistic "raid on the inarticulate" emerge impressively when we look at the late prose of *The Town* where the imagistic and the reflexive interpenetrate in a unique mode of expression that, despite putting off superficial readers, remains one of Faulkner's most original attempts to rescue the American novel from the dearth of Dreiser's naturalism. Chapter 5 of *The Town* unveils the inner relationship between psychology and literature in posing, right at the outset, the central aesthetic issue of the poet's relation to reality ("poets . . . are not really interested in facts; only in truth . . ." [*T* 88]), and then moves on to reveal, in the encounter with Eula, Gavin's sexual fears (the leitmotifs of the "blue envelopment" and of "the cold cloud lean[ing] in" [90-96]) as well as his attempts to outplay them in grand metaphoric gestures (Wagnerian passages) and in his mannered combinations of reflective and imagistic elements.

In the nervous seesawing of Gavin's Prufrockian style ("No: that's wrong . . . dont dare to hope, you are afraid to hope. Not afraid . . . but . . ." [*T* 88]), the image of "the frail web of bone and flesh snaring . . ." stands out as a metaphoric focus, establishing an overall metaphoric context, but without itself being imagistic. This image of the frustrated lover seeking to "ensnare" his boundless idealistic visions ("snaring that fragile temeritous boundless aspirant sleepless with dream and hope—cannot match it" [*T* 88]), which in itself is not very strongly visualized, becomes even more formulaic by being repeated twice, thus enhancing the vague and abstract quality characteristic of Gavin's style and his dilemma. It is all the more startling when the hero, suddenly expanding this imagistic formula "frail web of bone and flesh" into a whole metaphoric scene, portrays himself as the loving father and his fearful erotic vision as his baby: "peace in which to coddle that frail web and its unsleeping ensnared anguish both on your knee and whisper to it: There, there, it's all right; I know you are brave" (*T* 88). The sudden and vivid concreteness of this sentimental situation produces a manneristic quality that forcefully impresses on readers the bitter self-irony with which the speaker is ridiculing his attitudinizing as an erotic visionary. Associated with the sentimental vision is the word "peace" ("peace in which to coddle"), recognizable as a key word by its repetition.

This peace for which Gavin yearns is of the false and fatal kind, manifesting itself in *Flags in the Dust* in Horace's "decadent" vision of Oxford ("a perfect life, . . . into which the world's noises came only from afar" [191]), and, above all, in the association of his art and love (*"four mishaps* and . . . one *almost perfect vase . . .* called *by his sister's name"* [190, my emphasis]) with the image of an uncannily attractive cage: "At times he found himself suddenly *quiet,* a little humble in the presence of the happiness of his *winged and solitary cage.* For a *cage* it was, barring him from freedom with trivial compulsions; *but he desired a cage. A topless cage,* of course, that his *spirit* might wing on short excursions *into the blue,* but far afield his spirit did not desire to go: its direction was always *upward* plummeting, for a plummeting fall" (*FD* 191, my emphasis).

The cage, reminiscent of romantic metaphors for the poet as a "Poor captive bird! who, from thy narrow cage, / Pourest such music" in Shelley's "Epipsychidion," returns as a local leitmotif at the end of *Flags in the Dust.* There it occurs, at first pathetically, in Horace's letter to Narcissa and then, parodically, in the satiric scene in which the aesthete has to tote his weekly load of ill-smelling shrimp for Belle from the station: "But not those who carry *peace* along with them as the candle-flame carries light. I have always been *ordered by words,* but now it seems that I can even restore courage to my own cowardice by cozening it a little . . . But you will have served your purpose anyway, *thou still unravished bride of quietude. Thou wast happier in thy cage, happier?* Horace thought, looking at the words he had written and in which, as usual, he was washing one woman's linen in the house of another" (*FD* 398–99, my emphasis).

117

The peace which Horace finds so reassuring in his sterile relationship with Narcissa, and which he misses when he has allowed himself to be dragged into the "dirty and trivial" affair with Belle, is, as the highlighted phrases in the passages above suggest, a state in which the absence of erotic fulfillment constitutes the condition for the presence of poetic elevation. What makes this state so attractive to both Horace and Gavin is that their peculiar imaginative transcendence in idealistic sublimation also implies for them freedom from the threat of sexuality. After Temple Drake's account, in *Sanctuary*, of the psychoanalytic metamorphoses accompanying her rape, Horace Benbow, mindful also of Popeye's sexual problems and of his own daydreaming of Little Belle, is overcome by the death wish: "Better for her if she were dead tonight, Horace thought, walking on. For me, too. He thought of her, Popeye, . . . Removed, cauterised out of the old and tragic flank of the world" (*Sanctuary* 221). Nevertheless, sexual anxieties, despite all escapist efforts, prove persistent, in the early as in the late novel. In the passage quoted above we catch the sinister overtones of sexual fear and a latent suicidal urge in "the upward plummeting, for a plummeting fall" of the idealist poet all the better if we recognize the repetition compulsion and the symbolism of the fact that Horace, Gavin and the Quentin Compson of *The Sound and the Fury* all love—and suffer from having—*motherly sisters*.

This view of the hero of *Flags in the Dust* is enhanced by metaphors in which Horace's art work, associated with the love of the siblings, appears overshadowed by the association of sex and death in the presence of Belle as a femme fatale:

> At times the dark lifted, the black trees were no longer sinister, and then Horace and Narcissa walked the road in sunlight, as of old. Then he would seek her . . . bringing her the result of his latest venture in glassblowing . . . in his sooty hands in which the vase lay demure and fragile as a bubble . . . But then the dark would descend once more, and beyond the black and motionless trees Belle's sultry imminence was like a presence, like the odor of death. (*FD* 227–28)

> It was like a road stretching on through darkness, into nothingness and so away; a road lined with black motionless trees O thou grave myrtle shapes amid which Death. A road along which he and Narcissa walked like two children drawn apart . . . And somewhere, everywhere, behind

> and before and about them pervading, the dark warm cave of Belle's rich discontent and the tiger reek of it. (*FD* 223)

The tiger motif, associated with Belle, also plays a prominent role in Horace's affair with Belle's sister Joan, one of the sections discarded in the condensing of the novel. One can understand that Ben Wasson removed this episode for too closely doubling the thematics deployed in Horace's relationship with Belle, but the very repetitiveness of the Joan section is of interest to my line of argument as showing the author's urge to repeat the same psychological pattern. Faulkner, whose psychoanalytical interests are evidenced by Freudian touches in works as diverse as *Elmer* and *Light in August*, makes Horace introduce the leitmotif of the tiger, associated with Joan, as a revealing childhood memory ("He was five years old . . . his first circus . . . he raised his head and found a tiger watching him" [*FD* 341]). What seems more impressive than the traditional motif content tiger, cat-femme fatale (Baudelaire, Wedekind, et al.) is the young author's handling of it. In this early novel he employs a new metaphoric strategy of varying over a stretch of ten pages (*FD* 340–50) one basic metaphoric formula: "tiger, cat: lazy contemplation . . . calm lazy contemptuousness . . . carnivorous . . . cavernous . . . pink tongue, pink gullet." As a result the straightforward narrative takes on a metaphoric coloring which in turn causes the key words to affect the reader as much by a peculiar iconic quality as by their actual meaning. The constitution of this Faulkner mask through the metaphorization of the narrative provides a new kind of reading experience. Readers have to approach this type of fiction with the kind of attitude they would adopt in approaching poetry.

What makes a comparison with *The Town* relevant at this point is that Gavin's scene with Eula in chapter 5 features the same theme of sexual fear ("peace" and "serenity" are again key words [90, 92]) as Horace's account of his relation to Joan in *Flags in the Dust* and, in rendering it, displays the same kind of metaphorization of the narrative context. The considerable difference, however, lies in its much more intense degree of metaphorization. The leitmotif of the "blue envelopment," Gavin's fear of being "enveloped by Eula's blue eyes" (*T* 90–96), involves readers more radically than the motif of the tiger in Horace's memory of Joan, for both narrative and stylistic reasons.

The imagery in *Flags in the Dust* appears in a flashback of a fairly detached third-person narrative, while, in *The Town*, it is dramatically presented from Gavin's first-person point of view. The syntax in which the feline imagery emerges in *Flags in the Dust* is relatively balanced and orthodox, with the imagistic elements standing out as clearly recognizable units.

In contrast to Horace's more subdued tone of report and reflection, the lively oral quality of Gavin's discourse and the disturbed syntax characteristic of it cause the imagistic element to scatter, so to speak, over the whole passage, thus leading to a much more dynamic exchange between the metaphoric and the nonmetaphoric parts in the sentence. The dramatization of metaphor is both the distinctive stylistic feature and the essential theme of the passage. Gavin, in excitedly transforming observation (blue eyes) into imagery ("blue sea . . . blue envelopment" [92]), manifests himself not only as the fearful and evasive lover but also as a poet who uses the deferment of erotic fulfillment, the absence of love, to create the metaphoric presence of his poetic prose. The following passage shows that in doing so Gavin shares Faulkner's special stylistic gift of maneristic ingenuity as well as his urge to exorcize his fatal idealism by the distortive effect of his humorous imagery: "In fact I might have said she stood almost eye to eye with me if she had looked at me that long, which she did not: that one quick unhasting blue (they were dark blue) envelopment and then no more; no more needing to look—if she ever had—at me, but rather instead one single complete perception to which that adjective complete were as trivial as the adjective dampness to the blue sea itself; that one single glance to add me up and then subtract and then dispense as if that calm unhasting blueness had picked me up whole and palped me over front and back and sides and set me down again" (*T* 90).

Gavin, after magnifying the blue of Eula's eyes and metaphorizing it into the blue of the sea, attempts to express the inexpressible completeness of her "overpowering view" of him, by comparing the insufficiency of the term "complete" to that of "dampness" in defining the majestic sea. Then, nervously seeking a more appropriate metaphoric expression for her mythic superiority, itself the product of his creative imagination, he briefly interrupts his elaboration of the sea imagery by an abrupt and ironic shift to that of accounting (add, subtract, dispense), only to return in a detailed and comic anthropomorphism to Eula as a metaphoric sea picking him up, palping him over and setting him down again. What affects sensitive and intelligent readers of the passage is not only the content but the structure of the sea image in its expression of Gavin's sexual fears. He comes to realize that both the degree of imaginative elaboration of the grotesque leitmotif "blue envelopment like the sea" (92–93, 94–95) and the comic incongruities occurring in the process serve to characterize the dilemma of the hero as erotic idealist.

We should try not only to capture the effect of the persistent return to the core of the motif ("blue envelopment" suggests a force that is aloof and engulfing in a Freudian sense) but also to register the implications of the variations. In this context, the juxtaposition of allusions (Wagner, Prufrock's and Quentin's drownings), syntactical patterning, verbal content (waiting, calm, unfathomable), and audio-visual effects (watching, waiting) engages readers in symbolistic experiences. Gavin's excited syntax and his highly intelligent but erratic manner of metaphorical thinking are no less relevant in his role as idealistic lover and poet than the choice of words which his imagination makes for its metaphoric transformations. Finally, in gauging the effect of the synaesthetic leitmotif "blue envelopment" on readers, we should stress that it functions both as a parallel and counterpoint to the ludicrous action of the scene: Eula, Gavin's immortal beloved and Manfred de Spain's mistress, offering herself to Gavin "because he is unhappy" and Gavin, like Cyrano, failing to grasp this opportunity:

> I to be swept up as into storm or hurricane or tornado itself and tossed and wrung and wrenched and consumed, the light last final spent insentient husk to float slowing and weightless, for a moment longer during the long vacant rest of life, and then no more.
>
> Only it didn't happen, no consumption to wrench, wring and consume me down to the ultimate last proud indestructible grateful husk, but rather simply to destroy me as the embalmer destroys with very intactness what was still life, was still life even though it was only the living worm's. (91)

The passage, characteristic of Faulkner's unique poetic prose in which metaphor and reflection have become one, is no less characteristic in its answering an idealistic upward surge ("swept up as into storm") with a humorous countermovement ("Only it didn't happen, no consumption"). The concluding image ("embalmer . . . destroys with very intactness") opens a window onto the relationship between the psychological and the poetological aspect of Gavin as a mask of the writer. There is a negative and self-denigrating quality ("life even though it was only the living worm's") which is related to the suicidal and regressive urge as it emerges, for instance, in *The Sound and the Fury*. In this respect, the notion of "this embalmed life" reminds one as much of the negative aspect of virginity in *The Sound and the Fury* as of the "little life with dried tubers" in Eliot's *The Waste Land*. But there is also, as signalled by the striking structuring of the metaphoric content ("as the embalmer *destroys* with the very *intactness* what was *still life*, was *still life*" [my emphasis]), in the sinister term "embalmer," a suggestion of the preserving and "immortalizing" character of art as Faulkner had found it in his favorite Keats poem: "She cannot fade, though thou hast not thy bliss." Tragically (or ironically), Gavin's decisive weakness, his tendency to "spend too much time expecting" (*T* 94), and the resultant absence or deferment of erotic fulfillment, are also—as in the love scene of Keats's "Ode on a Grecian Urn"—the prerequisites for the presence of art.

Gavin's actual encounter with Eula, in which he reacts to the proffered favors of his beloved in a travesty of Christ's rejection of Mary Magdalen: "Dont touch me!" (*T* 93, 94),[4] undercuts the Swinburnian sound, the synaesthetic metaphors, and the whole operatic eroticism of his Wagnerian visions of her:

> . . . who should have moved like Wagner: not with but *in* the sonorous sweep of thunder or brass music, even the very limbs moving in tune with the striding other in a sound of tuned wind and storm and mighty harps. (*T* 89)

> But there was only the blue envelopment and the fading Wagner, trumpet and storm and rich brasses diminuendo toward the fading arm and hand and the rainbow-fading ring. (*T* 95)

Nevertheless Eula's urgent advice, "Dont waste time expecting" (94), "Stop being afraid of things" (95), does not fail to impress Gavin, and it makes him address the psychological problem that seems to be the cause of his metaphoric escapes—and of Faulkner's creation of such personae as Gavin or Horace. But, again ironically, this occurs in another exercise of his imagination: " 'So if I had only had sense enough to have stopped expecting, or better still, never expected at all, never hoped at all, dreamed at all, if I had just had sense enough to say *I am, I want, I will* and so here goes—If I had just done that, it might have been me instead of Manfred? But dont you see? Cant you see? I wouldn't have been me then?' No: she wasn't even listening: just looking at me: the unbearable and unfathomable blue, speculative and serene" (94). What Gavin is grappling with is his difficulty in establishing his identity through love and the encounter with the other, and, as his reference to Manfred and the return to his mythic vision of Eula herself humorously demonstrate, his compulsive role-playing and mask-bearing. The metaphors, "the cold invisible cloud leaning in again," leave no doubt that Gavin's role-playing, for all its humorous caricature, reflects a deadly serious game of the artist.

The study of Horace Benbow and Gavin Stevens as masks of the artist has revealed recurring major psychological patterns. To gain insight into Faulkner's participation in dominant international traditions and his use of central sociocultural themes of his time, one has to consider his fascination with history. After all, Quentin, one of his most important heroes, "was not a being, an entity, he was a commonwealth. He was a barracks filled with stubborn back-looking ghosts" (*AA* 9). In this obsession with the past, Quentin in *Absalom, Absalom!* is a characteristic southern hero and closer to the European than to the American mind, which tends to regard history as the fulfillment of a utopian vision rather than as a dilemma and an object for guilty reflections.

Obviously, one of the reasons for Faulkner's intense awareness of the importance of history is that he received his most important and seminal impressions at a time of great sociocultural changes in his family and his region as well as in the national and international world. As a writer, Faulkner experiences history concretely as family and regional history. Ike McCaslin's expiatory reconstruction of the fatal racial heritage from the plantation ledger (*Go Down, Moses*), and Aunt Jenny's retelling and glorifying family history (*Flags in the Dust*) are two of the many different projections of the author's own attitude toward the past. What characterizes his experience of the past in all these novels is that it holds no hope for the present and future. In fact, a closer look at Faulkner's fascination with family history reveals that it is in part a fascination with the experience of the decline of aristocratic families and their culture: the Sartorises, the Compsons, the Sutpens, in the last resort, the Falkners. A consciousness of decadence pervades Faulkner's rendering of family history and particularly of a type of hero that emerges as a persona of the artist in *Flags in the Dust*, *The Sound and the Fury*, *Sanctuary*, *Light in August*, and *Absalom, Absalom!*

Interestingly, Faulkner is far from alone among writers of the late nineteenth and early twentieth century in his preoccupation with the decadent aristocrat as a persona of the artist. In this regard, Thomas Mann's *Buddenbrooks*, a novel Faulkner had called "the greatest novel of this century" (*LiG* 49), constitutes a striking parallel to *Flags in the Dust* and *The Sound and the Fury*. Like Thomas Mann, Faulkner was very much attracted by the delicate sensibility of the fin de siècle. Moreover, his own social environment, the southern predilection for aristocratic role-playing (Gray, *Life* 2), its crisis at the rise of the rednecks and the waning political and sociocultural supremacy of the planter class, and, last but not least, the case of his own family explain why he should be interested in the theme of decadence. The goal of the following section is to examine Horace and other Faulkner characters as personae of the artist, particularly the decadent sensibility and related phenomena such as the split personality and the sibling motif. In this, Thomas Mann's *Buddenbrooks*, suggesting the international context, will prove a helpful subtext, demonstrating that Faulkner, in choosing the decadent aristocrat as persona, was following not a private nostalgia for a past order but critically responding to a major problem of his time. In the context of international cultural developments from romanticism through modernism, decadence appears as a major aesthetic concept.[5] The decadent aristocrat or aristocratic bourgeois as literary type of the fin de siècle reemerges as persona of the modern artist or as sensitive dilettante, as Hanno Buddenbrook or Horace Benbow. Apparently, the decline of the family firm, its disappearance as a factor in the respective local contexts, became for both Thomas Mann and William Faulkner the occasion of expressing their sense of the more far-reaching sociocultural changes of their time. It certainly made both writers open up more readily to the influence of a tradition of cultural pessismism that, running counter to nineteenth century progressivism, emerges in many different national variants, including such seminal texts as Arthur Schopenhauer's *The World as Will and Representation* (1819), Max Nordau's *Degeneration* (1892-93), and Oswald Spengler's *The Decline of the West* (1918–22).

As the end of the Buddenbrook dynasty clears the arena for the fatal ideological visions which in Mann's *The Magic Mountain* will bewilder poor Hans Castorp, the decline of the Sartoris and the Compson families appears as a tragic prelude to the arrival of the shabby new South of the Snopeses. In view of the demagoguery and brutal vulgarity of the emerging period of Hitler, Mussolini, Franco, and Stalin and their more local and less fatal American variants, Bilbo, Vardaman, Russell, and Huey Long, it seems hardly surprising that sensitive young artists like the Mann of *Buddenbrooks* and the Faulkner of *Flags in the Dust* should have celebrated their family history as the waning of aristocratic culture. Nevertheless, there is, at the center of both their family novels, a profound sense of conflict between deep-rooted loyalties to the aristocratic culture of their family and class and their equally pronounced awareness of differing from its values and traditions.

There was every reason why both Mann and Faulkner should develop a penchant for delicate heroes like Hanno Buddenbrook or Quentin Compson, for decadent and artistically sensitive siblings such as Siegmund and Sieglinde Aarenhold (Thomas Mann, "Wälsungenblut"), Horace and Narcissa Benbow. After the brashness of the Gilded Age and the *Gründerjahre*, in a milieu in which the Herman Hagenströms and Flem Snopeses counted for more than budding writers from decaying old families, Mann and Faulkner understandably affirm that the emergence of an artistic sensitivity in upper-middle-class business families is tied to the mellowness of decline. The concomitant aristocratic and decadent features are complementary and are used by the writers to symbolize the positive and negative aspects of their aesthetic and their societal experiences. Themes and motifs such as music and writing in *Buddenbrooks* or the identification of Horace's dilettantish art work with his incestuous love for his sister Narcissa in *Flags in the Dust* play themselves out against a background of sociocultural change.

Both Quentin Compson and Bayard Sartoris come, as Hanno Buddenbrook says, "from a family that has gone to rot" and share his death wish ("people should simply give up on me . . . I have so many worries, and it's all so difficult" [*Buddenbrooks* 772]). Both Senator Buddenbrook's Schopenhauerian pessimism ("Was not everyone a mistake, a faux pas?" [682]) and Mr. Compson's decadent cynicism ("no battle is ever won . . . They are not even fought" [*SF* 93]) create a deadly ambience for their sons. In a letter to his brother Heinrich (February 13, 1901), Mann, at this point the successful author of *Buddenbrooks*, speaks of "really severe bouts of depression with serious plans to do away with myself" (qtd. in Kurzke 14). Similar tendencies in Faulkner are latent but to the psychologist apparent enough. The sibling motif, with its aspects of doubling and splitting, of mirroring and distorting, illustrates well that narcissism in its psychological as in its aesthetic aspect plays a major role in Mann's and Faulkner's art and their stylized life. It is striking that, among the several masks they assume, both authors showed a marked predilection for the dandy and for the aristocrat, and that distance governed their social relations.

What the masks of dandy and dilettante, decadent and aristocrat have in common is that they imply roles allowing writers to gain the detachment, apparently necessary at the time, to establish their narrative discourse. This need to create distance would explain Thomas Mann's Goethean aloofness as well as Faulkner's privacy and anonymity complex, his notorious silences and his withdrawals into drinking.[6] Thomas Mann's Tonio Kröger offers pertinent reflections on the subject of the distance of the artist which constitute at the same time a crucial text on role-playing and the aesthetics of role-playing: "It is essential to be something extra-human and inhuman, and to stand in a strangely remote and distanced relationship to humanity in order to have the ability and the inclination to play it, play with it, and portray it effectively and tastefully. The talent for style, form and expression presupposes this cool and fastidious relationship to humanity, even a certain impoverishment and desolation of one's own human nature" (99). Isolation and narcissism then, even if they imply dangerous, potentially deadly withdrawal, regression, appear as the prerequisite of art.

There are several reasons why Mann and Faulkner, like other artists of their time, should each have been so strongly attracted by his family history. It was historically remote, yet of immediate autobiographical relevance, offering them the opportunity to identify with as well as distance themselves from the past. Furthermore, Mann and Faulkner discovered—or created—in their family histories certain recurring patterns, such as the configuration of the hostile brothers, suggesting the "eternal recurrence of the same." It is not only the ambiguity of their own individual psyches but also this more widespread sociocultural conflict that drives them to reactivate a major motif-complex of late romanticism and the decadence: that of the hostile siblings and the *Doppelgänger* or counterself.[7] The parallel between *Buddenbrooks* and *Flags in the Dust* in this regard is twofold: the analogy between the brothers Thomas and Christian and Bayard III and John III and the prefiguration of these two pairs in the ancestral pairs Jean and Gotthold and John I and Bayard I. What characterizes all four pairs is the hostile or negative quality of their relationships, the hostile or absent brother embodying the repressed antiself. This is forcefully impressed on the reader in Bayard's nightmare:

> Buddy breathed on in the darkness, steadily and peacefully. Bayard could hear his own breathing also, but above it, all around it, enclosing him, that other breathing. As though he were one thing breathing with restrained laboring, within himself breathing with Buddy's breathing; using up all the air so that the lesser thing must pant for it. Meanwhile the greater thing breathed deeply and steadily and unawares, asleep, remote; ay, perhaps dead. Perhaps he was dead, and he recalled that morning, relived it . . . and saw his brother's familiar gesture and the sudden awkward sprawl of his plunging body as it lost equilibrium in midair . . . seeking his brother who in turn was somewhere seeking him, never the two to meet. (*FD* 314–15)

In *Flags in the Dust* the traumatic consequences eventually leading to Bayard's alienation from home and to his death surface in the subsequent identity crisis. The uncanny atmosphere, *das Unheimliche* (Freud), emerging from the visionary setting and style of this scene and conveying the shock of Bayard's doubling and split of personality, makes this night scene at the McCallum farm a key to the understanding of the various other pairings in both Faulkner and Mann. What both Buddenbrook brothers experience and what they share with Faulkner's suicidal Bayard Sartoris is the disturbed relation of identity and otherness reflecting the sociocultural tension between

127

their bourgeois heritage and the artistic sensitivity of modernism. The motif of the twin brothers in *Buddenbrooks* and *Flags in the Dust* arises from the self-disgust and self-hatred characteristic of the late romantic/early modernist artists, of Baudelaire's *"L'Héautontimorouménos"* and the Prufrock figures of Eliot and Faulkner.

In view of the psychoanalytic dimension of the sibling motif, it is not surprising to find a similarly complementary relationship existing between Bayard Sartoris and Horace Benbow. Their juxtaposition and the symmetrical arrangement of the two plotlines evolving from them make it the more apparent that their double portrait contains the complementary features of one split personality. Bayard is a disturbed man of action, and Horace is an aesthete and dabbler in art, but both are decadent aristocrats. Bayard's cold violence and obsession with suicidal speed reflect the same sterile and deadly narcissism which surfaces in Horace's aestheticism, and one has no difficulty in interpreting Bayard's mad stallion ride and suicidal flying, as well as Horace's ineffectual glassblowing and furtive eroticism, as satiric projections of Faulkner's own antagonisms.

Considering Mann's and Faulkner's treatment of the sibling motif in connection with the experience of dominant mothers and absent fathers may help us to understand how in narrative discourse incestuous love between brother and sister comes to figure as a complement both to the antagonism between brothers (Thomas and Christian, Bayard and John, Jewel and Darl) and to the homoerotic relationship between friends (Hanno and Kai, Henry Sutpen and Bon).[8] Faulkner's preoccupation with the relation of strong sisters and weak brothers may be explained in terms of the strong attraction to his mother, the incest taboo, and consequent revision and displacement. A corresponding example in Thomas Mann to Faulkner's pairings or doublings of Narcissa-Horace, Caddy-Quentin, Margaret Mallison-Gavin Stevens is the incestuous love between the Aarenhold twins in "Wälsungenblut."

These parallels enable us to recognize in the structure of this configuration, in the coincidence of fatal attraction and essential narcissism, aspects of meaning which the motif of the siblings of different genders shares with the motif of the antagonistic brothers and with the motif of homoerotic friendship. The triangular relationship of the Sutpen siblings (Judith-Henry-Bon) in *Absalom, Absalom!* illustrates particularly well that the many variants of the sibling motif share one distinctive feature: they all symbolize the ambiguity of a desire for union which, although powerfully felt, must not or cannot be fulfilled (on account of socioreligious codes and the incest taboo). The sensibility of the Usher siblings, of Mann's Wälsungen, Siegmund and Sieglinde Aarenhold, yet also of Horace and Narcissa Benbow and Quentin and Caddy, may be a sign of decadence, but it is also what makes them special. Without the decadent sensibility and reflexivity preceding Quentin's suicide in *The Sound and the Fury*, he could not experience his resurrection in *Absalom, Absalom!* as the avatar of the modern narrator. In view of the sibling motif, one obviously has to widen the concept of doubling beyond Irwin's original meaning to do justice to the variety of expression which Faulkner gave the archetypal motif of the twins and the two friends or the mythic sister and brother relationship. The situation in *As I Lay Dying* where the antagonism of the brothers Darl and Jewel, the potential artist and the man of action, is juxtaposed with the problematic relationship of son and mother (Darl and Addie) demonstrates once more how subtly aesthetics and psychology in Faulkner's personae fuse.

Drawing inspiration from these psychoanalytic images in the study of the masks and metaphors of Faulkner's aesthetics ("It's a kind of dark thing . . . Freud and these other—" [*MOS* 248]), the portrait of the dying mother, Addie Bundren, in *As I Lay Dying*, can be recognized in the contours of an artist persona. However, her particular features emerge only fully when we study the heroine not merely by herself but also as a component in a constellation of characters, above all as a complementary projection to that of Darl, the most imaginative of her sons.

From one perspective, Addie belongs to the type of powerful mother figures in Faulkner of whom Noel Polk (*Children*) has made us aware. Moreover, reading her in terms of Judith Wittenberg's (*Transfiguration*) and Nancy Chodorow's (*Reproduction*) psychoanalytical approaches (cf. Lind, "Mutual Relevance" 32–39), we are able to experience her implications both as one of the several "male feminizations" (Frann Michel) in Faulkner and as a metaphoric projection of Maud Falkner's son trying to come to terms with the separation anxiety of his childhood. In conceiving of Addie and Darl as another complementary pair of personae, I am not suggesting that they should be simplistically taken as impersonations of Maud and her son William. Addie appears as both a reflection and a metaphoric transposition of Faulkner's experience of his mother and as marking psychologically and artistically an intermediary stage toward the male feminizations which Frann Michel (5–20) derives from male disempowerment in the twenties.

That it is indeed justified to consider Addie in this context can be seen from a striking parallel, in the only slightly later novel *Sanctuary*, in Temple Drake's male role-play. In her retelling, to Horace Benbow, of the night of horror at Frenchman's Bend, one of Faulkner's strikingly original explorations of the psychoanalytical repercussion of terror and rape, Temple mentions first how "I'd try to make like I was a boy" (*Sanctuary* 216), and then, after an intermediate stage of the "queen locked up with an iron belt" (217), draws a very vivid imaginary picture of a sadistic schoolteacher, resembling Addie—"in this passage Temple *becomes* Addie" (Polk, *Children* 36–37)—whom she in turn replaces by a father figure ("an old man, with a long white beard" [220]). There is a similarity in the traumatic father experience of Addie and Temple (but also of Quentin and Faulkner), and, moreover, there is the author's masochistic/sadistic invention of letting both women strive, by sadistic suppression of their students, to arrogate paternal power and, reflecting their inventor's anxieties, to leave the male disempowered: "then I was teacher in school and it was a little black thing like a nigger boy, kind of, and I was the teacher . . . So I was an old man, with a long beard, and the little black man got littler and littler" (220).

As one of Faulkner's "male feminizations" Addie is also herself depicted as imaginatively and erotically involved in unfulfillable relationships with the absent, with her students, with her trivial lover Whitfield, with her dumb husband, Anse, and ultimately with her cynical father. In regard to her function as one of Faulkner's artist personae, it is important to realize that Addie's frustrated love life corresponds with her skepticism about language, her experience of its insufficiency to communicate and to capture reality. Strangely enough, the negative implications of the symbolic title *As I Lay **Dying*** have so far received little critical attention.

Addie's status as absent mother and her inability to communicate with her students other than through sadistically punishing them seem to have originated under the impact of her life-denying father, whose nihilism corresponds with that of the father of another auto-biographical projection, Quentin Compson:

> I could just remember how my father used to say that the reason for living was to get ready to stay dead a long time. And when I would have to look at them day after day, each with his and her secret and selfish thought, and blood strange to each other blood and strange to mine, and think that this seemed to be the only way I could get ready to stay dead, I would hate my father for having ever planted me . . . My father said that the reason for living is getting ready to stay dead. (*AILD* 114, 118)

> It [the watch] was Grandfather's and when Father gave it to me he said, Quentin, I give you the mausoleum of all hope and all desire; . . . Because no battle is ever won he said. They are not even fought. The field only reveals to man his own folly and despair, and victory is an illusion of phi-losophers and fools. (*SF* 76)

Addie's negative artistic credo, "that living was terrible . . . that words are no good; that words dont ever fit," that words are a substitute for unlived life and absent reality is apparently connected to the persona of idealists Horace Benbow and Gavin Stevens. Here in *As I Lay Dying*, Faulkner captures the impossibility of communicating with others and of capturing life in words in the bitterly ironic image of the spi-ders: ". . . we had had to use one another by words like spiders dan-gling by their mouths from a beam, swinging and twisting and never touching, and that only through the blows of the switch could my blood and their blood flow as one stream. I knew that it had been, not that my aloneness had to be violated over and over each day . . . [Anse] had a word, too. Love, he called it . . . I knew that that word was like the others: just a shape to fill a lack; . . ." (115–16).

Addie's sadism makes it appear justified to relate the frustrating spider image from *As I Lay Dying* to the spider image in *Mosquitoes* with its femme fatale connotations. Obviously, both the spider image in Addie's sadistic reflections and the sadistic spider image in *Mosqui-toes* are projections of male anxiety distorting female sexuality. Equally important, both adumbrate metaphorically the aesthetic key issues of communication and expression. "The female is the larger, and when the male goes to her he goes to death: she devours him during the act of conception. And that's man: a kind of voraciousness

131

that makes an artist stand beside himself with a notebook in his hand always, putting down all the charming things that ever happen to him, killing them for the sake of some problematical something he might or he might not ever use" (*MOS* 320).

If "the dungeon was Mother herself" (*SF* 173), it is little wonder that the writer appears as transvestite and deadly female spider. The fact that we can also observe a fusing of the artistic with the voyeuristic and sadistic in "Artist at Home" confirms that we are indeed encountering behind several masks and metaphors a recurring psychoanalytic pattern. How intimately the aesthetic is interwoven with the experience of a disturbed sexuality becomes apparent when we witness Addie's imaginatively killing and re-creating Anse as "word": "Then I believed that I would kill Anse . . . He did not know that he was dead, then . . . and I would think: Anse, Why Anse. Why are you Anse. I would think about his name until after a while I could see the word as shape, a vessel, and I would watch him liquefy and flow into it like cold molasses flowing out of the darkness into the vessel, until the jar stood full and motionless: a significant shape profoundly without life like an empty door frame; and then I would find that I had forgotten the name of the jar. I would think: The shape of my body where I used to be a virgin is in the shape of a   and I couldn't think *Anse*, couldn't remember *Anse*" (116–17).

Again the image of the vessel, which in chapter 3 I discussed in connection with the shaping power of the artist as maker of a vase or urn and as symbolic expression of Faulkner's obsession with female sexuality, plays a major although somewhat different role. Addie, the artist as murderous transformer, metaphorically dissolves Anse's substance, observing how his depersonalized ("liquified") being flows into the emptiness of a mere name. What is new and original in this impersonation of the artist is that a disturbed sexuality expresses itself in her aesthetics and in a *nominalistic* quality of words: words are nothing but words and do no longer refer to substances conveyed through their metaphoric "liquefaction." Faulkner's artistic achievement lies in communicating this subtle psychoanalytic and aesthetic experience to the reader in very concrete, regionalistic terms: "cold molasses flowing." The jar standing "full and motionless"—and reminding one of Wallace Stevens's remarkable "jar in Tennessee"—suggests the uncanny identity of the perfection and the deadliness of

132

art before it transforms itself, in ways characteristic of Faulkner, into the iconic metaphor of female sexuality ("The shape of my body where I used to be a virgin is in the shape of a   " [117]).

That it is indeed appropriate to consider Addie not only as the mother of the Bundren family but also as an instance of "male feminization" and another of Faulkner's artist personae is confirmed by her reusing the metaphor of the wild geese, one of Elmer's central images of idealistic and narcissistic yearning. In *Elmer*, Faulkner's early fragment of an artist novel, the leitmotif-complex "keen bitter *blue*, heard geese *lonely and high, clean again*" (370) emerges in a contrapuntal development against the burgeoning artist's traumatic experience of sex. The young painter's decision, "He was through with women . . . He'd just be Elmer and paint pictures" (370), indicates the psychological origin of the narcissistic persona of the artist, throwing light on Faulkner's heroes, from the marble faun through the Quentins and Darl to the celibate Gavin Stevens.

The geese that Addie hears mark an important transitory stage in this development. In her case, the motif of the geese seems related to the motif of the spring and the experience of narcissistic reflection as well as cleansing after her sadistic encounter with her students. In the course of Addie's development, the motif of the geese (117) and its transmutation, "forlorn echo of the dead word high in the air" (118), gets caught up in the tension between the inarticulateness, "the dark land," of instinctive love and the narcissistic idealism of erotic refusal when the word appears as dead and nominalistic:

> instead of going home I would go down to the hill to the spring where I could be quiet and hate them. (114)

> I would lie by him in the dark, hearing the dark land talking of God's love and His beauty and His sin; hearing the dark voicelessness in which the words are the deeds, and the other words that are not deeds, that are just the gaps in people's lacks, coming down like the cries of the geese out of the wild darkness . . . (117)

> . . . in order to shape and coerce the terrible blood to the forlorn echo of the dead word high in the air. I just refused [Anse], just as I refused my breast to Cash and Darl . . . hearing the dark land talking the voiceless speech. (118)

If Faulkner, in an act of psychoanalytic justice or revenge, makes Addie, the matriarch of the Bundren family, represent the crisis of

133

the skeptical verbal artist, he lets her son Darl display his powers of morbidly close observer and of visionary "painter and sculptor." Addie's skepticism in regard to words and communication corresponds with her impaired ability to love. In turn, this absent maternal love stimulates Darl's powerful verbal imagination to the extent that he is exiled by his family as a madman. It is characteristic that his plastic imagination manifests itself particularly poignantly in his jealous admiration and mythologizing of his brother and counterself Jewel.

> With tossing mane and tail and rolling eye the horse makes another short curvetting rush and stops again, feet bunched, watching Jewel . . . Save for Jewel's legs they are like two figures carved for a tableau savage in the sun. (*AILD* 9)

> They are like two figures in a Greek frieze, isolated out of all reality by the red glare. . . . We watch through the dissolving proscenium of the doorway . . . the rain of burning hay like a portière of flaming beads, . . . so that he appears to be enclosed in a thin nimbus of fire. . . . This time Jewel is riding upon it [their mother's coffin], clinging to it, until it crashes down and flings him forward and clear . . . (149–50)

In contrast to Darl, who is marginalized and—as so many artists have been in modernism—finally exiled as mad, Jewel appears (in Darl's view) as a man of action and like one of the mythic heroes of ancient Greece: in the last of the quoted passages, Jewel emerges as triumphantly rescuing their mother's coffin and thus frustrating Darl's emancipatory attempt to burn it. However, it is Darl, the "madman" and compulsive maker of metaphors ("tableau savage," "torsos," "two figures in a Greek frieze"), who emerges as an artist of Faulkner's kind.

Metaphorizing and Role-Play in Narration and Reading

New Modes of Metaphor

The Sound and the Fury, Light in August,
and *A Fable*

In chapters 3 and 4, images of the artist have confirmed the profound affinity between masks and metaphors suggested by the introductory chapters on role-playing in photographs, letters, and interviews and also posited by the theoretical chapter. The analogy between the role-playing artist and the reader, who participates in the metaphorizing process, lies in the fact that both engage in an act of the imagination whose object is nothing less than to negotiate the tension between identity and difference.

As this *playful transcendence* is subject to the different historical conditions of each period—those of the twentieth century have been sketched in our reflections on theory—its manifestations are as various as the different historical art forms. The interest of our time in analogies between masks and metaphors and in identity as context-dependent has arisen with the emergence of openness as the dominant aesthetic category. Connected with this is the replacement of the work as ruling poetological metaphor by the image of the illimitable text. In turn, the reader reenacting the metaphorizing of the writer must exercise as flexible an imagination as the role-playing author.

This chapter, deriving its inspiration from the new aesthetics and the corresponding new sensibility, is dedicated to a study of what were considered in the early twentieth century new modes of metaphor. In the case of *The Sound and the Fury*, we shall focus on structural aspects of transcendence in metaphorizing; in the examples from *Light in August*, we shall explore the metaphor-creating tension between the realistic surface and its psychoanalytic implications; and finally, in *A Fable*, we shall study transcendence in allegory and in other modes of metaphorizing.

Our new sense of the text in its intertextuality and its contextuality also alerts us to a wider concept of metaphoricity, making us realize that the allusiveness of the titles *The Sound and the Fury* and *Absalom, Absalom!*, as well as the time shifts or the changes of narrators in these "open" novels, involve readers in an activity similar to the transfer within metaphor. Moreover, the new concept of discourse provides a much more comprehensive view than the traditional one of metaphor as either a rhetorical figure or an image content.

Readers, in realizing that the title of Faulkner's *The Sound and the Fury* is a partial quotation from Shakespeare's *Macbeth*, engage in a transgression between two contexts. The difference between the transfer in a metaphor and the transfer involving a quotation, however, lies in the fact that, in the latter case, readers are not faced with an imaginary but with a given context demanding of them a specific historical and stylistic consciousness. Accordingly, the experience of quotations produces a different, more detached attitude in readers than that of ordinary metaphors. One might say, in Wolfgang Iser's terminology, that metaphors, constituting wider "gaps," challenge readers to a more intense and less preordained imaginative activity than quotations. As we shall see, the time shifts in *The Sound and the Fury* appeal to readers in a similar way as quotations and metaphors. In both cases, readers create links between two different contexts and in doing so are aware, as in role-playing, of the fictive or imaginary nature of this transcending or linking (Iser). In doing so, they fulfill an essential prerequisite of metaphoric transfer.

The perspective of narrative openness and fictional context switching also throws new light on the metaphoric quality of well-known stylistic features of the several Compson stories. Thus, in the Benjy section, the absence of logical and temporal organization in the stream of consciousness of the retarded hero produces a distortion of perception that facilitates the metaphorization of reality. As a result, the mirror, the fighting, and the fire, to which Benjy keeps referring, without relating them "properly" in a causal, spatial, or temporal manner, take on the peculiar suggestiveness of Jungian dream images: "we could see Caddy fighting in the mirror and Father put me down and went into the mirror and fought too. . . . They were all out of the mirror. Only the fire was in it. Like the fire was in a door" (79). This effect is enhanced by the repetition of the motif after a brief shift from November 1900, the time when Benjy's name is changed from Maury to Benjamin, to April 7, 1928, the period of the telling of the story: "*You can look at the fire and the mirror*" (80). There are, on three pages (79–81), five shifts back and forth between 1900 and 1928, and what has been said about the complex "fighting-fire-mirror" also applies to the recurrence, after time shifts, of other phrases such as "hear the roof" and "cut up all Benjy's dolls" (79, 81, 82).

While the *metaphorical content* of motifs such as fire and water, Benjy's renaming, and his castration (anticipated in Jason's cutting up of Benjy's dolls) have received due attention, the equally important *structural aspect* of the metaphoricity emerging from the narrative mode has not. But the different ways in which Faulkner employs time shifts—their frequency and duration no less than their verbal texture—condition the metaphorization processes readers engage in. The eight shifts of time on two other pages (87–88) and the resulting segments, all short and of a factual nature, do not inspire readers to any clearly focused metaphorization, but, in forcing them to negotiate between the different time levels, provide the intense experience of a ruptured and metaphorically reestablished fictional reality. The intervals in the stream of consciousness make readers engage in imaginative transfers between the two contexts: between the child Caddy and her daughter Quentin, between the boy and the adult Jason, between the "unchanged" Benjy and Dilsey.

The Quentin section of *The Sound and the Fury* begins with three paragraphs that, in moving away from the present to the past, from realistic perceptions of passing time to the deadly cynicisms of what the father said, forecast the suicide of the hero. The narrative development of the novel, in other words, is adumbrated by the similarity of the structure of the first three paragraphs. They relate two contexts, of which, in the metaphoric experiences of readers, the second—that of the absent father inverting the values of the chivalrous South and orthodox Christianity—comes to overlay the first—that of the son relinquishing his hold on reality.

> When the shadow of the sash appeared on the curtains it was between seven and eight oclock and then I was in time again, hearing the watch. It was Grandfather's and when Father gave it me he said, Quentin, I give you the mausoleum of all hope and desire. . . . Because no battle is ever won he said. They are not even fought. The field only reveals to man his own folly and despair, and victory is an illusion of philosophers and fools.

> It was propped against the collar box and I lay listening to it. . . . then in a second of ticking it can create in the mind unbroken the long diminishing parade of time you didn't hear. Like Father said down the long and lonely light-rays you might see Jesus walking, like. And the good Saint Francis that said Little Sister Death, that never had a sister.

> Through the wall I heard Shreve's bed-spring . . . Father said that. That Christ was not crucified: he was worn away by a minute clicking of little wheels. That had no sister. (*SF* 93ff.)

The structure of metaphoric transfer helps to integrate the sociocultural theme of the disappointed southern idealist turned nihilist and the psychological theme of the repetition compulsion apparent in the insistently returning father and sister motifs. This metaphoric deep structure plays an important role in grounding readers' experiences of the metaphors emerging at the verbal surface: the realistic "shadow of the sash" whose metaphoric quality is confirmed by its repetition in the third paragraph; the heirloom watch that appears as the "mausoleum of all hope and desire"; the painterly vision, alliteratively emphasized, of a receding figure of Christ ("down the long and lonely light-rays"); and the parody of his salvation ("[Christ] worn away by a minute clicking of little wheels").

The two phrases "that had never a sister" and "that had no sister," concluding paragraphs two and three respectively, illustrate once more that the traditional meaning of the term *metaphor* is only of limited use in assessing the metaphoricity of narrative contexts. The phrase is basically a nonmetaphoric statement. What makes it metaphoric is the suggestiveness arising from its repetition and its ambivalent semantic relation to the rest of the passage. Ostensibly, "no sister" refers to St. Francis, whose "sister" is metaphoric in nature; it may also refer to Shreve and other college friends who have no sisters. But, in the metaphoric context and in the open space of Faulkner's syntax, "no sister" becomes, as it were, a Freudian image for Quentin's troubled relation to Caddy.

As this first example has shown, the gaps in the Quentin section, demanding of readers that they engage in imaginative transfers, are as extensive and frequent as they are in Benjy's narrative. But the important point is that they are of a different kind and consequently have a different effect on readers, eliciting a different response from them. Moreover, in assessing the impact of the imagery in the Quentin section, we should—as our next example demonstrates—allow for a wide variety of metaphoric modes as well as for different degrees of intensity of the metaphoric transfer.

> A sparrow slanted across the sunlight, onto the window ledge, and cocked his head at me. His eye was round and bright. First he'd watch me with one eye, then flick! and it would be the other one, his throat pumping faster than any pulse. *The hour began to strike.* The sparrow quit swapping eyes and watched me steadily with the same one until the chimes ceased, as if he were listening too. Then he flicked off the ledge and was gone. It was a while before the last stroke ceased vibrating. It stayed in the air, more felt than heard, for a long time. Like all the bells that ever rang still ringing in the long dying light-rays and Jesus and Saint Francis talking about his sister. *Because if it were just to hell; if that were all of it. Finished. If things just finished themselves. Nobody else there but her and me.* If we could just have done something so dreadful that they would have fled hell except us. *I have committed incest I said Father* . . . (*SF* 97–99, my emphasis)

It is probably the reoccurrence of the leitmotif "the hour began to strike" that makes readers begin to realize that this apparently straightforward description of the sparrow on the window ledge is really *metaphoric*. But the metaphoric process thus initiated is then considerably extended. One is struck by the smallness of the sparrow, the uncanny, pathological preciseness of Quentin's perception of the bird's behavior. His concentration on detail is expressive of his inability to organize a comprehensive, integrative view of life. The anthropomorphic vision of the sparrow "as if he were listening too" is suggestive of Quentin's isolation. Time is registered in terms of the sparrow's movements and final departure. The synaesthetic metamorphosis "more felt than heard" announces a change in Quentin's mental state: he becomes excited, he drifts off, his associations start getting tangled and confusing for readers. At the same time, the synaesthetic crossing over or metamorphosis "more felt than heard" signals and prepares for the generalizing shift caused by the motif "Like all the bells. . . ." Verbal leitmotifs demand of readers a special mode of negotiating between several contexts and establishing metaphoric relations. In the development of leitmotif-chains, the phenomenon of repetition, the subject of Richard C. Moreland's *Faulkner and Modernism*, is as important as Iser's gaps. Given the obfuscated temporal and spatial organization in the stream-of-consciousness novel, these recurring words or phrases of leitmotifs have an important function as a structuring device. A particularly interesting example of this is the leitmotif "gray" in *The Sound and the Fury*.

Readers, led on by the ostinato of the color gray, experience its frequent recurrence within a limited space (pages 149–57) and the implications of the sameness and difference of the collocations. In the reading process, we register synaesthetic clusters ("the gray it was gray with dew slanting up into the gray sky" [153]) and crossovers of the gray light, the gray honeysuckle, the gray grass, and the gray dew (150, 154, 155, and two times on 157). However, in the reading process, readers are exposed not only to the groundswell of these synaesthetic transfers but also to the poignancy of metaphoric foci expressly introducing into the nature scenery the theme of mutilation and death: "the ditch was a black scar on the gray grass" (153) and "outside the gray light the shadows of things like dead things in stagnant water" (157). The result of the experience of this metaphorized context or of the metaphorizing reading experience is our increased awareness of the symbolic relationship between the color gray and the fate of the hero.

However, what keeps us from putting Quentin's fate down as just an individual case of adolescent suicide is another act of metaphorizing reading, in which we relate the synaesthetic symphony in gray, with its thematic focus mutilation and death, to grandfather's watch as "the mausoleum of all hope and desire," and to the battles that, according to the decadent heir of the chivalrous southern tradition, "are not won and not even fought" (97). Indirectly, Quentin's tragedy demonstrates the sinister effect of southern myths on family relations, the perverseness of his erotic idealism appearing as the counterpart and consequence of fatal cultural patterns such as the cult of the sexless southern lady. More specifically, his suffering and suicide reflect on his father, whose cynicism is a means for masking his disillusion with the false political idealism of the South and the socioeconomic dilemma of the outgoing planter class. In negotiating the gap between the two contexts, we establish a metaphoric relationship between the melancholy impressionism of the nature scenery and the sociopolitical background surfacing in Mr. Compson's cynicism. From this perspective, the symphony in gray appears as the metaphorical echo of a specifically southern tragedy.

The example of the symphony in gray and its combination with historical references shows that in the adequate response to the pattern of gaps and repetitions and the metaphoric experience of leitmotifs, memory plays an important role. The role of an imaginatively active memory in the metaphoric experience is particularly important in regard to the sphere of intertextual relations and the metaphorization involved in quotation and allusion: the phrase in the passage from *The Sound and the Fury* (97–99) discussed above—"if it were just to hell; if that were all of it . . ."—sounds like a vague and juvenile reminiscence of the more impressive ramblings of Shakespeare's *Hamlet*, another great suicidal hero. The expression "finished," combined with it, seems to refer to Christ's famous last words on the cross. Readers' metaphorizing memory makes them ironically associate Quentin's suicide with Christ's salvational death and thus realize the full measure of the novel's modernist despair. Clearly, the metaphoric transcending taking place when readers experience structural features such as time shifts and leitmotifs ("gray") demands of them a reenactment or form of "role-play" other than that involved in linking the surface and deep structure of psychoanalytical metaphors.

I propose to discuss as examples of the particular experience of psychological metaphors some passages from the Joe Christmas plot-line in *Light in August*, because their psychological content has been clearly established in an impressive body of recent research, particularly by feminist critics.[1] Images, metaphors, and also irony play a major role in psychoanalytic theory. In fact, because of the dominance of the concept of transference, psychoanalytic theory might altogether be regarded as a theory of metaphor or mode of metaphoric thinking, continuing in a modified form the comprehensive role of allegory from the Middle Ages through the seventeenth century. The point of similarity between medieval allegory and the metaphorics of psychoanalysis is that both constitute systems of ordering experience by relating it to levels of otherness containing the real but hidden—in any case more profound—"meaning" (Hönnighausen, *Faulkner's Discourse* 3–54).

However, in the present study, the focus will not be on the transformation of the *contents* of psychoanalytic images, but on how their *forms* in given Faulkner texts might affect readers, or, more basically still, how readers can recognize their specific appeals and adequately respond to them. For instance, the leitmotif *"Something is going to happen to me. I am going to do something"* (475, 486) in chapter 5 of *Light in August*, presenting Joe before the murder, signals *aboulia* or will-lessness, thus suggesting a context in which readers are likely to encounter psychoanalytical imagery. Although they have no difficulty following Joe's actions in every detail, they will note that all his movements are rendered in such a way as to give them a nonrational somnambulistic quality. Even those readers who do not immediately associate Joe's cutting off the buttons on his clothes (477) with the cutting of all female contacts and his symbolic self-castration are aware of the suicidal antifemininism[2] of his iconic key phrase *cut off*: "With his pocket knife and with the cold and bloodless deliberation of a surgeon he would cut off the buttons which she had just replaced" (477).

There are metaphorized sentences that in their syntactical clearness echo the clearness of the allegorical act. But, more often, the metaphoric leitmotifs undergo modulations that—thanks to Faulkner's unique verbal genius—convey indirectly the complexity of Joe's violent and confused sexuality, its erotic trance and perverse liberation, through the finessing of sensuous acoustics and anthropomorphic images: "Edgewise it struck the remaining button a light, swift blow. The dark air breathed upon him, breathed smoothly as the garment slipped down his legs, the cool mouth of darkness, the soft cool tongue" (477).

The kind of metaphorizing in which readers in these instances participate is of a tentative, groping kind, but there is no doubt that both the vocabulary ("gutter filth . . . thick still black pool") and the acoustic emphasis on the keywords "watch, whispering, water" a bit earlier in the scene, turn Joe's act of self-observation into a sinister encounter with his wraith: "he appeared to be *watch*ing his body, seeming to *watch* it turning slow and lascivious in a *whispering* of gutter filth . . . a *thick still black* pool of more than *water*. He touched himself . . ." (477, my emphasis). That Joe's act of self-observation does indeed imply narcissist preoccupation with an infantile self and a deadly split personality or doubling (Irwin) is confirmed by the insistent, modernist metaphor of the emerging photo print: "He watched his body grow white out of the darkness like a kodak print emerging from the liquid" (478).

Readers, who in *Go Down, Moses* have been witness to Ike McCaslin's confrontation with the intertwining and doubling of his black and white family tree (Williamson 22–32), understand what drove Faulkner to dramatize in Joe Christmas the tragedy of the mutually reflective but irreconcilable black and white self and antiself. They will know why in *Absalom, Absalom!* the fatal flaw of Sutpen's design and the evolving tragic identity crisis is both social and psychic, and derives as much from the inability to integrate the black and the white soul of the South as from Faulkner's individual family dilemma (Bleikasten, "Fathers" 133–35).[3]

In *Light in August*, the social drama of race and gender flares up in dramatic acts, such as when Joe, after cutting off all the buttons on his clothes and exposing his nakedness, provokes the white occupants of a passing car (" 'White bastards!' he shouted. 'That's not the first of your bitches that ever saw . . .' "), or when, in the Freedman Town episode, his awareness of black female power escalates and turns into panic. What, in these instances, makes Joe's exhibitionist act emerge as a symbolist epiphany or later, in the Freedman Town episode, keeps his hysterical flight from becoming melodrama, is the rich metaphoric contextualization of the narrative.

145

As from the bottom of a thick black pit he saw himself enclosed by cabin-shapes, vague, kerosenelit, so that the street lamps themselves seemed to be further spaced, as if the black life, the black breathing had compounded the substance of breath so that not only voices but moving bodies and light itself must become fluid and accrete slowly from particle to particle, of and with the now ponderable night inseparable and one. He was standing still now, breathing quiet hard, glaring this way and that. About him the cabins were shaped blackly out of blackness by the faint, sultry glow of kerosene lamps. On all sides, even within him, the bodiless fecundmellow voices of negro women murmured. It was as though he and all other manshaped life about him had been returned to the lightless hot wet primogenitive Female. He began to run, glaring, his teeth glaring, inbreath cold on his dry teeth and lips, toward the next street lamp. (483)

In the "Augusttremulous lights" (484) of this scene, key word repetition ("black pit . . . black life, the black breathing . . . blackly out of blackness"), and imagist acoustic clustering, intensified in compound forms ("fecundmellow voices of negro women murmured"), function contrapuntally with the clear and simple action ("standing still now . . . glaring this way and that . . . He began to run, glaring, his teeth glaring"). The experience of such a metaphorized context in which space and action lose their surface solidity enables readers to transcend the realistic topography and to transform it into a symbolist landscape of the social and individual subconscious ("bottom of a thick black pit") and of atavistic gender antagonism ("he and all other manshaped life about him had been returned to the lightless hot wet primogenitive Female"). Furthermore, these parts of the narrative, which can only be assimilated if read connotatively as poetry, affect readers' perceptions of other so-called realistic scenes. In fact, their psychoanalytic metaphors tend retroactively to influence readers' memory of scenes which at the time may have appeared to them only as part of a straightforward narrative.

The suggestive stillness of the Edward Hopper-like scene ("standing outside the barbershop, looking through the window at the man whom he had taken for a partner" [482]), and, above all, the recurring mirror scenes begin in retrospective rereading to display fully the psychoanalytic symbolism of their deadly narcissism: "Nailed to the wall was a shard of mirror. In the fragment he watched his dim face as he knotted his tie" (479); "Kneeling beside the spring he shaved, using the water's surface for glass, stropping the long bright razor on his shoe" (480). When readers reencounter this leitmotif towards the end of the novel ("But it is still too dim to see his face clearly in the water, so he sits beside the spring and waits until he can see better" [647]), they have been exposed, in Hightower's story as well as in Christmas's, to many instances of southern self-contemplation, and, through the interplay of metaphors, have been confronted with forms of deadly narcissism, inaccessible in direct speech:

> . . . he appeared to be *watching his body, seeming to watch . . . whispering* of gutter filth . . . *thick still black* pool of more than *water.* He touched himself . . . (477, my emphasis)

> He watched his body grow white out of the darkness like a kodak print emerging from the liquid. (478)

In some cases, as at the beginning of chapter 6, the first of the flashback chapters, readers are even alerted to the psychoanalytic dimension of the narrative by direct announcement of the famous formula "Memory believes before knowing remembers" (487) and its variants (505, 507, 568). However, this sentence should not be read as an abstract philosophical proposition since it straightaway reveals itself a verbal leitmotif, undergoing ingenious musical as well as intellectual modulations: "Believes longer than recollects, longer than knowing even wonders." Moreover, initiating one of the processes of Faulkner's characteristic *metaphorizing thinking* or *thinking in metaphors*, this philosophic and, at the same time, iconic motif introduces the hero characteristically "like a shadow . . . quiet as a shadow." The iconic memory-definition initiates the remembrance of a specific real corridor, but it also calls up in readers, alerted by the metaphorics of chapter 5 ("Something is going to happen"), the psychoanalytic connotations of the corridor image, particularly since the word is repeated four times on the first page alone.

What follows is the *ur*-scene (the coupling of the dietitian and the doctor, respectively, little Joe's surrogate enjoyment of the phallic toothpaste and his trauma of deferred punishment), which, because of an unfortunate tradition of reductive reading of the psychological content, is rarely given its due as an artistic achievement. We appreciate the performative power of Faulkner's prose when we expose ourselves to its rhythm and acoustics, to its alliterations and compound forms and, above all, when we do not substitute the experience of metaphor by a Freudianizing allegory of its abstracted theme. The verbal leitmotifs "clean" and "polish," in what purports to be a straightforward description of the Presbyterian Sunday in the McEachern household, because of their repetitions, their negative contextualization, and acoustic-thematic interlacing ("*polished* . . . would *p*olish . . . dull *p*atches . . . the *p*olish . . . a *P*resbyterian catechism" [507, my emphasis]) tend to lose their originally positive meaning and, especially through this inversion, reveal metaphorically the sociopsychic origins of Joe's trauma. Joe appears as "a Catholic choir boy" (509) and "with a rapt, calm expression like a monk in a picture" (509) while he is beaten by McEachern for not learning his catechism. Ironically, McEachern, the exponent of Presbyterianism, is characterized by exactly the same inverted Catholic imagery. Faulkner's satire of the role of religion in southern culture could hardly be more devastating. By combining psychoanalytic imagery of male paralysis and isolation with inverted religious similes, Faulkner makes the scene of Joe's corporal punishment metaphorically reveal that the hero as murderer and martyr is a reaction to the dilemma of the rigidly patterned pre-civil rights South as a white, male, puritan culture: "Perhaps he was thinking then how *he and the man* could always *count upon one another, depend upon one another*; that it was the *woman alone who was unpredictable.* . . . McEachern did not rise. He *still sat, stolid and rocklike*, his shirt a white blur in the door's black yawn. 'I have milked and fed,' he said. Then he rose, *deliberately*. Perhaps the boy knew that he already held the strap in his hand. It *rose and fell, deliberate, numbered, with deliberate, flat reports*. The *b*oy's *b*ody might have been *wood or stone; a post or a tower* upon which the sentient part of him mused like a *hermit, contemplative and remote with ecstasy and selfcrucifixion*" (516–17, my emphasis).

As in these perverted rituals of male dominance—the pendant scene to McEachern's beating of his son is that in which Joe knocks down his adoptive father with a chair (550)—metaphor plays an essential role in the respective rituals of male mythicization of woman.

In the ensuing discussion, we shall focus only on some ideological aspects of *metaphoric form*, since Doreen Fowler and Noel Polk have already convincingly dealt with the psychoanalytic *content*. However, I should mention in passing that such scenes as Joe's washing of his hands in the blood of a sheep (535)—to exorcize his hysterical horror at ordinary facts of female biology—are characterized by the obtrusive ritualization and myth making (Igor Stravinsky, T. S. Eliot, and John Steinbeck) that was part of the modernist period style.

More revealing in regard to the psychoanalytical motives of Faulkner's role-playing are the involved and mannered metaphorics conveying Joe's shock at the supposed contradictions of female nature, "the smooth and superior shape in which volition dwelled doomed to be at stated and inescapable intervals victims of periodical filth" (535), especially if we relate the fear and sadistic perversion of Joe's sexual encounter with the "womanshenegro" (leitmotif: "kicked her. He kicked her hard, kicking into . . . hitting at her . . . striking at . . . enclosed by the womanshenegro and the haste" [514]) to the southern cult of ideal womanhood (Scott; Roberts) and its refractions in Faulkner's autobiographical masks: Quentin, Horace, and Gavin.

The respective ambivalences appear encapsulated in the surrealistic, de Chirico-like vision of "suavely shaped urns in moonlight" from which "issued something liquid, deathcolored, and foul" (538). The metaphorics in this passage illustrate well the particular challenges readers have to meet in encountering psychoanalytic imagery, e.g., in the case of the surrealistic passage of the cracked urns. The scene is concrete and detailed. However, the meaning of all the clearly depicted details is anything but clear and rational. Readers, in trying to make sense of the scene, have to bring to bear outside information (e.g., the knowledge of Freudian or Jungian imagery) on the iconography of the cracked urns. In this, the only criteria to guide their choice of interpretative aids and associations are the dreamlike, nightmarish mood of the scene and the antagonism between the surface beauty of the "suavely shaped urns in moonlight, blanched" and the more powerful impact of their cracked state and the "issuing deathcolored and foul liquid." The shape of the urns puts one in mind of that very famous Grecian one in Keats's ode that had become the chief icon of Faulkner's aesthetics and was so much in his mind that he even used it in a rather surprising manner in *Light in August*, giving timelessness to the regionalist context of Lena Grove and the Mississippi mule wagons: "like something moving forever and without progress across an urn" (404). That Faulkner would use the same symbol as icon of his sexual trauma and of his art throws light on both his role-playing and his aesthetics.[4]

In the famous "the dungeon was Mother herself" passage (Polk, *Children* 32–40), the context (the memory of a picture in one of his children's books), the dreamlike quality of the images and the motif content (she was "never a queen or a fairy . . . always a king or giant") suggest to readers the psychoanalytic dimension of these images. Again, our interest is not in the particular psychological *content* of the imagery, the painful remoteness of the parents, or the striking mother-complex, but in the *stylistic features*, marking them as psychoanalytic. "When I was little there was a picture in one of our books, a dark place into which a single weak ray of light came slanting upon two faces lifted out of the shadow. *You know what I'd do if I were King?* she never was a queen or a fairy she was always a king or a giant or a general *I'd break that place open and drag them out and I'd whip them good* It was torn out, jagged out. I was glad. I'd have to turn back to it until the dungeon was Mother herself she and Father upward into weak light holding hands and us lost somewhere below even them without even a ray of light. Then the honeysuckle got into it" (*SF* 215).

Perhaps the surest signs that the reader's transcendence here must indeed be that between surface and psychoanalytic deep structure are the rhetoric of anamnesis ("When I was little") aided by the stream-of-consciousness style, the interpretive stance of the narrative voice ("she never was . . . she was always"), and, finally, the sadism suggesting Addie's in *As I Lay Dying* and the sense of urgency in the reenactment of the childhood experience: "*I'd break that place open and drag them out and I'd whip them good* It was torn out, jagged out. I was glad."

In its prototypical use of Christ's Passion story and its tendency toward moral and sociopolitical allegory, *A Fable* testifies to the spirit of the thirties and the wartime trauma of the forties—with the didactic juxtaposition of simple country life and evil military apparatus recalling the affirmative post office art of the Works Progress Administration. This dimension of *A Fable* will remain foreign to readers expecting the subtle exploration of streams of consciousness as in *The Sound and the Fury*, the sophistication of self-reflexive narrative as in *Absalom, Absalom!*, or the rich regionalism in *The Hamlet*. Rather, readers reenacting this allegorical "transcendence" in *A Fable* have to draw on their ability of didactically rationalizing its biblical Passion story and of intellectually appreciating its sociopolitical satire.

In *A Fable*, Faulkner, visibly under the impact of World War II, portrays a triangular tension between the authoritarian power structure of the military regime, the idealistic rebellion of the individual, and the shifting loyalty of the passive crowd. Given the potentially traumatic development of this power triangle, he affirms his own brand of existentialist stoicism and a patriotic belief in the basic rightness of the ordinary American people. However, neither the formulation of the dilemma nor the affirmation of values comes across easily in the Christian imagery, so that the most convincing scenes are those in which he digresses the furthest from the biblical prototype. However, what is of interest in connection with our inquiry into the modes of Faulkner's metaphor is that the typological use of the Passion Week as the structuring pattern of *A Fable* affects not only the development of the theme but also the novel's style and its impact on readers.

Obviously, *A Fable* aims neither at the excitement of psychological exploration nor at narrative suspense. Like mystery plays, moralities, and political parables, it comprises a series of didactic units or stations, unfolding not in narrative progression but like *tableaux vivants* or film stills. Their sequence clearly is determined by abstract considerations. This holds true even for those episodes which are not modelled on the typological pattern, such as the marshal's conversations with the quartermaster, with Marthe, and with the corporal, or the Gragnon and Levine episodes. Within a typological system, the arrangement of single episodes is not a matter of the artist's imagination but of moral purpose. It is this that gives *A Fable* its rigid and contrived quality. The dilemma becomes apparent in Faulkner's own schematic comments on the allegories of moral consciousness which he sees in *Moby-Dick* and which he claims to have depicted in *A Fable:* ". . . the trinity of conscience: knowing nothing, knowing but not caring, knowing and caring. The same trinity is represented in *A Fable* by the young Jewish officer . . . the old French quartermaster . . . and the English battalion runner" (*LiG* 247). Of course, some of this abstractness disappears in the actual novel, but the tendency towards calculating and contriving an allegorical master plan manifests itself in a system of multiple, essentially static symmetries and in purposeful parallels and contrasts: the savior-like features of father and son and the pageantry of the introductory and concluding tableaux in Chaulnesmont and Paris.

Readers react to a structure of stationary panoramas and typological design with a specific response. They are not carried along by a flowing narrative; instead, they are exposed, as in a series of monumental murals, to the iconic language of didactic tableaux, at times reflecting and rationally allegorizing, at times sensuously and only half-consciously registering the symbolic implications. It is this demand for a shifting sensibility and a flexible response to shifting metaphorizing attitudes that apparently has been too great a challenge for many critics. Since diverse typological relationships and a number of the telling names (De-mont or Mor-ache) can indeed be deciphered with some intellectual ingenuity, such critics feel tempted to devise a total allegorization of the work. But Faulkner's *A Fable* is not Spenser's *Faerie Queene*. The novel's finest sections, which probably *are* the crowd scenes, inspired by films like Eisenstein's *Potemkin* (1925), the theater of Erwin Piscator, and Faulkner's own Hollywood experience, reveal themselves more readily to a sensitive apperception of their image patterns. Even in these multivalent, sensuous contexts, however, readers are often expected to engage in the discursive metaphorizing of allegory (for instance, the child's appropriation by the evil "messenger" Angelique). Such "vacillations" between allegoric and symbolic transcending and linking of contexts place high expectations on the flexibility of readers' aesthetic sense.

In some of the most convincing tableaux and panoramas of *A Fable*, Faulkner has created a new medium hovering between novel, essay, and prose poem, a medium which recalls the American novel Faulkner admired most, *Moby-Dick*. Chapter 7 of *A Fable*, for instance, consists almost exclusively of tableaux and panoramas focusing on the crowd and the marshal. The opulent decor of a rococo boudoir, "princely insensate opulence," unfolds symbolically in a sentence bursting with the terminology of interior decoration: "In fact, it had been merely a boudoir back in the time of its dead duchess or marquise, and it still bore the imprint of that princely insensate (and, perhaps one of the duchesses or marquises had thought, impregnable) opulence in its valanced alcoves and pilastered medailloned ceiling and crystal chandeliers and sconces and mirrors and girandoles and buhl etageres and glazed cabinets of faience bibelots, and a white rug into which war-bleached boots sank ankle-deep as into the muck of trenches say in the cold face of the moon, flooring bland and soft as cloud that majestic vista at the end of which the three old generals sat" (876). Sharply contrasting with the rococo decor as an expression of the ancien régime are the brutal boots belonging to the new absolute military power of modern warfare. At the end of the magnificent vista of feudalism and its amassed interior decoration, the breathless reader perceives the three old generals whose static trinity is underscored by the repetition of key words. As the background for modern military high command, the rococo interior appears grotesque and unreal, like opera scenery. The artificiality is also emphasized by the tableau-like arrangement: "Backed by a hovering frieze of aides and staff, they sat . . ." (876).

The grotesqueness of the military appears particularly conspicuous in the tension between realistic features and bizarre images. On the one hand, the generals are bespectacled old men, bending over military documents; on the other, the table is like "a knight's or a bishop's sarcophagus" (877), and the entire group like the illustration for one of Aesop's fables, "a pack of tameless forest beasts dressed in the regalia" (877). What lends the scene an additional touch of the morality play, such as *Everyman* or Calderon's *The Great Theatre of the World*, is the crowd. In accordance with the nature of the ceremonial, it is not directly present, but the impact of its existence is conveyed by subtle, symbolist images. Along with the afternoon light and air, some of the city's tumult enters through the open windows, but: "It was rather a sense, a quality as of the light itself, a reflection as of light itself from the massed faces below, refracted upward into the room through the open windows like light from disturbed water, . . ." (877). Similarly, the theatrical quality of the scene finds expression when the marshal's aide brings about the scene's transition "like Harlequin *solus* on a second- or third-act stage" (884). This theatricality is but one aspect of the ritual of power which is *A Fable*'s major theme.

The emphasis on rituals of power, not surprising in a period that had witnessed the uncanny art of Hitler's political shows, takes a wide variety of metaphoric forms ranging from typological episodes to the ritualization of otherwise banal occurrences, for instance, the repeated opening and closing of doors in the scene following Gragnon's official meeting with the marshal (882–85). The predilection for ceremonial effects is also evident in the staging of the arrival of the marshal and the corporal at the beginning of the novel, and the state funeral and the anticlimactic runner episode at the conclusion. A striking example of the tendency to ritualize secular events is the use of the sacred number three, especially in the depiction of flags: "the three flags broke simultaneously from nowhere and climbed the three staffs" (670). The ceremonial, which also imposes its order on the masses, reflects the philosophy of the marshal, who observes all occurrences with godlike detachment, since they are all part of an unchanging pattern. The ritual element apparent in scenic composition finds its stylistic counterpart in the long philosophical passages dominated by word and image clusters. Since in these sections narration is replaced by reflection, they constitute a static element in the novel. In this regard, the contemplative panoramas correspond to the tableau-like scenic compositions.

Readers wishing to share fully in Faulkner's novelistic prose poetry should have a sense of appreciation for the ironic intelligence apparent in the handling of the ceremonial theme. Faulkner amasses titles of military and civilian rank and satirically combines this litany with images from the elaborate rituals of Catholicism. Before actually understanding their significance, readers visually register both the symmetries and the incongruities:

. . . but their staffs and secretaries and clerks, and the commanders of divisions and brigades and their staffs . . . (878)

. . . the Prime Ministers and Premiers and Secretaries, the cabinet members and senators and chancellors; . . . (880)

First and topmost were the three flags and the three supreme generals who served them: a triumvirate consecrated and anointed, a constellation remote as planets in their immutability, powerful as archbishops in their trinity, splendid as cardinals in their retinues and myriad as Brahmins in their blind followers; next were the three thousand lesser generals who were their deacons and priests and the hierarchate of their households, . . . (887)

Here Faulkner satirically combines the leitmotif of the three flags with the Roman institution of the triumvirate and the Christian concept of the Trinity. From the peak of this hierarchy, emphasized by images of stars and consecration, the movement proceeds downward. The irony in this image pattern shows in heterogeneous combinations of cardinals and Brahmins, acolytes and colonels, and in the threefold repetition of portfolios, which in this way become ritualistic objects like "monstrance, host, and censer."

Even more insidious is the satire inherent in Gragnon's subtle equation of the military code with a bullet: "analogous and coeval" (880). Faulkner's originality manifests itself in both the scientific accuracy of the imagery and its rhetorical patterning. The careful symmetries of content and sound—"precipitate of earth's and air's primordial motion, the two condensed and combined"—point back to the painstaking artistic exercises of the young Faulkner. Readers can only do justice to this kind of text if they are able to combine, as in the reading of poetry by T. S. Eliot or John Donne, both sensibility and intelligence. Indeed, there is a cerebral quality in Faulkner's imagery deserving closer attention, because metaphoric ingenuity as a characteristic of his particular genius has largely been ignored. Even some of his more sensitive readers fail to appreciate this achievement of his manneristic satire, perhaps because their attention is so fully claimed by his other stupendous linguistic gifts, particularly that of realistic portrayal. The multiplicity of Faulkner's metaphorizing attitudes demands readers who on their part are able and willing to engage their imagination in equally various role-play. The interaction of different kinds of image making and image receiving in *Absalom, Absalom!* and *The Hamlet* will confirm what this introductory discussion of his new modes of metaphor suggests, that his artistic challenge to the reader lies as much in the creativeness of his imagery as in his narrative invention.

Metaphor and Narrative in
Absalom, Absalom!

Absalom, Absalom! has been studied as much for its psychoanalytic prose poetry as for its sophisticated narration.[1] Among the several narrative voices in the novel, Rosa Coldfield's is easily the most poetic. However, critics have not been much impressed by Rosa's richly metaphoric idiolect. They tend to find her rhetoric overblown and her metaphors mannered, and, consequently, her demonizing view of Thomas Sutpen distortive and in need of correction by more balanced narrators. In contrast, the following reflections on some examples of Rosa's metaphorics assume that this patriotic poetaster of the antebellum South, together with her "spokesman," Quentin, functions as a projection of the artist, her frustrated ravings and his melancholy ruminations supplementing each other as do Addie's and Darl's voices in *As I Lay Dying*. Further, the contents and forms of the imagery through which Rosa expresses her outrage at Sutpen's obscene marriage proposal refer to major aspects of Sutpen's guilt-tainted, but nevertheless heroic, cultural productivity. If Rosa and Quentin are embodiments of the artist as suffering reflector and probing narrator, Sutpen is an avatar of the artist as demonic demiurge, a frustrated version of the romantic creator: "this Faustus, this demon . . . this Faustus who appeared suddenly one Sunday" (*AA* 145). Indeed, the contents and forms of the imagery through which Rosa expresses her outrage at Sutpen's obscene proposal to marry her only after she has borne him a male heir convey major aspects of the novel: *"my presence was to him only the* **absence of black morass and snarled vine and creeper to that man who had struggled through a swamp** with nothing to guide or drive him—**no hope, no light: only some incorrigibility of undefeat** . . ." (137, my emphasis). The indirectness of the metaphors leads readers to the sociopolitical as well as psychoanalytical deep structure of the theme: the *motives* for Sutpen's inhuman design and the nature of the harm it causes Rosa and others. Sutpen appears no longer as magically pulling the plantation from the swamp but as barely managing to extract himself from it. Still, there is a positive element in the victory of his peculiar kind of civilization over wilderness that is different from the merely exploitative colonialism in the Haiti episode, with its echoes of Joseph Conrad's *Heart of Darkness*. Moreover, what the imagery also conveys is that this frontier Faustus bases his specifically southern version of the American dream on the total instrumentalization of others. Rosa's striking opposition of the abstract terms "my presence was to him only the absence of," and her combining them with the vividly concrete "black morass and snarled" impress forcefully upon readers her resentment that she was relevant to Sutpen only as a means for socially reestablishing himself.

However, as Rosa indicates, Sutpen shares with his fellow southerners a specific, bitter determination not to surrender which Faulkner conveys in terms ("no hope, no light: only some incorrigibility of undefeat") that, without being concrete images, achieve a peculiar kind of visibility on the page that is independent of their precise meaning. This iconicity, resulting from the mannered phrasing, or, in the case of the ensuing verbal leitmotif "mad, madness," from repetition, demands a special kind of response. *"If he was mad, it was only his compelling dream which was insane and not his methods: it was no madman, who bargained . . . it was no madman who kept clear . . . it was no madman's plan or tactics which gained him at the lowest possible price . . ."* (137–38). Readers have to react both to the imagery of the swamp, which appeals to their visual imagination, and to the icons "incorrigibility of undefeat" or "mad, madness," which address their intellect. Furthermore, they have to register the indirectness of the graphic effect of the recurring words "mad" and "madness" that betray

Rosa's own visionary hysteria as much as Sutpen's, while at the same time appreciating Rosa's well-balanced rhetoric and her penetrating sociopolitical analysis. The achievement of Faulkner's metaphoric narrative lies in part in its imperceptible fusing of the several thematic strands. Thus, the sociopolitical aspect of Sutpen's liaison with Rosa is also related to the novel's subtle theme of potentiality and impotence arising from Faulkner's profound study of southern idealism, as metaphors like the following indicate: *"O furious mad old man, I hold no substance that will fit your dream but I can give you airy space and scope for your delirium"* (139). The metaphoric phrase continues the motif of madness begun on page 137, but relates it through its diction (*"no substance . . . dream . . . airy space"*) to the philosophic problems of *reality and vision* and the equally sinister fatalities of *action and impotence* of which Sutpen, on the one hand, and Rosa and Quentin, on the other, are the avatars. The tension between the *actual* and the *possible*, between Sutpen's doing and Rosa's and Quentin's reflecting, has been established earlier in the novel through parodic references to *Hamlet*, and readers who allow themselves to be guided by the style of Rosa's metaphorics as well as by their content will appreciate the pseudo-Shakepearean lingo (*The Hamlet*, part 3, sections 1 and 4) and its uncomfortable wavering between prose and blank verse as serving this thematic purpose:

> that living is one constant and perpetual instant when the arras-veil before what-is-to-be hangs docile and even glad to the lightest naked thrust if we had dared, were brave enough . . . to make the rending gash. (118)

> the might-have-been which is the single rock we cling to above the maelstrom of unbearable reality. (124)

If we approach this novel as a poem, we will understand that such obtrusive sound and image clusters as *"the meed and due of all mammalian meat,"* or such recherché words and iconic phrases as *"all polymath love's androgynous advocate"* (121) arise as an adequate means of expression from Rosa's erotic longings and immature voyeurism as well as from her considerable but cramped intelligence. We shall understand how Rosa's involved and unbalanced syntax, her argumentative and hysteric tone, her pedantic and over-sophisticated manner of thinking are part of Faulkner's very original mode of creating another of his monstrous and at the same time profoundly human characters. As with similar human borderline cases, such as Benjy Compson and Ike Snopes, Horace Benbow and the Reverend Hightower, Joanna Burden and Joe Christmas, who helped Faulkner bring the *conditio humana* into focus, Rosa's fate, for all her piteous mannerisms, remains deeply moving, particularly if we allow the tragic determinants of her life, her loveless childhood and her maimed emotional growth—surfacing, for instance, in her hopeless worship of Charles Bon—to reach us.

> me, who had been born too late, born into some curious disjoint of my father's life and left on his (now twice) widowed hands, I competent enough to reach a kitchen shelf, count spoons and hem a sheet and measure milk into a churn yet good for nothing else, yet still too valuable to be left alone. I had never seen him (I never saw him. I never even saw him dead. I heard a name, I saw a photgraph, I helped to make a grave: and that was all) . . . it was as though that casual pause at my door had left some seed, some minute virulence in this cellar earth of mine . . . that June gave substance to that shadow . . . that shape without even a face . . . because I who had learned nothing of love, not even parents' love . . . became not mistress, not beloved . . . I became all polymath love's androgynous advocate. (120–21)

Readers who catch the gist of this passage will not fail to grasp the sad irony of its involved style and understand that in Rosa's frustrations and overblown rhetoric Faulkner was also exorcizing his own.

The last we hear of Rosa in the novel is "her whimpering panting" before the closed door, which is guarded by her black antagonist, Clytie, and opened through Quentin's mediation. Rosa's situation at the closed door, a leitmotif in the novel (*AA* 112–18, 123, 124, 299), encapsulates her lonely and sterile existence, movingly attested to by the lampooning rhyme *"'Rosie Coldfield, lose him, weep him; caught a man but couldn't keep him' "* (139) or other local leitmotifs such as the exculpatory phrase *"they will have told you."* However, Rosa Coldfield's (*nomen est omen*!) inability to cross sexual and sociocultural thresholds is not only her personal fate but is also grounded in the moral and racial codes of the antebellum South. In view of her racism and her role as local poetess laureate of the Confederacy, it is particularly ironic that she herself should fall victim to Sutpen's exploitative design that is rooted in plantation feudalism whose ideology she propagates in her second-rate verse.[2] Nevertheless, there is no doubt that

160

Rosa's racist frustrations, when earlier in the novel, Clytie bars her entry (*"the face stopping me dead"* [113]; *"hurling myself into that inscrutable coffee-colored face"* [114]) are suffused with her sociosexual outrage at Sutpen's demeaning proposal, as the reference to Clytie as Sutpen's daughter and the outcome of miscegenation illustrates: *"that cold implacable mindless . . . replica of his own which he had created and decreed to preside upon his absence"* (138). Obviously Rosa *ante portas* constitutes a structurally important parallel to the sociocultural *ur*-scene of Sutpen's boyhood when he is sent away from the door of the big house by a black slave, and as a reaction against that sociopsychic trauma conceives his redneck vision of a planter-aristocrat.

In contrast to Quentin, the narrator-hero who recovers the guilty southern past by making narration a work of mourning, Rosa remains psychologically and socially paralyzed. This paralysis early announces itself in her portrait that provides such an appropriate opening to the novel. Her strange, stunted quality, a reminder of the paralyzed marble faun as a persona of the artist, is both stated directly ("that air of impotent and static rage," "her impotent yet indomitable frustration") and conveyed through imagery ("like children's feet" and "as if she had iron shinbones and ankles" [5]). Moreover, it is the result of the metaphoric assimilation of Rosa's legs and her chair ("straight hard chair . . . legs hung straight and rigid") and of startling compounds, alliterative linkages and other lexical or phraseological means of cramming ("nothusband none knew," "at last listening would renege and hearing-sense self-confound") that swell the lengthy and relentlessly insistent sentence in which "Miss Coldfield in the eternal black which she had worn for forty-three years now . . ." (5) evokes "her demons." That the frustrated and bigoted spinster Rosa should be Quentin's Clio and initiate him into the Sutpen parable of southern history is very fitting and reflects Faulkner's view, in works such as *Absalom, Absalom!* and *Go Down, Moses*, of southern culture as essentially flawed by its association with slavery.[3]

However, we must not overlook that Rosa's persona, besides opening a historical perspective, also enables Faulkner to present a fascinating study of female self-awareness and through it of artistically unmapped areas of the human psyche. Her speech may sound like a mix of Shakespeare, Rossetti, and Faulkner's own epigonic early poetry (*"That was the miscast summer of my barren youth"* [119]), but to sensitive and intelligent readers the hybrid and warped style of her grotesque metaphorics and her slips into blank verse are as revelatory of her tragic sexual and social inhibitions as the image contents: *"But it was no summer of a virgin's itching discontent; no summer's caesarean lack which should have torn me, dead flesh or even embryo, from the living: or else, by friction's ravishing of the male-furrowed meat, also weaponed and panoplied as a man instead of hollow woman"* (120). Moreover, Rosa's language never remains exclusively "literary" for long, but again and again provides sufficient forthright information, as, for instance, in the case of the reference to her sexual ambivalence (*"I lived out not as a woman, a girl, but rather as the man which I perhaps should have been. I was fourteen then"* [119]), enabling us to make sense of the puzzling phrase *"I became all polymath love's* **androgynous** *advocate"* (121, my emphasis). After directly stating her age and psychological situation, Rosa's discourse becomes more intensively metaphoric—her prolonged puberty appearing as a dim prenatal world—because her peculiar experience of deferred womanhood, being exclusively sensuous (*"that blind subterranean fish," "light," "smell," "touch"* [119–20]) is not accessible to the more direct mode of rational representation. It is only through the indirectness of his metaphoric language that Faulkner can suggest the in-between state of the hermaphrodite or of "love's *androgynous* advocate" (*AA* 117, my emphasis) and, as a male, can project his sexual frustrations into a female mask such as Rosa, who, in one phase of her development, appears to herself *"weaponed and panoplied as a man instead of hollow woman."*

One of the prominent yet little-studied characteristics of Faulkner's metaphorics is the rich diversity of their forms and their complex and synergic effect. The sense-impressions "oversweet . . . twice-bloomed wistaria" (5) and "September sun," on the first page of the novel, appear as straightforward descriptions, but the striking word and phrase formations "coffin-smelling" and "impacted distilled and hyperdistilled" involve readers in a metaphorizing activity. However, while this metaphorizing takes place, as it were, instinctively or imperceptively, the transgression in the case of the ensuing simile "flutter of the sparrows . . . like a flat limber stick" demands a more conscious imaginative effort on the reader's part. Moreover, this transfer coincides with a syntactical caesura ("into which came now and then"), is acoustically prominent ("loud cloudy"), and involves a linkage, suffused with an element of synaesthesia, of fairly remote semantic fields: "loud flutter of the sparrows . . . stick whipped."

The unit "rank smell of female old flesh long embattled in virginity," again taking off from a descriptive base, introduces acoustically aided ("*f*emale, *f*lesh") imagery that allegorically forecasts the thematic complex "virginity, impotence, frustrated love." The alliterative phrasing of the description of Rosa's face, through its position within a context marked by strong metaphorizing impulses, also takes on an imagistic suggestiveness: "embattled in *v*irginity *w*hile the *w*an haggard face *w*atched him." The syntactical and lexical signal "in which she resembled" alerts readers to the central importance of the image of the "crucified child," epitomizing Rosa's painful and maimed state.

The narratological reference to the slow and intermittent beginning of Rosa's storytelling, "the voice not ceasing," illustrated with epic gusto by a leisurely unfolding simile, "like a stream, a trickle . . . sand," prepares the ground for the introduction of the Faustian hero. Thanks to Faulkner's novelistic inventiveness, Sutpen's entry is filtered through the irony of a detached storyteller whose metaphoric ingenuity is tempered by humor (the hysteric voice of Rosa's narrative is not a comfortable dwelling place even for a ghost): "the ghost mused with shadowy docility as if it were the voice which he haunted where a more fortunate one would have had a house" (6).

The close interaction of the storyteller's narrative and metaphoric irony, its detachment serving as a contrastive foil to Rosa's wild mannerisms, continues into the next imagistic unit, the painting of Sutpen's triumphal entry. The very mode of narrative presentation here, that of showing a picture, produces a sliding of contextual boundaries (between the world depicted and the world shared by the narrator and readers) that is similar to the transcendence of metaphor. The narrator reveals with glee the contradictoriness of this imagistic painting: "the thunderclap" is "quiet," the scene, in which Sutpen is the "supposed" demon, the "faint sulphur-reek"—in Rosa's description—"still in hair clothes and beard," does not enter but "erupts," is "peaceful and decorous as a schoolprize water color." The conjunctions (as, like) of the similes "as a schoolprize," "like beasts . . . like men" are strong reminders to readers of the wholly imaginary nature of the scene.

The narrator, using a museum guide's syntax of description, "immobile, bearded and palm-lifted the horseman sat," produces the effect of arrested movement, an iconic quality that is, as many critics have attested, a striking and appropriate feature of this novel of mournful historic and psychoanalytic anamnesis. The experience of being confronted with a painting is enhanced by the framing of the iconic impression with a phrase that, through its alliterative insistence ("carrying in bloodless paradox the shovels and picks of peaceful conquest") as well as through its lofty abstractions "bloodless paradox" and "peaceful conquest," suggests Currier and Ives's chromolithographs such as *Westward the Course of Empire Takes Its Way* (1860) and legends such as "The Arrival of Sutpen, or The Paradox of Peaceful Conquest." The unreal quality of Sutpen's peaceful conquest forecasts the tragic failure of his design.

One major difficulty with the *experience* of Faulkner's metaphors, which so far has received little critical attention, is that readers of *Absalom, Absalom!* not only have to consider from which perspective metaphors are presented but also to adjust to the different intellectual, emotional, and aesthetic claims of the metaphors employed by the different narrators. These difficulties are compounded when there are changes between narrators or narrative levels and when these changes take place frequently, as, for instance, in chapter 7 with its Chinese box-like arrangement of frames. In the following instant, the image of language as "that meager and fragile thread" (208), which inspired the title of Donald Kartiganer's Faulkner study, occurs on the level of Grandfather's commentary on Sutpen's telling, while the image of the volcano, a bit further on in the same sentence, occurs on the level of his retelling of Sutpen's tale. The language-fragile thread image, occurring as a narratological aside, is discursive, appeals to readers' philosophic reflectiveness and, on account of its expansion, demands a sustained intellectual effort: ". . . while he learned the language (that meager and fragile thread, Grandfather said, by which the little surface corners and edges of men's secret and solitary lives may be joined for an instant now and then before sinking back into the darkness where the spirit cried for the first time and was not heard and will cry for the last time and will not be heard either), not knowing that what he rode upon was a volcano, hearing the air tremble and throb at night with the drums and the chanting and not knowing that it was the heart of the earth itself he heard, . . ." (208). The brief metaphoric reference to "a volcano," initially equipped only with the very limited visualness and denotative quality of images in proverbs, is, retroactively, supplied with additional suggestiveness by the ensuing scenic description "hearing the air tremble," eventually involving readers in a metaphorizing process: "the heart of the earth itself is heard." But only after they have passed well beyond this particular passage will readers realize that the Conradian darkness, which Sutpen experiences in the sinister Haitian fighting, and that "darkness" in Grandfather's commentary from which "language rescues us only for instants," are of the same kind.

A successful reading of *Absalom, Absalom!* demands of the reader the adoption of an amazing range of metaphorizing attitudes. For one thing, there is the obvious difference between the primarily sensitive or sensuous response requested, for instance, in the case of the great opening passages of the novel, with its "dim coffin-smelling gloom sweet and oversweet." For another, there is the predominantly intellectual reaction necessary in the reflective parts, for instance, in the passages on Mr. Coldfield's conscience. Here, a kind of allegorical imagery with hardly any visual appeal serves to critique the South in terms of Coldfield's Yankee puritanism: ". . . that day when the South would realize that it was now paying the price for having erected its economic edifice not *on the rock of stern morality but on the shifting sands of opportunism and moral brigandage*" (215, my emphasis). In contrast to the discursive nature of this imagery and its functioning as part of the novel's cultural criticism, the imagery, illustrating two pages earlier the background of the narrators and their narrative situation, shows a playfulness reminiscent of the metaphysical poets and of T. S. Eliot, one of their rediscoverers and one of Faulkner's masters: ". . . born half a continent apart yet joined, connected after a fashion in a sort of geographical *transubstantiation* by that Continental Trough, that River which runs not only through the physical land of which it is the geologic *umbilical*, not only runs through the *spiritual lives* of the beings within this scope, but is very *Environment itself which laughs at degrees of latitude and temperature*, . . ." (213–14, my emphasis).

Clearly, in following the play of Faulkner's metaphors, readers have to take on many roles. They have to assume the part of the sensitive impressionist, assimilating atmospheric nuances ("... their quiet regular breathing vaporising faintly and steadily in the now tomblike air" [247]) as readily as that of the subtle intellectual and aesthetic explorer, tracing the intertwining sexual and narratological aspects of Quentin and Shreve's relationship and its implications for the novel's theme of ambivalence: "not at all as two young men might look at each other but almost as a youth and a very young girl might out of virginity itself—..." (247).

In studying the disconcerting impact of manneristic imagery, I have so far left out the important countervailing factor of the narrative stance which provides guidance to readers in their effort to accommodate the diverse images. In the case of the sherbet leitmotif, for example, the narrative stance informs not only the scenic starting point but also, as the emphasized passages in the following quotation show, the variations of the motif:

> *... like when you have left* the champagne on the supper table and *are walking* toward the whiskey on the sideboard and *you happen to pass a cup of lemon sherbet* on a tray and *you look at the sherbet* and *tell yourself,* That would be easy too *only who wants it.*— (265)

> *It would be like you* passed that sherbet and maybe you knew you would even reach the sideboard and the whiskey, yet you knew that tomorrow morning you would want that sherbet, ... *and all of a sudden you knew you didn't want to go back there even. It would be no question of choosing, having to choose* between the champagne or whiskey and the sherbet ... (266)

> ... all the other cups that had been willing and easy for him to take up hadn't contained sherbet but champagne or at least kitchen wine ... *And who to say if it wasn't maybe the possibility of incest, because who (without a sister: I dont know about the others) has been in love and not discovered the vain evanescence of the fleshly encounter* ... (266–67, my emphasis)

Initially, Shreve's demeaning comparison of Charles Bon's lukewarm feelings for Judith Sutpen to a cup of sherbet, which one may or may not take at a dinner party, serves to emphasize by contrast Bon's desperate yearning for his white father's recognition. But in the course of the narrator's speculations, he becomes more and more intrigued by the possibility that Bon may have developed an interest in Judith after all. However, Quentin, his narrative partner and the focus of the ambiguous virginity and incest theme, expresses reservations about Shreve's suggestions: "Quentin could have spoken now, but Quentin did not . . . 'I dont know,' Quentin said . . . 'I dont know,' Quentin said" (267).

What is of interest here in connection with the interaction of narration and metaphor is that the development in the passage is predominantly one of narrative reflexion, not of metaphoric expansion. However, there is a counterforce, and the numerous repetitions of the formulaic sherbet imagery reminding one of Faulkner's diverse experiments with repetition effects in his playlet *The Marionettes* as well as in his realistic short story "Dry September" have a metaphorizing impact on the narrative context. As a consequence of this acoustic as well as graphic effect, readers apprehend the novel's psychological ambivalences and its complex thematics of incest ("without a sister") and Manichaean fear of the body ("the vain evanescence of the fleshly encounter"), of virginity and hermaphroditic neutrality (". . . that state of virginity which is neither boy's nor girl's" [267]) not so much intellectually as *aesthetically.*

Paradoxically, the central image of sherbet, although used by the narrator in a strictly functional manner, through its very stereotypicality takes on the nonverbal symbolic referentiality of signs. Although readers would be hard-pressed to define precisely its symbolic contents, they can safely say that the cup of sherbet is certainly more than a sexist symbol of woman and also more than a metaphor of the absence or presence of Bon's affection for Judith. Instead of looking for a single and definite meaning, we should recognize that the sherbet image functions in an open field as a focus for the various metaphorizing efforts of the readers and the respective symbolic constellations occuring to them in their evolving and waning experience of the sentence.

Among the several forms and modes of metaphor, recurring word patterns, which in the open contexts turn into icons, are particularly characteristic of the prose in *Absalom, Absalom!* Even unimaginistic words such as "know" and "do" (282) or the phrases "saw . . . face" (264) and *"was all finished now"* (287) and their variants become metaphorizing vehicles of such psychoanalytic and sociocultural motifs as the hostile brothers and the quest for the father, which evolve against the background of the final defeat and collapse of the South:

167

Because Bon would *know* what Henry was *doing*, just as he had always *known* what Henry was thinking . . . Maybe he would *know* all the better what Henry was *doing* because he *did not know* what he himself was *going to do*, that he *would not know* until all of a sudden some day . . . (282, my emphasis)

Then for the second time he looked at the expressionless and **rocklike face** . . . **the face in which he saw his own features,** *in which he saw recognition, and that* **was all** . . . *because it* **was all finished now,** *that* **was all** *of it* **now** *and at last* . . . **"Not God;** *evidently we have done without Him for four years . . . and* **not only not shoes and clothing** *but* **not even any need** *for them, and* **not only no land nor any way to make food,** *but* **no need for food."** (287–88, my emphasis)

In *Absalom, Absalom!* the sense of the end of a social order—after the Civil War and after World War I—is adumbrated by the clustering of negative forms. They negate not only particular aspects ("Not God . . . No land . . . no shoes") but make the whole passage with its repetition pattern à la Gertrude Stein become one comprehensive, annihilating sociocultural metaphor: "it *was all finished now*, that *was all* of it *now* and at last" (287). It is this substitution of individual metaphors or similes by the metaphorization of whole sentences or rather a whole context that constitutes the most striking characteristic feature of Faulkner's imagery.

The close interrelationship between metaphor and narration does not simply derive from the fact that the style of *Absalom, Absalom!* is richer in metaphors than that of *Vanity Fair* or *Gone with the Wind*. Rather, it lies in an essential affinity between the hypothetical or conjectural nature of the narrative in *Absalom, Absalom!* and the structure of metaphor. As the narrators of *Absalom, Absalom!* are always toying with several possibilities, the readers following them have also—as in metaphor—to negotiate among several interacting contexts.

The *interaction model* of metaphor (Black)—in contrast to the more traditional one of *substitution*—seems also appropriate for describing the impact on one another of the several retellings in *Absalom, Absalom!* Mr. Compson's version does not *substitute* for Rosa's story; rather their narratives coexist and *interact* with the several others and with the hypothetical tellings or interpretations of Shreve and Quentin. Moreover, such multiple and conjectural narration, like the essentially dynamic structure of metaphor, incites readers to move imaginatively beyond the interacting contexts and devise ever new ones. Finally, the element of imaginative movement between modes and levels of discourse, their mutual mirroring and interaction, constitutes the link not only between hypothetical narrative and metaphor but also between multiple narration and the concept of masks and role-play.

In regard to the relation between narration and metaphor, not only the frequent occurrences of the formula "Maybe" (253–54) but also the numerous references to narrative framing, for instance, in the Haiti episode ("That was how he [Sutpen] told it" [185]) are relevant because they create in readers distance to the told story and with it also a challenge to relate it to other versions of the narrative, to metaphorize the story material. It seems quite characteristic that many of the narrative "maybe" formulae do not really introduce narrative alternatives but fulfill themselves in metaphorizing gestures: "*Maybe* before she even got started telling it good that gentle white glow began *like when you turn up a wick; maybe* he could even *almost see his hand writing out into space*" (254, my emphasis).

The hypothetical mode of narration and the frequent narratological interruptions are supported by and in turn give support to two further devices characteristic of the synergetic relationship between narrative and metaphor in *Absalom, Absalom!*: the repetition of events, facts, or motifs which makes these narrative units (for instance "that Christmas morning") function like musical leitmotifs and the momentary arrest of actions, movements and gestures which gives them the picture-like effect that has been commented on by several critics.

Concentration on the moment is a reaction of late romanticism and early modernism (Walter Pater, Henri-Louis Bergson) to the perception of life as a flow of becoming.[4] What is important in the present context is that the presentation of Sutpen in arrested movement facilitates his metaphorization: "that maybe there broke free and plain in midgallop against the yellow sky of dawn the fine proud image of the man on the fine proud image of the stallion and that the fumbling and the groping broke clear and free too, not in justification or explanation or extenuation or excuse, Father said, but as the apotheosis lonely, explicable, beyond all human fouling: *He is bigger than all them Yankees that killed us and ourn*" (237). Why he should appear transformed into "the fine proud image of the man on the fine proud image of the stallion" is clarified by the text in italics, the beginning of Wash's admiring commentary.[5] In view of the "revolt of the rednecks" in his own time,[6] Faulkner explores the hero worship of "white trash" like Wash who, forgetting the sociopolitical dilemma of their class, looked upon Sutpen and other plantation owners as their born leaders and splendid redeemer figures.

In Haiti, Sutpen both makes the fortune he needs and prepares for its ruin by fathering the black son he will later refuse to acknowledge. Yet, if we try to register our first reaction, we find that the episode appears not so much as an integral part of the novel and itself a coherent story but as a series of picture fragments or film stills:

> . . . the horses' eyes shining in the torch light . . . the dogs and the niggers . . . the red light on their round heads and arms . . . (203)

> . . . [a man] crouching behind a window in the dark and firing the muskets . . . someone else [a girl] loaded and handed to him . . . (203)

> . . . a little island . . . (207)

> . . . [a man and a woman] walk[ing] across the burned land with the bright sun shining . . . (210)

The details are already quite expressive in themselves, but their selected, isolated presentation makes them still more intensive. Above all, the central elements are focused on and diversely repeated: the man with the musket and the dimly visible girl appear seven times on seven pages (203–10), and the uncanny tropical island is described three separate times in three pages (206–9).

Instead of following the continuous plot of an adventure story, readers can only catch glimpses of the plot in segments that are focused and condensed and function like a musical leitmotif. They are not carried along by a suspenseful story, but are transposed into a lyrical state by images in the form of a chain of leitmotifs. Paradoxically, the lyrical appeal of the text is generated by narrative strategies, a multiple-frame structure (Sutpen telling Grandfather telling Quentin telling Shreve) with frequent interference by the narrators ("Grandfather said"). What is new about such strategies in *Absalom, Absalom!* is the radicality of the interruptions in time and plot. The ensuing disorientation of the readers' sense of time and place reflects the unsure grasp on reality of the characters in the novel. But the evaporation of the firm structures of epic time and action facilitates the interaction of the narrative strands, their metaphorization.

Metaphor is relevant to the problem of character drawing in *Absalom, Absalom!* in a double sense: the narrators, and consequently the readers, develop a projective and, in that sense, a metaphoric relationship with their characters. As a consequence, they tend to vest these characters, who exist only as their imaginings, with extravagant, often ironic or parodic metaphors such as would not be used in a straightforward realistic narrative.

In the following passage the narrative stance is Shreve's communication with Quentin: "so your father said . . . didn't your father say?" (264). The imagery, echoing Mr. Compson's fin de siècle mannerism, is applied by Shreve as narrator to Charles Bon. To reflect Shreve's parodic view of the two differing visions of Bon, he links with Henry and Judith several literary associations: Henry's Bon is representative of a dandy in the tradition of Beau Brummel, Baudelaire, and Oscar Wilde ("the esoteric, the sybarite, the steel blade in the silken tessellated sheath" [264]), and Judith and her Bon are conceived as characters from the Arthurian world of Tennyson and the Pre-Raphaelites ("what maiden meditative dream ridden up out of whatever fabulous land . . . the silken and tragic Lancelot" [264]). Both of their visions are ironically contrasted with the view of Mrs. Sutpen, their matchmaking mother, who, as wife of the north Mississippi country potentate ("would have purchased him and paid for him with Judith even" [264]) sees in the New Orleans-born Bon the apogee of sophisticated city elegance and a desirable husband for her wealthy but countrified daughter. To what extent character drawing in *Absalom, Absalom!* is inspired by the principle of metaphor becomes strikingly evident from the fact that the narrators themselves, at particular moments in the process of their conjectural narrative, display the same malleability and also elusiveness as the characters they create. "It did not matter to them (Quentin and Shreve) anyway, who could without moving, as free now of flesh as the father who decreed and forbade, the son . . . be already clattering over the frozen ruts of that December night and that Christmas dawn, . . . not two of them there and then either but four of them riding the two horses through the iron darkness, and that not mattering either: what faces and what names they called themselves and were called by . . ." (243–44). A metaphor of imaginative empathy, "as free now of flesh as," foregrounds the analogical or metaphoric relation between narrators and narratees. There is little doubt that the fluidity and unstable identity of the characters, resulting from the narrative stance, is the concomitant of what in the biographical context has appeared as a predilection for masks and role-play.

The evanescence of characters enables readers to reenact more easily psychoanalytical and sociocultural constellations. From Quentin and Shreve's narrative perspective Bon was unlike "other children [who] had been made by fathers and mothers . . . he had been created . . . between this woman and a hired lawyer" (252), almost as if his birth was his mother's revenge weapon, "like the dynamite that destroys the house and family," to use against his father. The reiteration of the narrative formula "created between woman and a hired lawyer" stresses the fact that the narrators also create Bon as an "invention" of his mother and, in turn, as "inventing" her. They let him achieve only a conditional and precarious reality, because, as the "black" son, he fails to win the acknowledgment of his white father. The impression of Bon's hypothetical reality is conveyed by a fusion of narrative and metaphoric strategies, which expresses ingeniously both the psychoanalytical and racial aspects of Bon's quest.

Yet Charles Bon, his shifting identity notwithstanding, for moments and in specific situations does assume amazingly concrete postures and presences which then serve to project or metaphorize major aspects of the novel's themes. In the following miniature, Bon, in a dandy-like pose, observes his mother's attempts to turn him into an instrument of her hatred against his father. Bon's detached and ironic view of his mother has an affinity with some of the other negative portraits of mothers in Faulkner's fiction—in particular, Mrs. Compson and Mrs. Boyd, the mother in "The Brooch"[7]—springing from Faulkner's love-hate relationship with his mother. Perhaps Gwin's concept of "feminine difference . . . dissolving boundaries . . . between author and character [respectively] . . . between text and reader" (238–58) can be fruitfully applied to this constellation: ". . . [Bon] watching her, lounging there against the mantel maybe in the fine clothes, in the harem incense odor of what you might call easy sanctity, watching her looking at the letter, not even thinking *I am looking upon my mother naked* since if the hating was nakedness, she had worn it long enough now for it to do the office of clothing like they say that modesty can do, does—" (253).

The images of harem incense and of nakedness/clothing underline the sexual implications of Bon's feeling of male superiority over his mother. His allegorizing interpretation of the central image, *"I am looking upon my mother naked,"* seems to be a case of what Freudianism would call secondary revision, an avoidance of the violation of the sexual taboo by an abstracting reinterpretion, as "if the hating was nakedness." The reader, in registering the oedipal impact of the images of harem incense and "my mother naked," may indeed see the boundaries between author and character dissolve, and imagine how Maud's eldest son may have shared and yet resented her moves against her disappointing husband. From this perspective, Bon's quest could also be read—in Chodorow's sense—as autobiographical role-play and the projection of Faulkner's own yearning for a more loving, congenial, and impressive version of Murry Falkner. Given the multidimensional quality of *Absalom, Absalom!*, such a psychological reading would not substitute for but would only supplement the sociological reading of this metaphoric narrative as a white version of a "black" son's quest for his white father.

In fact, a sensitive response to the metaphorics of the novel confirms that all major thematic developments of *Absalom, Absalom!*—from the contrast between the quest for the absent father to the archetypal confrontation between the hostile brothers—evolve from a racial context (291, 293) as well as from a particular historical situation of Faulkner's own time: the "revolt of the rednecks" (see chapter 8) and their political supplacement of plantation aristocrats like the Percys (*Lanterns on the Levee*) with such figures as Theodore Bilbo, James K. Vardaman, Lee Russell, and Huey Long. Joseph Blotner and, more recently, Walter Taylor and Joel Williamson have informed us about the involvement of the Falkner family in this takeover. Our concern here is with the impact of this sociopolitical change on Faulkner's rendering of history. In a sense both *Absalom, Absalom!* and *The Hamlet* are redneck novels: Sutpen, Labove, and Flem, like Willie Stark in Robert Penn Warren's *All the King's Men*, all rise from the same social background.

Faulkner indicates his own split feelings about the inescapable advance of the rednecks and the doom of the plantation aristocracy by

173

portraying both classes critically but with occasional sympathetic touches. He yearned for the old aristocratic plantation culture but knew perfectly well that it was based on a slave economy and, later, on the exploitation of black and white sharecroppers. He knew about the rising rednecks' toughness and stamina but also of their ruthlessness, bigotry, and vulgarity. It is therefore characteristic that Faulkner's greatest novel presents the tragedy of the redneck Sutpen, who seeks to found a plantation dynasty but fails because he gets caught in the same web of social and racial patterns which had instigated him to his rise to power. In contrast to the rising rednecks, the decadent aristocrat, Mr. Compson, and his son, Quentin, suffer under the burden of history. Mr. Compson thinks nostalgically of the pioneer period of Sutpen and of Mississippi between 1833 and 1865 when, he wants to believe, people were "simpler . . . larger, more heroic too, not dwarfed and involved but distinct, uncomplex" (74). Quentin suffers an identity crisis and his narrative role-playing evolves under the onslaught of the many-voiced past: "his very body was an empty hall echoing with sonorous defeated names; he was not a being, an entity, he was a commonwealth" (9). This hyperconsciousness of the decadent and outgoing elite of Faulkner's time (*"I have heard too much, I have been told too much; I have had to listen too much"* [171–72]) makes him very sensitive to the sociocultural changes that Judith Sutpen and Rosa Coldfield experienced during and after the Civil War: *"what hurdling of iron old traditions since she had seen almost everything she had learned to call stable vanish like straws in a gale"* (172). In the guise of his narrators, Faulkner tracks to its very core the repercussions of the revaluation of sociocultural values in the thirties, in the course of which the will to live overcomes the trauma of the lost cause and initiates a vitalistic countermovement. *"I believed that there were things which still mattered just because they had mattered once. But I was wrong. Nothing matters but breath, breathing, to know and to be alive"* (172). Passages like this one demonstrate that *Absalom, Absalom!*, for all of its historical details, is not a historical novel but a novel of historical consciousness subjected to the critical probe of art.[8] This makes Faulkner's chef d'oeuvre, and also *Light in August*, *Go Down, Moses* and *Intruder in the Dust*, profoundly interesting to German critics of my generation for whom the study of history has been primarily a work of mourning. Faulkner uses the masks of the narrator and that of the young southerner Quentin—in his narratological interplay with his ludicrously remote Canadian counterpart—to scrutinize southern history and to explode the lost cause and other mystiques of his region. In this effort, his new critical language, combining metaphoric reflection ("transmogrified into" [284]) and metaphoric narration, plays a major role.

> They both bore it [the cold in their room at Harvard] as though in deliberate flagellant exaltation of physical misery transmogrified into the spirits' travail of the two young men during that time fifty years ago, or forty-eight rather, then forty-seven and then forty-six, since it was '64 and then '65 and the starved and ragged remnant of an army having retreated across Alabama and Georgia and into Carolina, swept onward not by a victorious army behind it but rather by a mounting tide of the names of lost battles from either side—Chickamauga and Franklin, Vicksburg and Corinth and Atlanta—battles lost not alone because of superior numbers and failing ammunition and stores, but because of generals who should not have been generals, who were *generals not through training in contemporary methods or aptitude for learning them, but by the divine right to say "Go there" conferred upon them by an absolute caste system*; or because the generals of it never lived long enough to learn how to fight massed cautious accretionary battles, since they were already as obsolete as Richard or Roland or du Guesclin, who wore plumes and cloaks lined with scarlet at twenty-eight and thirty and thirty-two and captured warships with cavalry charges but no grain nor meat nor bullets, who would whip three separate armies in as many days and then tear down their own fences to cook meat robbed from their own smokehouses, who on one night and with a handful of men would gallantly set fire to and destroy a million dollar garrison of enemy supplies and on the next night be discovered by a neighbor in bed with his wife and be shot to death; . . . (284–85, my emphasis)

This long passage, illustrating Faulkner's perceptive study of the Civil War as a southern dilemma, is not an excursus but is closely related to the novel's plotting, which shows that Sutpen is indeed one of the confederate leaders "who should not have been generals, who were generals by" the aristocratic principle of the plantation culture. A grotesque example of this is the episode of the two thousand-pound-marble tombstones which Sutpen has transported with his ragged and starving regiment (157). The final proof of the failing leadership of the plantation barons is the gruesome contrast between Sutpen's idealized picture as gallant feudal master on his black stallion and his shabby and brutal death by the scythe of his disillusioned and outraged retainer.

The study of the historical metaphorics of *Absalom, Absalom!* shows that Faulkner is interested not so much in political as in sociocultural history, again focused on the rise of rednecks. Iconographically, Sutpen appears modelled on the prototype of the romantic superhero, displaying features of Melville's Ahab and Faust ("this Faustus, this demon . . . who appeared suddenly one Sunday with two pistols" [148]). However, in his social characteristics he is above all a *redneck* Faustus of Andrew Jackson's brand who "skulldugged a hundred miles of land out of a poor ignorant Indian and built the biggest house on it you ever saw." Sutpen's returning from one of his "foraging expeditions" with six wagons loaded with "the crystal tapestries and the Wedgwood chairs [sic!]" is a vitriolic caricature of the social climber as well as a successful stroke of frontier humor; it may also reflect the self-irony of the would-be aristocrat Faulkner.

His subtlety in creating this redneck tragedy is apparent in Sutpen's stilted language, which becomes a central metaphor of his inhuman design: "the bombastic phrases with which Grandfather said he even asked you for a match for his cigar" (198). A particularly striking example is Sutpen's ludicrously detached way of stating in legal terminology and with breathtaking soberness why he had to rid himself of his first wife, Eulalia Bon, who turned out to be "racially tainted": "I found that she was not and could never be, through no fault of her own, *adjunctive* or *incremental* to the design, which I had in mind, so I provided for her and put her aside."

Sutpen's fondness for the "hard words" of lawyers' English and his obsession with the ideal of a stately home and formal gardens (the grotesque motif of the French architect) are characteristic of autodidacts and social climbers who, like Fitzgerald's Gatsby, seek to bolster their socially unfortified egos through the masquerade of the paraphernalia of culture. Faulkner's great creative idea was to use a peculiar artificial language as a metaphor for the artificiality of Sutpen's *design* and the inhumaneness of his *innocence*. Sutpen's use of English as a dead language is symbolic of his pioneer monomania and utter unconcern for the feelings of others, which culminates in his denial of his son, Bon, his ruthless proposal to Rosa, and his callousness towards Milly that makes Wash Jones kill him.

The racial metaphors in Mr. Compson's analytic narrative of Sutpen and Wash are of considerable sociocultural interest because they project a positive relation between the self-made frontier aristocrats and their redneck retainers, one that was based on a precarious alliance: plantation aristocrats were to keep blacks in their inferior position to help poor whites keep their self-esteem. The poor white retainers paid back through their loyal and self-redeeming hero worship.

> But they [Sutpen and Wash Jones, master and retainer] would drink together under the scuppernong arbor on the Sunday afternoons, and on the week days he would see Sutpen (the fine figure of the man as he called it) on the black stallion, galloping about the plantation, and Father said how for that moment Wash's heart would be quiet and proud both and that maybe it would seem to him that this world where niggers, that the Bible said had been created and cursed by God to be brute and vassal to all men of white skin, were better found and housed and even clothed than he and his granddaughter—that this world where he walked always in mocking and jeering echoes of nigger laughter, was just a dream and an illusion and that the actual world was the one where his own lonely apotheosis (Father said) galloped on the black thoroughbred . . . (232–33)

Metaphoric phrases such as "this world where he walked always in mocking and jeering echoes of nigger laughter" illustrate the essential sameness of Wash's racial attitude and the young Sutpen's. Sutpen's rise to baronial splendor as well as his fall and the failure of his design are caused by the racism of his redneck origins. This is confirmed by the psycho-social *ur*-scene in which the thirteen-year-old Sutpen is turned away from the door of the big house by a black butler and told to use the back door. Under the impact of the pervasive metaphorization of the language, readers witness the origin of Sutpen's lasting psychic trauma that will govern both his social ambitions and—as an integral part of it—his racial attitudes.

The twofold frame of the narrative (Sutpen via Quentin's grandfather via Quentin) provides the stylistic flexibility necessary for Faulkner's treatment of the difficult task of rendering the boy's initiation into social stratification (poor white/black house slaves of the white aristocracy) and of capturing, in a manner fitting the hero's age, his emerging racial hatred. Details of the experience that Sutpen cannot rationally articulate are mirrored in certain groups of syntactical, verbal, and auditory repetitions and image clusters. Frustrated aggression, for example, is expressed in the patterns of repetition "could hit . . . not hit . . . did hit," and the qualities of the contemptuous, the sarcastic, and the unassailable are conveyed in the auditory images of the metaphoric terms "child's toy balloon . . . slick . . . smooth . . . distended . . . burst . . . loud laughing": ". . . you knew that you could hit them, he told Grandfather, and they would not hit back or even resist. But you did not want to, because they (the niggers) were not it, not what you wanted to hit; that you knew when you hit them you would just be hitting a child's toy balloon with a face painted on it, a face slick and smooth and distended and about to burst into laughing and so you did not dare strike it because it would merely burst and you would rather let it walk on out of your sight than to have stood there in the loud laughing" (190–91).

The significance of this fusion of narrative and metaphor manifests itself in the repercussions of the door episode and the balloon motif in the passage where the thirteen-year-old Sutpen comes to view the miserable situation of his family and class from the assumed perspective of a plantation owner:

> . . . seeing his own father and sisters and brothers as the owner, the rich man (not the nigger) must have been seeing them all the time—as cattle, creatures heavy and without grace, brutely evacuated into a world without hope or purpose for them, who would in turn spawn with brutish and vicious prolixity, populate, double treble and compound, fill space and earth with a race whose future would be a succession of cut-down and patched and made-over garments bought on exorbitant credit because they were white people, from stores where niggers were given the garments free, with for sole heritage that expression on *a balloon face bursting with laughter* which had looked out at some unremembered and nameless progenitor who had knocked *at a door* when he was a little boy and had been *told by a nigger to go around to the back* . . . (194, my emphasis)

In the image of the miserable white lower class as "cattle," Faulkner emphasizes the main thematic aspects through a diversified orchestration: animality is stressed by the alliterative grouping of "cattle, creatures, evacuated into a world" as well as by the word repetition "brutely, brutish." The image of meaningless, mass procreation ("evacuated into a world, spawn") receives acoustic as well as optic stress in the alliterative group "prolixity, populate, double treble and compound." These key words symbolize both acoustically and graphically their content through their latinate heaviness. A new sense of language expresses itself here: a sensitivity to words as words, their iconicity, which was unknown in the nineteenth century novel.

The reading of *Absalom, Absalom!* as a metaphoric narrative also provides insight into the unadmitted and unconscious ideological motifs of the artist, particularly through the magnificent prose poem describing the descent of the miserable Sutpen family to the lowlands. As in Walker Evans's moving photos and James Agee's beautifying prose (*Let Us Now Praise Famous Men*, 1941), the social misery of these deprived rednecks appears aesthetically transformed, although they are not yet endowed with the human dignity and monumental quality that Mrs. Armstid will achieve in *The Hamlet*. The rendering of the Sutpens' descent from the mountains promises further clues to the artistic and ideological direction into which Faulkner as writer was heading. A close look at the text shows that it was not yet the direction of postmodernism, as our present-day preoccupation with the narratological aspect of *Absalom, Absalom!* has led some contemporary critics to assume, but of contemporary regionalism. What makes the Sutpens' trek appear to anticipate that of the Joads in John Steinbeck's *The Grapes of Wrath* (1939), or of Flem and the Snopeses at the end of *The Hamlet* (1940) is its character as sociocultural ritual or saga.

In contrast to Lee Smith's *Fair and Tender Ladies* (1988), where a comparable migration from the mountain farms to the mining areas of Virginia is pragmatically rendered as a socioeconomic development, the "translation" of the Sutpens strikes readers as a mythic and monumental event. The trek of the Sutpens, like that of the Snopeses in *The Hamlet*, seems to breathe the same kind of inspiration as the contemporary murals of José Clemente Orozco, Diego Rivera, and Thomas Hart Benton, where events and characters derived from social and regional history are given a timeless and universal quality.

He didn't remember if it was weeks or months or a year they traveled (except that one of the older girls who had left the cabin unmarried was still unmarried when they finally stopped, though she had become a mother before they lost the last blue mountain range), whether it was that winter and then spring and then summer that overtook and passed them on the road or whether they overtook and passed in slow succession the seasons as they descended or whether it was the descent itself that did it and they not progressing parallel in time but descending perpendicularly through temperature and climate—a (you couldn't call it a period because as he remembered it or as he told Grandfather he did, it didn't have either a definite beginning or definite ending.) (186)

The impression of timelessness and universality results not from individual metaphors so much as from a peculiar kind of comprehensive metaphorizing force that informs and transforms the entire passage. What makes readers realize that this is a migration of a peculiar kind, a "translation" as one of the apt mannerisms puts it, are not vivid images but the repetition of narrative formulae ("He didn't remember"), inverting references to time ("if it was weeks or months or a year") and the representation of their "not *progressing parallel in time but descending perpendicularly* through temperature and climate" (my emphasis).

Like other writers and artists of the thirties who had witnessed the breakdown of traditional socioeconomic and cultural values after World War I and the bank crash, Faulkner must have felt a specific urge to register the changes in social philosophy. In the face of the collapse of the old leadership—his fascination with decadent aristocrats like the Sartorises and Benbows, or the Compsons and Drakes, is striking—Faulkner, for all his sophistication, seems to have toyed with a belief in "good, simple people," particularly women of an underprivileged, tough, natural, motherly type (Ruby Lamar, Dilsey and Lena Grove). As we know from the study of Faulkner's self-stylizations in chapter 1, the role of a protopopulist, anti-intellectual writer ("I was just trying to write about people . . . Just the human heart, it's not ideas" [*FU* 10]) was one he particularly enjoyed and stressed. Moreover, without subscribing to anything like socialism or national socialism, Faulkner, like Erskine Caldwell, John Dos Passos, and John Steinbeck, felt that the fates and the history of simple people, the social progress and racial conflict of the Yoknapatawpha rednecks or the lives of the peasants and of the city masses in *A Fable*, deserved to be artistically reenacted. In pursuing this goal, he, through his metaphoric language, managed to transform an event in regional history, such as the migration of the poor white hillbilly family and their emerging racial conflict with low-country blacks, into a mythic dimension. Like Joyce and T. S. Eliot and so many other modernists, Faulkner was convinced that to reveal the mythic patterns in the historical or actual might provide aesthetic and moral redemption. Readers who are not so dazzled by the narrative and stylistic sophistication of *Absalom, Absalom!* as to overlook this dimension in the novel will also see that the break between it and *The Hamlet* is less total than many critics have made out. The two novels present different artistic solutions to the problem of accommodating the contemporary tension between modernism and regionalism.

The author of these poems is a man steeped in the soil of his native land, a Southerner by every instinct, and, more than that, a Mississippian. George Moore said that all universal art became great by first being provincial.

   —Preface to Faulkner's *The Marble Faun* (1924)

Beginning with *Sartoris* I discovered that my own little postage stamp of native soil was worth writing about.
—Faulkner, interview with Jean Stein Vanden Heuvel (1955)

I believe it is war and disaster which remind man most that he needs a record of his endurance and toughness. That is why after our own *disaster* there rose in *my country, the South, a resurgence of good writing*, writing of a good enough quality that people in other lands began to talk of a *"regional" Southern literature* even until I, *a countryman*, have become one of the first names in our literature which the Japanese people want to talk to and listen to.

   —Faulkner, "To the Youth of Japan" (1955, my emphasis)

In fact, there are people in the South, Southerners born, who not only believe they can be reconciled but who *love our land—not love white people specifically nor love Negroes specifically, but our land, our country: our climate and geography, the qualities in our people, white and Negro too, for honesty and fairness, the splendors in our traditions, the glories in our past*—enough to reconcile them, even at the cost of displeasing both sides: the contempt of the Northern radicals who believe we dont do enough, the contumely and threats of our own Southern reactionaries who are convinced that anything we do is already too much.

   —Faulkner, "On Fear: Deep South in Labor: Mississippi"
            (1956, my emphasis)

SEVEN

Faulkner and the Regionalist Context

In the past, the term *regionalism*, particularly in literary studies, has often been understood as denoting a short-lived, reactionary movement of the thirties. However, the study of a wider range of contemporary texts shows that *regional* is closely interrelated with the term *national* and occurs in a central debate (not just in *The Nation* but also in *The New Republic* and in the African American *The Messenger*) on American identity and values at a time of fundamental crisis. The complexity of regionalism can be seen from the fact that it appears as often in the political and economic context of Roosevelt's New Deal measures (e.g., TVA) as in the nostalgic manifestos of the Agrarians. It is a key concept of the new sociological schools not only at the University of North Carolina at Chapel Hill (Howard W. Odum, Rupert B. Vance) but also at the University of Chicago (Roderick D. McKenzie, Robert E. Park, Ernest W. Burgess) and has led to *The Index of American Design* as well as to the WPA Guide Series and to the several great photo projects of the time. The focus on the regional element is as important in Lewis Mumford's *The Culture of Cities* as it is in Donald Davidson's *The Attack on Leviathan*. Finally, the context in which we have to see regionalism comprises the western school of painting, including Thomas Hart Benton of Missouri, John Stuart Curry of Kansas, and Grant Wood of Iowa, and western writers such as Willa Cather and Sherwood Anderson, as well as the centrally conceived, but in its goals decentralist, Federal Theater movement. The cultural impulse bringing forth regionalism also manifests itself in the new appreciation of Native American and African American culture as well as in the discovery of American folk art and folk music. It inspired Constance Rourke's exploration of a genuinely American literature (*American Humor, The Roots of American Culture*) no less than the American studies movement. Moreover, regionalist impulses fuse with left-wing interests (the art of the people) and with right-wing nostalgia for a true American culture undiluted by foreign influences.

Obviously, regionalism is a contradictory umbrella term. In its close alliance with primitivist elements, it appears as part of modernism. However, it is also set against the internationalist aspect of modernism. In the neorealism of Grant Wood and Thomas Hart Benton, regionalism appears as opposed to modernist abstraction, while in Faulkner's specific exploration of the oral tradition, it is again close to the modernist spirit. The following quotation from a standard book of the time aptly summarizes the complexity of the phenomenon: "This regional variety and dilemma have been emphasized of late not only in the numerous legislative issues at Washington and in widely distributed newspaper editorials, but have been well described in the last few years in a large number of excellent books on America and Americans. Perhaps a hundred volumes could be listed from which authentic pictures of America's diversified culture can be had. More than a thousand titles of fiction have attempted to picture the several regions, the land and people, their culture and folkways" (Odum and Moore 425).

In the spirit of the new historicism, this chapter seeks to resituate Faulkner in a context that is as much informed by regionalism as by modernism. Henry Nash Smith, in his remarkably perceptive review of *The Sound and the Fury*, recognized that this modernist stream-of-consciousness novel "is also distinctly related to provincialism," but, being a great critic, he also emphasizes the universal dimension of this regional novel: "In short, by the only definition that means very much, Mr. Faulkner is a provincial writer. He belongs to the South, if not to the Southwest. Though he is not a folklorist, though he is more concerned with life than with regionalism, his book has shown unguessed possibilities in the treatment of provincial life without loss of universality" (Inge, *William Faulkner* 34).

The four epigraphs to this chapter all attest to the continuity and

184

diversity of Faulkner's rural and regionalist preoccupations, with the quotation from "To the Youth of Japan" indicating his awareness of the inner relationship between his "countryman" role and southern "regional" writing as a literature sui generis. The first epigraph, from Phil Stone's preface to his friend's poetry volume of 1924, suggests that Faulkner, even before producing, under the auspices of the regionalist ideologue Sherwood Anderson, pieces like "Out of Nazareth," was aware of the contemporary predilection for regionalist ideals.[1] For more than one reason these pronouncements by Faulkner's friend, the small-town Mississippi lawyer with sophisticated artistic tastes, constitute a major turn in the history of literary theory. Why Faulkner let himself be presented in *The Marble Faun* preface in the role of southern regionalist becomes clear when we collate the publication date of his poetry volume, 1924, on the one hand, with Willa Cather's regionalist *O, Pioneers!* (1913), *My Ántonia* (1918) and *Death Comes for the Archbishop* (1926), and, on the other, with that of Frederick Jackson Turner's landmark essay "The Significance of the Section in American History," published in 1925. That the book version, *The Significance of Sections in American History* (1933), was to become a posthumous recipient of a Pulitzer Prize illustrates that regionalism was at the fore, a fact further documented by the appearance in 1930 of the essays of twelve southern agrarians, *I'll Take My Stand*, in 1936 of Howard Odum's sociological standard book on southern regionalism, *Southern Regions of the United States*, and in 1938 of Donald Davidson's anticentralist *The Attack on Leviathan*.[2]

Phil Stone's preface to Faulkner's *The Marble Faun*, particularly by referring to George Moore and the provincial origin of all universal art, reveals the continuity from nineteenth century naturalism through early twentieth century regionalism, allowing us to situate America's greatest novelist in this context. This should not offend critics who have stressed Faulkner's internationalist characteristics and have rejected his regionalist features because they feel that affinities with regionalism might make his genius appear limited and dated. George Moore's formula, "the provincial as prerequisite of the universal," suggests not only the internationality of regionalism but also the possibility of the highest aesthetic achievement in this mode of art. Finally, the fact that Faulkner knew George Moore both as the author of *The Confessions of a Young Man* (1888) and through Phil Stone as proclaimer of the regionalist gospel indicates the overlapping of the decadence movement and the naturalist/regionalist tradition as well as the diverseness of Faulkner's literary roots. The exploration of the regional and its transfiguration into the universal, which in the Faulkner of the early poems of 1924 remains but a wishful assertion, was to become a distinctive feature of his major works. After his encounter with late romanticism and modernism had taught him the decisive role of stylization in art, regionalism—as this chapter tries to show—provided the young writer with both an aesthetic base and personal encouragement to deal with his native South and to render its tragic and mundane features. Yet the great artistic problem was how to reconcile regional materials—a southern cow or a dirt road, a woman in a man's brogans without shoelaces or an old man's sloppy habits of eating—with the sophisticated sensibility elicited by late romanticism and with the narrative techniques and the style evolved in connection with the internationalist themes of modernism. The study of metaphor in *The Hamlet* (chapter 8) will reveal the progress beyond the early experiments ("The Hill," "Nympholepsy") and the first serious achievements (*The Sound and the Fury, As I Lay Dying, Sanctuary, Light in August*).

The image of the "little postage stamp" in the second epigraph, from the Jean Stein interview of 1955, easily represents Faulkner's most popular poetological statement; however, its full implications and its commitment to the poetics of regionalism are less often recognized. Both the sociocultural and the psychoanalytical dimensions of the regionalistic metaphor "postage stamp of native soil" are of interest here. Faulkner's central motive for transforming his native region into his special symbolic space must have been the urge to distance and focus his experience of a world of shifting values and the need to come to terms with the disturbing relativism of the ironic twenties. Characteristically, the emphasis on the importance of place is already among the literary goals affirmed in *Mosquitoes* (1927) ("Clinging spiritually to one little spot of the earth's surface so much of his labor is performed for him" [*MOS* 184]), and, as the Mississippi essay and the interviews in Japan and with Jean Stein confirm, remains dominant through his last phase. The land, which he came to call Yoknapatawpha, and which he rendered with all its agonizing qualities (*"I dont hate it! I dont hate it!"* [*AA* 311]) in such a rich concreteness, provided more than the material for his comedies and tragedies. The Yoknapatawpha region also represented, for the writer whose work grew, as powerful strains of his imagery suggest, from a persistent and determined effort to fight the death instinct, a reassuring home base. My third and fourth epigraphs, coming from the same late period and displaying the same continuing regionalist thrust, however, have very different sociopolitical implications. While the association in "To the Youth of Japan" (1955) of the striking "resurgence of good writing" in the South with the lost cause mystique of the Civil War has some plausibility, the idea in "On Fear: Deep South in Labor: Mississippi" (1956) that the "love [of] our land" would reconcile the suppressed blacks of Faulkner's time with the supremacist whites strikes one as preposterous. "Endurance and toughness" may indeed have been qualities that made the cultural survival of the South and its literary bloom in Faulkner's own time possible, but it is not very likely that "the splendors" of the southern tradition appealed to African Americans who had been the victims of white hegemony underlying these "splendors."

However, more important is that the appeal in "On Fear: Deep South in Labor: Mississippi" to the myth of the land is sociopolitically charged in a way that Phil Stone's fashionable reference to George Moore's praise of provincialism is not. The strength of his regionalist commitment is borne out by the fact that he appealed to the "love [of] our land" when the conflicting claims of the civil rights movement and his Mississippi loyalties put him under extreme social and psychological pressure. In fact, to appreciate the full impact of regionalism on Faulkner—as on many other contemporaries—we had better realize that the notorious pronouncement in the Russell Howe interview occurred in the same year, 1956, as the appeal to "love our land" in "On Fear: Deep South in Labor: Mississippi." Both are variants in extremis of the regionalist identification, in 1924, as "a Southerner by every instinct, and, more than that, a Mississippian" and of the idyllic apostrophe to "the postage stamp of native soil" in 1955.

The intertwining of the political and the cultural motives in Faulkner's regionalism is apparent in his answers to the Japanese interviewer, Sakanishi, whose perceptive question (on the limitation of regionalism to rural communities) Faulkner does not really respond to. Instead, he identifies regional loyalty as a mythic gut feeling, independent of profession or social class and associated with "blood" and "clan": "No, it is regional. It is through what we call the 'South.' It doesn't matter what the people do. They can be land people, farmers, and industrialists, but there still exists the feeling of blood, of clan, blood for blood" (*LiG* 191). To a German reader, repeated references, in such a context, to blood call up fatal associations of the "blood and soil" art of the Nazis,[3] and of the amazingly similar art of the Stalin era and its full-bosomed and well-muscled working-class heroines and heroes. More awkward still, the striking family likeness between these politically discredited art forms and regionalist art produced during the same period in many democratic countries has embarrassed scholars for some time and has made them sigh at the unfortunate period style of the thirties and shun the field. However, present-day critics, convinced of the ideological implication of artistic forms, cannot let the matter rest at that, particularly since the new culturalist and historicist approaches offer critical tools to deal with such intractable matters as ideology and aesthetics and with regionalism as the period style of the thirties.

In view of Faulkner's continuous regionalist sympathies in both his fiction and literary reflections from the *Marble Faun* preface and "Out of Nazareth" through *The Town* and *The Mansion*, the question is not whether regionalism plays a role in his oeuvre, but *what* role it plays in particular works and phases of his career and how it relates to his other aesthetic commitments—above all, to his internationalist and modernist orientation that in recent Faulkner criticism has been exclusively foregrounded. There are certainly varying degrees of intensity with which the regionalist element expresses itself in his works of the thirties, forties, and fifties. Moreover, regionalism functions differently in the early prose poem "Nympholepsy" (early 1925), where it is laced with fin de siècle features, and in the fragment *Father Abraham* (late 1926), which anticipates the regionalism of the Snopes trilogy. Of particular interest in this regard are works such as *The Sound and the Fury, Sanctuary*, and *Light in August* as well as *Soldiers' Pay* and *If I Forget Thee, Jerusalem* where regionalist and modernist features appear, in varying degrees, side by side and whose strength derives in large part from the synergic effect of the two elements.

While in *Soldiers' Pay* the regionalist element is limited to the ethnic context (for instance, the vitalistic singing in the black chapel [319] in contrast to the postwar malaise informing the center of the novel), and in *Mosquitoes* it only occurs as a subject of the aesthetic debate among the literati, in works such as *Go Down, Moses* and *Intruder in the Dust* it dominates. Here, however, it does so in very different ways: *Go Down, Moses* is characteristic of the tendency of artists in the thirties and forties to combine the exploration of atavistic, primitivistic and historical roots with regionalist features, while *Intruder in the Dust* fuses regionalism with civil rights concerns, thus anticipating the political themes of the fifties and sixties.

Faulkner scholars, having discarded his regionalist dimension as limiting and irreconcilable with his international stature, will be surprised to note that in *Revolt of the Provinces: The Regionalist Movement in America, 1920–1945* (1993), Robert L. Dorman blithely numbers *Absalom, Absalom!* among the regionalist works of the thirties (184–85). This should not create an outcry, however, since anyone familiar with Dorman's comprehensive yet subtle study will appreciate the regionalist aspect in Faulkner's masterpiece which we literary critics may indeed have read too exclusively as the ultimate in postmodernist narrative strategies. Still, *The Hamlet* is probably a more pronounced example of the regionalist impact on Faulkner's writing despite the fact that, in light of Sonja Bašić's subtle narratological investigation (41–55), this novel, nowadays, also appears closer to the literary avant-garde and *Absalom, Absalom!* In fact, if we try to relate *The Hamlet* to other regionalist Faulkner texts such as "Out of Nazareth," *Go Down, Moses* or *Intruder in the Dust*, we note that its emphasis is more on regional features than on regionalist values, although ideology is not totally absent from this novel, as its metaphoric deep structure will reveal. The interplay of modernist and regionalist metaphors, in particular, demonstrates that the regionalism in *The Hamlet*, as in *Flags in the Dust, Sanctuary*, or *Light in August*, is not of an affirmative but of a critically probing or problematic kind.

The regionalist dimension in Faulkner's work has not received much scholarly attention in the last decades except, more recently, in some presentations by Europeans or by Americans at European symposia.[4] A major reason for this neglect seems to have been that any study of regionalist features of the great southerner would have appeared as a remnant of the reductive picture of Faulkner as an untutored genius close to the southern soil. However, as Faulkner's literary sophistication has meanwhile been established so clearly and our methodological awareness of sociocultural phenomena has sharpened so considerably, it seems time to reopen the debate concerning the regionalist aspect in Faulkner. The main motive for such a new approach derives from our new historicist or culturist view of literature, demanding that we contextualize such an exceptional writer and establish a vantage point beyond that of the postmodernist Faulkner.

One of the main differences between the old regionalism of the thirties and the new interest in regionalism that has emerged since the eighties is that we no longer see terms such as "regionalism" or "modernism" as defining essences but as metaphors and elements of discourse suggesting viewpoints. In a variation of Edward W. Said's definition of the Orient as one of "the deepest and most recurring images of the Other" (1, 5, 12), one might say that the region is one of the deepest and most recurring images of the desire for a world of one's own. The fact that the concept or discourse of region and regionalism seems to be bound up with the definition of identity explains why it is highly value charged. Further, there is no doubt that the concept of region arises as much from a sociocultural as from a psychological context and, as the war-torn Balkans have again confirmed, cannot be understood without studying its configurations of economic and political power.

In Faulkner's case, his strong regionalist commitment arises from the wider context of his time, as well as from his individual attempt to overcome personal difficulties by impersonating a pastoral role. As we shall see, both Faulkner's regionalist mask and his related organicist metaphors emerge as part of a situation dominated by the decline of the South, the local variant of Oswald Spengler's international myth, *The Decline of the West* (1926). Against this background, the new impulses, movements, and terms such as *primitivism, regionalism, modernism,* and *agrarianism* have appeared to critics in complementary or polar arrangements, and, more recently, in a complex and shifting interplay. I have chosen "regionalism" as a key term because it allows me to focus more easily on the internationality of the phenomenon and its relationship with modernism. This does not mean that I find other terms such as "agrarian" or the "southern renaissance" less suitable for contextualizing Faulkner.[5]

While it is not difficult to define the three terms "modernism," "primitivism," and "regionalism" on the basis of contemporary evidence in such a way that they seem to refer to three distinct phenomena, "modernism" may be taken as a more comprehensive term than the two others and one which focusses more on the formally innovative aspect of writing. Although "primitivism" and "regionalism" both have an important formal dimension—I shall deal with some of these aspects later in this chapter—the emphasis seems to be more often on content. In this situation one can perhaps do no better than simply state one's definition in the given case, as, for instance, in using the term "primitivist" in discussing Faulkner's—or the expressionists'—fascination with the prerational emotionalism of Benjy Compson and Ike Snopes, and the term "regionalist" in evaluating his use of tall tale and southwestern humorist motifs.

It seems essential, above all, in dealing with the terminological field primitivism-regionalism-modernism not to denigrate the regionalist element as reactionary and bad and to focus solely on the modernist forces as forward oriented and good. This kind of allegorizing and moralizing has in the past seriously impaired our perception of the transitions or interrelationship between such phenomena as primitivism and regionalism, in turn limiting our understanding of the role of the respective forces in modernist literature and art. As we shall see, Faulkner's rendering of Dilsey or the anonymous black mule rider whom Quentin befriends shows the same tendency towards monumentalization that characterizes the regionalism of John Steinbeck's *The Grapes of Wrath* (1939) and the contemporary murals of José Clemente Oroszco and David Alfaro Siqueiros.[6] Only when we no longer identify regionalism as inferior and primitivism as good can we understand why the author of the modernist classic *The Waste Land* (1922) is also the author of the reactionary *After Strange Gods—A Primer of Modern Heresy* (1934), why Kandinsky and the German expressionists withdrew to the country to study folk art in Murnau, and why their American contemporaries found such an inspiration in Taos and its regional Native American and Hispanic cultures.

In suggesting this approach to regionalism, I have drawn inspiration from previous criticism as diverse as Steiner/Mondale's multidisciplinary bibliography and Norbert Mecklenburg's comparatist approach to German regionalism, as well as the international context in which Faulkner and Steinbeck appear beside Herman Broch, Thomas Hardy, C. R. Ramuz, J. Giono, Cesare Pavese, F. A. Abramov, D. Aitmatov, J. Amado, and C. G. Rosa, with G. Freyres's "Regionalist Manifesto" and the Latin American "Centro Regionalista" (1926) as important ideological manifestations.[7] Robert L. Dorman's recent groundbreaking intellectual history of American regionalism has proved an important supplement to the studies of the South by Tindall, O'Brien, King, and Gray as well as to the comparatist essays by Nicolaisen and Inge respectively on Faulkner and Hamsun, and on Faulkner and Sholokhov. What emerges from such studies is an understanding of regionalism as an international phenomenon with sociopolitical as well as sociocultural aspects, appearing before and after the turn of the century and observed in many disciplines from many different angles and very often more concerned with *universal values* than with *regions* in the geographic sense. While related to the international romantic tradition, it manifests itself in various national, geographic, and historical formations such as the art work of Grant Wood and Thomas Hart Benton (Gillen 236–68) and the fiction of Willa Cather, Sherwood Anderson, Faulkner, and Steinbeck. Sociologists may insist that the West or the South as "fact" is not significantly different from the rest of the nation, or may prefer to concentrate on particular localities and groups, but the polling results evaluated in John Shelton Reed's several books all demonstrate that the *region* as *concept, image*, or *ideal* continues to exist (*Southern Folk*). However, the fact that a writer chooses his particular region as his main theme does not automatically make him a regionalist. The term is value charged, carrying emotional overtones and implying a positive attitude to the particular region and perhaps to all regions as embodying pastoral ideals, and thus as different from and opposed to other entities such as metropolitan areas and international centers. Moreover, the term carries connotations of simplicity, organicism, healthiness, of agrarianism in the sense of subsistence farming rather than of agribusiness, an inviolate ecology and landscape, and, perhaps most important, an attachment to a specific place as a basis of identity.

One of the regionalist axioms is the intimate connectedness of the regional and the national, and it thus comes as no surprise that Faulkner, like Sherwood Anderson, but also like Gertrude Stein (*The Making of Americans*, 1925) and William Carlos Williams (*In the American Grain*, 1925), felt called upon to emphasize the Americanness of the American literary tradition from which he excludes Poe, Hawthorne, and Henry James as "primarily European . . . not true Americans in the sense that I mean—indigenous American writers who were produced and nurtured by a culture which was completely American such as Whitman and Mark Twain, the poet Sandburg. They were products of a nation which did not develop, did not begin to develop, until after the eastern seaboard was a cultured region, where the tradition (which after all, to me) was a European tradition" (*LiG* 95, 168). It seems revealing in connection with the projection of Faulkner's own literary persona that when asked to name the five greatest American writers he mentions Mark Twain, Herman Melville, Theodore Dreiser, Willa Cather, Sherwood Anderson, and Sinclair Lewis ("the ones that I was impressed with and that probably influenced me . . ."). While all six authors are writers whose Americanness is identifiable with their regionalism, Willa Cather and Sherwood Anderson as declared regionalists are particularly relevant to the question of Faulkner's place in this context.

Apparently, his contact with Willa Cather was limited to his reading experience, but Sherwood Anderson, whom he called, somewhat overgenerously, "the father of all of my works" (*LiG* 101), was his mentor and friend in his crucial New Orleans phase. In fact, Faulkner's early story "Out of Nazareth" (1925), featuring a hero from the Middle West, reads like an echo of Sherwood Anderson's description of the writing of *Mid-American Chants*. Faulkner's story, the work of a beginner, has the advantage, in our discussion, of displaying its regionalist features very directly. The first striking characteristic is that the text serves more to transmit moral or spiritual values than to communicate actual regional features. Associated with this hero are peace and simplicity. There is the same emphasis, as in "The Hill" and "Nympholepsy," on the simple and healthy life of farm labor, "of long, peaceful lands where the compulsions of labor and food and sleep filled men's lives" (*NOS* 47).

However, the most important trait is the closeness of the hero to the earth, an affinity providing an existential basis for spiritual values and a natural sense of direction ("was serving his appointed ends" [*NOS* 48]). The striking absence of this direction was what Gertrude Stein really meant by her ironic commentary on Hemingway and his contemporaries: "You are all a lost generation." Related to this identification of the young regional writer in "Out of Nazareth" with the "eternal" earth are the organicist metaphors in the preface to *The Marble Faun* (1924) and in the somewhat grandiloquent retrospective essay "Verse Old and Nascent: A Pilgrimage" (1925):

> These are primarily the poems of youth and a *simple heart*. They are the poems of a mind that *reacts directly* to sunlight and trees and skies and blue hills, *reacts without evasion or self-consciousness* . . . He has *roots in this soil as surely and inevitably as has a tree* . . . The author of these poems is a *man steeped in the soil of his native land*, a Southerner by every instinct, and more than that a Mississippian. (*MF & GB* 7)

> I have this for which to thank whatever gods may be: that *having fixed my roots in this soil* all contact saving by the printed word, with contemporary poets is impossible . . . I discovered there the secret after which *the moderns course howling like curs on a cold trail* . . . the splendor of fortitude, *the beauty of being of the soil like a tree* . . . (*EPP* 116–17, my emphasis)

Phil Stone's preface, besides illustrating the affinity between regionalism and organicist imagery ("roots in this soil . . . the soil like a tree"; "soil of his native land"), exhibits some of the collocations of the complex "regionalism-organicism" such as the terms and phrases "youth," "simple heart," "without evasion or self-consciousness," "muscularity of wrist and eye," "by every instinct," "the varied outdoor experience," "his quick humor," "the usual Southern alertness and flexibility of imagination," "so shrewdly and humorously honest" (7). Interestingly, those connotations also remain the same in Faulkner's retrospective essay of the subsequent year.

In these early attempts at defining an aesthetics, he not only combines regionalist concepts and vitalistic imagery (soil, tree) (Dorman 113) with the ideal of simplicity, naiveté, and spontaneity, but also displays a decidedly antimodernist stance. His attitude resembles the antipathy of regionalist painters to the internationalist modernism of the Armory Show—despite their own avant-garde techniques. Such an antimodernist attitudinizing appears particularly strange in Faulkner, for whom Eliot and Joyce were revelations even if he did not admit it. Organicism and closeness to the earth—Mecklenburg identifies this trait in connection with "primitivism-elementarism" as "terrism" (64–70)—will remain a characteristic feature of Faulkner's heroes whether we think of Joe Christmas or Lena Grove in *Light in August* or Mink Snopes in *The Hamlet* and *The Mansion*. However, the relation to the soil of these latter figures tends to be more problematic and also less directly stated than in this early story ("I seem to be in true communion with nature" [51]). Still, "Out of Nazareth" is far from a simple story, with Faulkner's aesthetic consciousness and narrative sophistication marking an important step beyond the earlier cubist-regionalist hybrid, "The Hill." On the one hand, there is, in "Out of Nazareth," the direct affirmation against the contemporary malaise of life as a central regionalist value: "But seeing him in his sorry clothes, with his clean young face and his beautiful faith that life, the world, the race, is somewhere good and sound and beautiful, is good to see" (54). On the other hand, there is the sophisticated style of the narrative frame ("no one since Cézanne" [46]) in which the artistic friends Spratling and Faulkner situate the simple hero from the Middle West and his story in a regionalist context, and wonder whether he, along with A. E. Housman's *A Shropshire Lad*, has also read the American regionalist Robert Frost.

This capability of artistic distance is a first indication that Faulkner as a writer would get further than his master Sherwood Anderson. Another mark of Faulkner's superiority is that he, in contrast to Cather and Anderson, who consoled themselves with the dichotomy of a positive regional and a negative metropolitan world,[8] harbored no such illusion. While both Cather and Anderson counterpoint Chicago as the embodiment of the urban dilemma with the regional ideal of the Southwest and the West, Faulkner has the Memphis gangsters in *Sanctuary* gain a foothold in the "pastoral" country because the corrupt and decadent elite (Judge Drake, his daughter Temple, and Horace Benbow) are unable to avoid complicity with them; the simple country folk become their mutual victims. That Faulkner, as we shall see, had his own regionalist illusions about the "goodness" of "simple" people, particularly about women of the earth-mother type, is another matter. However, *Sanctuary* illustrates that the terms "regionalist" and "modernist" do not simply refer to opposites but to a much more complex and ambiguous phenomenon in which both interact. While Anderson's more narrowly circumscribed talent is really definable in terms of the regionalism movement, the regionalist impulse, in Faulkner's case, provided only a departure point and aesthetic basis to be transcended. Yet the great southerner, in emphasizing the importance of Sherwood Anderson's influence, was thinking not only of himself but of his generation. This self-characterization in terms of national-regional features may not do justice to himself or to Hemingway or Fitzgerald, but it does illustrate my point that regionalism and cultural nationalism are closely related: "[Sherwood Anderson] was the father of all of my works, of Hemingway, Fitzgerald, etc. all of them—we were influenced by him. He showed us the way, because up to that time the American writer had been an easterner— he looked across the Atlantic, to England, to France, but only in Anderson's time had we had an American who was primarily American. He lived in the big central part of the Mississippi valley, and wrote what he found there. Hawthorne, the others they were Europeans, they were not Americans" (*LiG* 101).

Essential in Faulkner's argument and confirming the identification of the national with the regional is the supposition that to be a truly American writer one must not come from the Europe-oriented East Coast, but, like Sherwood Anderson, be from "the big central part of the Mississippi valley." Transitions from a regionalist to a nationalist commitment and vice versa apparently come easily. This might seem surprising if it were not for the strange tendency of regionalism towards the universal and its preoccupation with the affirmation of basic values. What facilitates the transition from regional to national assumptions is the philosophical need to assert, in a period of change and shaken value systems, a firm and healthy ideological basis. This merits attention, since Faulkner's patriotism, to which the subtitle of Karl's biography, *William Faulkner: American Writer*, is one of the few references, tends to be overlooked because of both the author's pronounced southernness and the internationalism of his reception. However, what matters in the present context is that Faulkner's patriotism seems to derive from the special regionalist-nationalist brand of the twenties and thirties, and is characterized by the suffusion of soil imagery: "He [Anderson] is American, and more than that, a middle westerner, of the soil: he is as typical of Ohio in his way as

196

Harding was in his. A field of corn with a story to tell and a tongue to tell it with" (*NOS* 139).

The following text from Faulkner's "A Note on Sherwood Anderson" (1953), spelling out the holistic vision of the regional as integral part of the national ("like when you prize a brick out of a wall"), clearly indicates that regionalism implied for him more than rendering regional details, let alone regional clichés ("Iowa corn or Mark Twain's frog"):

> I learned [from Sherwood Anderson] that, to be a writer, one has first got to be what he is, what he was born; that to be an American and a writer, one does not necessarily have to pay lip-service to any conventional American image such as his and Dreiser's own aching Indiana or Ohio or Iowa corn or Sandburg's stockyards or Mark Twain's frog. You had only to remember what you were. "You have to have somewhere to start from: then you begin to learn," he told me. "It dont matter where it was, just so you remember it and aint ashamed of it. Because one place to start form is just as important as any other. You're a country boy; all you know is that little patch up there in Mississippi where you started from. But that's all right too. It's America too; pull it out, as little as it is, and the whole thing will collapse, like when you prize a brick out of a wall."
>
> "Not a cemented, plastered wall," I said.
>
> "Yes, but America aint cemented and plastered yet. They're still building it . . . That's why ignorant unschooled fellows like you and me not only have a chance to write, they must write. All America asks is to look at it and listen to it and understand it if you can. Only the understanding aint important either: the important thing is to believe in it even if you dont understand it, and then try to tell it, put it down." (*ESPL* 8)

What regionalism, in contrast to his region, meant to Faulkner can only partly be elicited from that anti-intellectual, pioneer posturing of Faulkner's Anderson persona ("ignorant unschooled fellows like you and me"; "still building the new America"). But one should note how, already in "Out of Nazareth" and in the early Sherwood Anderson essay of 1925, organicism and anti-intellectualism are linked, and how the syndrome of region-organicism functions as focus for a whole context of related concepts and metaphors, with "simplicity" and the "earth," "corn," and the "land" playing dominant roles.

> One thought of wheat slumbrous beneath a blue sky and a haze of dust, along the land; of long, peaceful lands where the compulsions of labor and

> food and sleep filled men's lives. But he could have come *from anywhere, and he probably had. He was eternal, of the earth itself.* (*NOS* 47, my emphasis)

> And behind all of them a ground of fecund earth and corn in the green spring . . . Here again is the old refulgent earth and people who answer the compulsions of labor and food and sleep, whose passions are uncerebral. (*NOS* 134–35)

The vitalistic implications of the motif are confirmed by the fact that the regional artist is mythicized ("He was eternal, of the earth") and—like the several Faulkner characters who feel the "fecund" earth beat under them—gets into physical contact with it: "In this book he seems to get his fingers and toes again into the soil, as he did in *Winesburg*" (134).

These organicist metaphors characterizing the artist make readers realize how among Faulkner's several masks, his regionalist persona offered a viewpoint opening up a whole new dimension of "earthy" perceptions previously unknown to literature. The representation of the seasonal changes in terms of sexual tension ("the slow, full hot summer and the rigorous masculine winter") heralds the vitalist quality permeating the seasonal and other natural descriptions in Faulkner's own works from *Flags in the Dust* through *Light in August* and *The Hamlet*. A concomitant of this is the emphasis on the unconscious, the "uncerebral," and the "inevitability" of sexual maturing: "[people] whose passions are uncerebral. A young girl feeling the sweet inevitability of adolescence, takes it as calmly as a tree takes its rising sap" (135). What Faulkner registers here in his sensitive appraisal of the regionalist features in Sherwood Anderson is an inspiration which he himself will fully realize in his mythic transformation of the regional features in Lena Grove and Eula Varner.

One more characteristic in Faulkner's Sherwood Anderson portrait—one which he shares with his mentor—needs special mention here, and this is his populist fascination with people, which critics with an internationalist-modernist perspective of Faulkner tend to neglect. But Warren I. Susman, in his *Culture as History*, has emphasized the central role of "the people" in contemporary texts: "The most persistent symbol to emerge from the bulk of the literature of the period, however, was 'the people.' It was the theme of Burke's lecture on 'Revolutionary Symbolism in America.' In 1936 Carl Sand-

burg insisted, at extraordinary length and with much sentimental-
ism: *The People, Yes*" (178). Apparently, this fascination with people
derives from the same source as cultural nationalism, which is more
intimately related to the regionalist faith than one should think. The
urge towards both "the people" and "the nation" coincides with the
regionalist aspiration in expressing the need of a generation longing
for a collective experience that would fortify their identity: "A fascination with the folk and its culture, past and present, aided many to
find a collective identification with all of America and its people"
(205).

The linkage of people and earth remains a recurring feature of
Faulkner's early and late pastoral role-play, with its affinity to the
Walt Whitman quotation indicating the wider regionalist context of
this specific "populism":

> In this book there are people, people that walk and live, and the ancient
> stout earth that takes his heartbreaking labor and gives grudgingly, may-
> hap, but gives an hundredfold. (*NOS* [1925] 137)

> I don't know too much about ideas and ain't really interested in ideas, I'm
> interested in people, so what I speak from my experience is probably a
> limited experience. But I'm interested primarily in people, in man in con-
> flict with himself, with his fellow man, or with his time and place, his
> environment. (*FU* [1957] 19)

> Everything comes out of the dirt,—everything;
> Everything comes out of the people, the everyday
> people, the people as you find them and leave them:
> not university people, not F.F.V. people: people,
> people, just people! (Whitman qtd. in Dorman 81)

It seems important not to lose sight of this populist feature in the
regionalist persona of the writer, because it provides the theoretical
basis for those richly detailed low-class descriptions that Henry James
or Joseph Conrad as yet knew little of. The fascination of Faulkner
and other middle-class authors in the twenties and thirties with simple people, with their ideolects (for instance, Anse Bundren's speech
in *As I Lay Dying*) and eating habits (Lena Grove eating the sardines
in *Light in August* [419–20]) informs much of the description in these
novels and announces itself already in "Out of Nazareth." David's
simplicity is as evident from the naiveté of his reactions as from his

table manners; the comparison here, "like an animal," is meant to be as positive as his delight in pictures "when there were people like you see every day in them, or trees." "He ate frankly, like an animal and though he employed his cutlery as one should not, there was nothing offensive about it—it was exactly what he should have done. No, he told Spratling, he hadn't seen many pictures. But some he liked, when there were people like you see every day in them, or trees. Trees were nicer than flowers, he thought" (*NOS* 48). Like land, labor, and earth, the references to animals and trees serve as means of identifying with the permanence of nature ("eternal, of the earth") and are thus counterpointed to the hectic rhythm and superficial elegance of the Jazz Age that Faulkner would caricature in the scenes at the Mitchells' in *Flags in the Dust*. However, just as important in Faulkner's regionalist treatment of simple people as the detailed rendering of their behavior is the monumental quality of the setting in which they appear.

This tendency announces itself already in the highly stylized landscapes and visionary experiences of the early prose sketches "The Hill" and "Nympholepsis," where anonymous peasant heroes ("his heavy shapeless shoes were gray in the dusty road, his overalls were gray with dust" [*US* 331]; "blue shirt wet with sweat" [*US* 333]) experience a symbolist ecstasy. In *Light in August* Faulkner brings this regionalist combination of monumentalized setting and detailed rendering of manners to perfection. As the following texts show, the regional serves as departure point for a moralizing idealization of simple people and basic situations. In view of a shaken sociocultural order, this dedication to essentials and the corresponding *transformation of the regional into the universal* ("enormous land . . . beyond all time") is to help assess and affirm a new and wholesome philosophy of life: "The wagon moves slowly, steadily, as if here within the sunny loneliness of the enormous land it were outside of, beyond all time and all haste . . . Then she stops, not abruptly, yet with utter completeness, her jaw stilled in midchewing, a bitten cracker in her hand . . ." (419–20). What makes Lena stop eating is the first spasm of the birth of her baby, and the prominent role of such an *ur*-myth as motherhood is typical of the author interested in people. No less characteristic of Faulkner's regionalist role-play is that in "Out of Nazareth" he associates the image of a pregnant woman with the writer: "He reminded one of a pregnant woman in his calm belief that nature, the earth which had spawned him, would care for him, that he was serving his appointed ends, had served his appointed end and now need only wait. For what? He had probably never thought of it. As all the simple children of earth know, he knew that even poverty would take care of its own" (*NOS* 48).

However, Faulkner, self-critical genius that he was, did not naively abandon himself to the regionalist tendencies of the period. Instead, he uses Horace Benbow's relation to Ruby Lamar to make his own tendency to sentimentalize simple, low-class people the subject of ironic portrayal. Yet this self-castigation in Horace, one of his chief personae, did not keep him from turning Ruby Lamar into a secular madonna and an icon of that basic rightness that he was missing in his own class. How far-reaching the implications of the phenomenon—for which "regionalism" is only an approximative term—really are becomes clear from *A Fable*, where Faulkner's fascination with "simple people" (in the Marya plot) fuses with his predilection for the staging—in the manner of Eisenstein and Piscator—of anonymous masses and their movement. The combination of detailed, and, at the same time, monumental renderings of people in *Light in August* as well as in *A Fable* seems to be a reaction by an American writer with a democratic background to sociopolitical tendencies, also manifesting themselves in the preoccupation with people and soil in Knut Hamsun's *Growth of the Soil* and Mikhail Sholokhov's *Virgin Soil Upturned* and *Quiet Flows the Don*. The manifold repercussions and complex consequences of Faulkner's creation for himself of a regionalist persona leave no doubt about the fact that Sherwood Anderson's regional gospel was of prime importance to the young, uncertain writer. It provided the aesthetic formula and sesame for his artistic breakthrough, the conviction that "that little patch up there in Mississippi" was worth writing about.

As the regionalist orientation allowed the westerner Sherwood Anderson to identify with the South—Faulkner would gently poke fun at this in *Sherwood Anderson and Other Famous Creoles* (1926)—it also made the southerner John Crowe Ransom involve himself with the Southwest. Like the consideration of the Anderson connection, a comparative glance at Ransom's "The Aesthetic Regionalism" (1934) provides an opportunity to see Faulkner's southern regionalism in a broader perspective. John Crowe Ransom's enthusiasm about the Indian culture of the Southwest was in line with that of many other modernist painters and writers—Willa Cather, D. H. Lawrence, and Georgia O'Keeffe merely the best known among them—who found the landscape and Indian-Hispanic cultures of the Southwest a congenial counterworld to the "evil and spoilt" civilization of their time.[9] What makes these artist colonies in Taos or those in Worpswede and Murnau in Germany relevant to the theme of regionalism is that the writers and painters, in creating their new surroundings as imaginary regions, were inspired by the same kind of sociocultural and psychological motives manifesting themselves in regionalist aesthetics.

The quest for a new sociocultural order to replace the American way of life, obviously discredited by the 1929 crash ("without that special insecurity which white men continually talk about"), is unmistakable. In fact, the crash, adumbrated in Faulkner's *The Sound and the Fury* (published in October 1929, the month of the crash) in Jason's worried and frustrating financial speculations, is expressly referred to in Ransom's essay.[10] The key demands of the new sociocultural order are a subsistence economy (still dear to environmentalist reformers) and the socially oriented arts and crafts aesthetics of the Ruskin and Morris tradition, which at the time was also very much cherished in the United States.[11] The following passage is of particular interest because it reveals the conglomerate of anxieties which contemporaries sought to exorcize with their regionalist gospel: "The superiority of Indians, by which term the philosophical spectator refers to the obviously fuller enjoyment of life, lies in their regionalism. Regionalism is as reasonable as non-regionalism, whatever the latter may be called: cosmopolitanism, progressivism, industrialism, free trade, interregionalism, internationalism, eclecticism, liberal education, the federation of the world, or simple rootlessness; so far as the anti-regional philosophy is crystallized in such doctrines. Regionalism is really more reasonable, for it is more natural, and whatever is natural is persistent and must be rationalized. The reasonableness of regionalism refers first to its economic, and second to its aesthetic" (Ransom 294).

In view of the gaudy newness of the Jazz Age culture and its economic unreliability, Ransom in his essay and Cather in her Indian-Hispanic novels express special appreciation of the fact that the "Indian culture *goes back to the Stone Age,"* and that these Native Americans "live as they always have lived." There is obviously a point of similarity in Faulkner's taking up the Indian theme in his stories "Red Leaves" (1930), "Justice" (1931), "Lo!" (1934), and "Courtship" (1948) and the fascination with mythicizing history in the prose poems of *Requiem for a Nun* (1951). However, there is also the decisive difference that Faulkner's interest in the Native American history of his region did not lead to a nostalgic affirmation of an inimitable Indian lifestyle but to the critical and grotesque rewriting of Native American history in the South.[12] Perhaps the closest affinity between Ransom's and Faulkner's regionalism lies in their concept of nature as an integral part of the region, exemplified by Faulkner's authentic though strictly functional descriptions of the regional flora and fauna which find an aesthetic justification in Ransom's tenet: "Coming to the theory, the first thing to observe is that nature itself is intensely localized, or regional" (295). Instead of embracing the American pioneer ideal and its metaphors of military conquest, Ransom, like Cather ("It was the Indian's way to pass through a country, without disturbing anything" [*Death* 271]), praises the harmonious relation between Native Americans and nature: "It is as if man and nature had declared a truce and written a peace . . ." (297). The connection in this regard to Faulkner is twofold. First, there is the affinity with Faulkner's sociocultural criticism in *Go Down, Moses*, and his adoption of the Native American view that land cannot be owned as "things" can ("[the land] belonged to no man. It belonged to all; they had only to use it well, humbly and with pride" [*GDM* 261]). The second connection is his experience of the inevitable destruction of the wilderness as a symptom of a more comprehensive human decline ("Now a man drove two hundred miles from Jefferson before he found wilderness to hunt in . . ." [*GDM* 251, 253]).

Sherwood Anderson's 1925 lecture "The Modern Artist," particularly as it is reprinted in the congenial Lantern Press edition,[13] illustrates well the inner connection of regionalism and the arts and crafts ideals, and the context in which we have to situate the Faulkner of the New Orleans period. Anderson's intermingling of regionalist and arts and crafts impulses confirmed Faulkner's appreciation of regional architecture. It manifests itself in his purchasing and restoring the Shegog house as well as in his subtle counterpointing, in *Flags in the Dust*, of the aristocratic Sartoris mansion ("... the white simplicity of it dreamed unbroken amid its ancient sunshot trees" [11]) and the plutocratic villa of the Mitchells ("an architectural garbling so imposingly terrific as to possess a kind of chaotic majesty . . ." [25]), where the embarrassing love scene between Belle and Horace takes place. Faulkner's interest in regional architecture is part of his more comprehensive fascination with both white and black folk culture. Again Ransom's "The Aesthetic Regionalism" provides a helpful perspective, making Faulkner's sense of cultural regionalism stand out: "Cookery is one of the activities which go by regions" (298). Memorable manifestations of regional culture in Faulkner are the Thanksgiving dinner as well as Elnora's singing "Sinner riz fum de moaner's bench" in *Flags in the Dust*, Reverend Shegog's famous Easter sermon in *The Sound and the Fury*, and the tall tales in the horse-swapping episode of *The Hamlet*.

Faulkner's essay "Mississippi," written in March 1953, one year after the Sherwood Anderson essay, demonstrates that he remained committed to the regionalist outlook with which he had become acquainted through his mentor during his 1925 stay in New Orleans. But as a consequence of the changed political situation and the impact of the civil rights movement on societal life in Mississippi, Faulkner's regionalist outlook underwent a considerable modification; above all, it becomes more politicized. However, there is no thirties "blood and soil" and earth-mother cult here. Instead, we find, in what appears at first sight a rambling essay, a very discriminating sociocritical assessment of the region, from its "mythic past" to the author's own memories. It extends from the observation of the wastefulness of the pioneer, in the essay's first section, through the satiric commentary on such heterogeneous matters as northern colonialism, the federal agricultural subsidy policy, and the polluted southern landscape of Faulkner's present.

Informing the gist of the "Mississippi" essay is Faulkner's experience of the socio-political-cultural change from the hegemony of the planter-lawyer-banker aristocracy to that of the redneck class, a great theme that occupied him from *Father Abraham* through *Absalom, Absalom!*, *The Hamlet* and beyond: "because by the beginning of the twentieth century Snopeses were everywhere" (*ESPL* 12). The essay refers in detached terms to the names of the redneck politicians Vardaman and Bilbo, whom the author had introduced into his fiction both as realistic reflection of regional politics (*As I Lay Dying*) and as political grotesques ("... twins, already named Bilbo and Vardaman" [*T* 37]): "These [the Snopeses] elected the Bilboes and voted indefatigably for the Vardamans, naming their sons after both; their origin was in bitter hatred and fear and economic rivalry of the Negroes who farmed little farms no larger than and adjacent to their own ..." (*ESPL* 13). Like his master, Balzac, Faulkner sympathized with the decaying aristocratic culture, and, like him, he registered with the kind of objectivity, which Lukács had found so impressive in Balzac, their replacement by the Snopeses. Moreover, the aristocratic Falkners, as we know from Blotner (I: 144), had no difficulty in working closely together with redneck politicians. Faulkner captured the regional political climate with absolute authenticity when he made Miss Jenny, otherwise the spokeswoman of the aristocratic ancien régime in *Flags in the Dust*, express her sympathy for Mr. Vardaman's racial views in regard to the "uppity" blacks, Caspey and Isom, in the Sartoris family: " 'Who was the fool anyway, who thought of putting niggers into the same uniform with white men? Mr. Vardaman knew better; he told those fools at Washington at the same time that it wouldn't do. But politicians!' " (68) The full implications of this instance of regional and national politics are borne out when we adopt a new historicist view and contextualize the issue by juxtaposing a quotation from one of Vardaman's speeches with a characteristically supercilious description of Vardaman from the viewpoint of William Alexander Percy as a representative of the outgoing plantation aristocracy:

> The Negro is necessary in the economy of the world, but he was designed for a burden-bearer ... Then why squander money on his education when the only effect is to spoil a good field hand and make an insolent cook? (qtd. in Blotner, *Faulkner* [1974] I: 129)

> Father rather liked Vardaman—he was such a splendid ham actor, his inability to reason was so contagious, ... Father considered his Negro-baiting mischievous and his proposed changes in the Constitution impractical and undesirable; he was not a moral idiot of genius like Huey Long; he was merely an exhibitionist playing with fire. So Vardaman announced his candidacy for the United States Senate while Father was hunting quail in Arkansas. (143–44)

The most impressive regionalist aspect of "Mississippi" is Faulkner's courageous stand in 1953 on the race question through an attack against educational, religious, and economic inequality: "But most of all he hated the intolerance and injustice: the lynching of Negroes not for the crimes they committed but because their skins were black" (37). This is in contrast to the unacceptable way in which Ransom and other southern regionalists of the thirties (also Cash in his *Mind of the South*) had idealized ("a spiritual continuity")—or ignored—the racial aspect: "New England had achieved a rather strong regionalism. The South had done about as well, or if anything better. The peculiar institution of slavery set this general area apart from the rest of the world, gave a spiritual continuity to its many regions, and strengthened them under the reinforcement of 'sectionalism,' which is regionalism on a somewhat extended scale . . . The darkey is one of the bonds that make a South out of all the Southern regions. Another is the climate" (Ransom 303–8). Unlike Ransom, with his odd reference to slavery as giving "spiritual continuity" to the South, Faulkner, in *Absalom, Absalom!*, *Go Down, Moses*, and *Intruder in the Dust*, probes the psychology of the guilty racial past as an essential element of his regional heritage. His close ties to individuals such as Mammy Callie and Ned confirmed him in his conviction that African Americans were as integral a part of southern culture as whites and that this should also be reflected in their political and socioeconomic equality. The qualification by one of Faulkner's favorite personae in declaring his love for his region ("*I dont hate it! I dont hate it!*" [*AA* 311])—was in large part caused by the past and present racial attitudes of the South. It is this critical historical consciousness we have to bear in mind when we say that in contrast to his many changing and ephemeral roles, Faulkner's regionalism remained continuous because it concerned his life as much as his art: "Home again, his native land; he was born of it and his bones will sleep in it; loving it even while hating some of it" (*ESPL* 36).

What is most striking in regionalist paintings and writings is not so much the contents as the peculiar modes and forms of their presentation. There is obviously a kind of regionalist ideology inspiring this style of writing that matters much more than the accidental fact of artists being born in a certain region and for that reason depicting regional features. These artists are clearly inspired by the intention to make regional settings convey what they regard as basic human values. As a reaction to the crisis of Victorian beliefs after World War I and after the stock market crash of 1929, artists and writers began looking for lasting values, no longer finding them in the antiquated, "Genteel Tradition" exploded by George Santayana; thus, they turned to the "simplicity" of regional or black life and to primitive or archaic qualities. Willa Cather's novel *O Pioneers!* (1913) and her story "Neighbor Rosicky" (1928) about Nebraska farm life are, at their centers, characterized by a healthy simplicity and a mystical closeness to the earth, while cities like London and New York appear as tainted environments in both the social and the ecological sense. Sherwood Anderson's novel *Dark Laughter* (1925) depicts African Americans representing primitivist values—invoked under the headings of both modernism and regionalism—in contrast to the inhibited whites.

In view of the neo-Rousseauist or populist faith in "the people" of regionalists like Anderson, Cather, and also Faulkner, it is not surprising that the regions where populism had emerged most forcefully, the West and the South, were also those where cultural regionalism particularly flourished. Obviously neither Ruby Lamar in *Sanctuary* nor Lena Grove in *Light in August* is a paragon of southern womanhood (Scott 3–21); indeed, Ruby, as a woman with a past and a sickly baby, and Lena, as an unwed mother, are conceived as inversions of the traditional ideal and embody the new populist ideals of the thirties that combined low social status with the positive qualities of vitality and an unorthodox moral stamina.

In this regard both appear as counterweights to the spoilt or decadent representatives of the outgoing upper class, Temple Drake and the Reverend Hightower, the one depending on the status of her father, the Judge, and the other obsessed with the false glamor of a heroic southern past. That the contemporary hopes in the redemptive quality of a simple, natural and lowly life eventually had a politically conservative rather than an emancipatory impact is another matter. There is no doubt that Faulkner's regionalist leanings are of a problematic and probing kind, as the study of metaphor in *The Hamlet* will show. Nevertheless, he shared—and in parts of such works as *Sanctuary, Light in August, Go Down, Moses,* and *Intruder in the Dust* also expressed—the regionalist yearning for timeless values, for the heroism of common people, for the redemptive qualities of the land. This

207

can be seen from the modes of representation as well as from the contents of such motifs as sculptures and gods, the plow, the house, the regionalist madonna, and Lena and Dilsey as monuments. The contrary tendencies toward minutely rendered regionalist details and toward a stylized, monumental presentation have considerable relevance in terms of the semiotics of culture: the populist motives arise as symbols of Faulkner's attempt to exorcize the decline of the old aristocratic order as well as his own disgust at the vulgar modernity of Snopesism.

Apparently, Faulkner's problem was one confronting other writers of his time as well; for instance, James Agee, who together with the photographer Walker Evans produced a documentation on the impoverished rural South of the thirties in *Let Us Now Praise Famous Men* (1941), refers to the same issue of combining the realistic with the aesthetic element, "finding a diction proper to the so-called simple folk" as "one of the most embarrassing, not to say hopeless, literary problems we have set ourselves" (qtd. in King 204; 213–14). The problem is in part that of the equally pressing claims of *regionalist realism* and *regionalist idealism*. Both Agee and Faulkner, in their attempts to "elevate" regional material, have recourse to the arts and to Egyptian or Greek sculpture in particular:

> These two sat as if formally, or as if sculptured, one in wood and one in metal, or as if enthroned, about three feet apart in straight chairs tilted to the wall . . . (Agee and Evans 32)

> They are like two figures in a Greek frieze, isolated out of all reality by the red glare. (*AILD* 149)

The same tendency reveals itself in *Sanctuary* in the stylized description of the anonymous country people whom the sinister events attract to the town. "The square was lined two-deep with ranked cars, while the owners of them and of the wagons thronged in slow overalls and khaki, in mail-order scarves and parasols, in and out of the stores, soiling the pavement with fruit- and peanut-hulls. Slow as sheep they moved, tranquil, impassable, filling the passages, contemplating the fretful hurrying of those in urban shirts and collars with the large, mild inscrutability of cattle or of gods, functioning outside of time, having left time lying upon the slow and imponderable land green with corn and cotton in the yellow afternoon" (86).

208

What Faulkner provides here is undoubtedly a richly concrete, authentic picture of his region. But neither term, "realism" nor "regionalism," enables us to do full justice to this text. What informs the metaphoric phrasings such as "mild inscrutability of cattle or of gods," "outside of time," or "having left time lying upon the slow and imponderable land" is an urge—as in the paintings of Thomas Hart Benton and Grant Wood—to widen the scope of reference and to reveal the universal meaning inherent in regional features. It is worth noting that these phrases are far from alone in having this effect. Rather, they act as a focus for several other stylistic features, too, like the leitmotif "slow," which recurs in striking configurations ("slow overalls," "slow as sheep they moved," "the slow and imponderable land"), and the bold mythicizing of the country folks ("with the large, mild inscrutability of cattle or of gods"). These metaphors structure and symbolically charge their whole context. In its combination of realistic and stylized features, the harmonious prose evoking the permanence and beauty of a southern landscape ("the slow and imponderable land green with corn and cotton in the yellow afternoon") is a characteristic example of Faulkner's contribution to regionalist art. If Cleanth Brooks falsely identified this side as the solely important aspect of the South, his successors, in an understandable reaction, have tended to err on the other side and have too exclusively focussed on Faulkner's critical assessment of the "negative" South.[14]

How important regionalist values were to Faulkner is demonstrated by the fact that seventeen years after *Sanctuary* (1931), in *Intruder in the Dust* (1948), he would similarly cite them, in view of still more strained race relations, of an urgent need to reform, and of fear of white supremacist resentment. In the following description of a car ride with his progressive uncle Gavin, the boy narrator, Chick Mallison, notes how the black population neglects their pressing field work because, after the murder of Vinson Gowrie, they fear reprisals by the Gowrie clan and other white supremacists. The thrust of the stylized description and iconic evocation is racial oppression (leitmotif: "empty") against which Faulkner sets, in symbolic counterpoint, the image of one intrepid black plowman embodying what in Cleanth Brooks's day one called "the lasting order" of the rural South. The outcome is a landscape painting in the style of the symbolically over-charged realism and ideological insistence of WPA murals:

> now he could see the white bursts of dogwood in the hedgerows marking the old section-line surveys . . . and *always* beyond and around them the *enduring land*—the fields geometric with furrows where corn had been planted . . . *but empty, vacant of any movement and any life.* (*ID* 394)

> . . . and in the back yards the pots sitting *empty and cold* among last Monday's ashes among the *empty* clotheslines and as the car flashed past the *blank and vacant* doors . . . but most of all, the *empty fields* themselves in each of which on this day at this hour on the second Monday in May there should have been fixed in *monotonous* repetition *the land's living symbol—a formal group of ritual almost mystic significance identical and monotonous* as milestones tying the county-seat to the county's ultimate rim as mile-stones would: *the beast the plow and the man integrated in one foundationed into the frozen wave of their furrow* tremendous with *effort* yet at the same time *vacant of progress,* ponderable *immovable and immobile like groups of wrestling statuary* set against the *land's immensity.* (395)

> . . . he and the Negro behind the plow looked eye to eye into each other's face before the Negro looked away—the face black and gleamed with sweat and passionate with effort, . . . *the man and the mule and the wooden plow* which coupled them furious and solitary, *fixed and without progress in the earth,* leaning terrifically against nothing. (395–96, my emphasis)

Faulkner, employing the populist motif of the plow twice in connection with the central concept of his aesthetics, the coincidence of rest and movement, evokes in the verbal sculpture of "the man and the mule and the wooden plow" the absent but imaginatively present other black plowmen and their teams. The monumentality of this vision ("against the land's immensity"; "terrifically against nothing") is enhanced through the silhouette effect, the association of the Laocoon group and the anonymity of the plowmen, and in this way suggests universality and depth of meaning. The symbolic quality does not reach readers indirectly but is expressly stated; in fact, the narrator informs readers that the appearance of the plowmen ought to be captured as "ritual of mystic significance," "it should have been fixed" as "the land's living symbol." The ideological and didactic overemphasis, which strikes modern readers probably as aesthetically dubious, is a characteristic, if belated, feature not only of regionalist but also of socialist and fascist art of the thirties.

In view of Faulkner's sympathy for the archregionalist Willa Cather, it is not surprising that they both turn plows into monuments.[15] As in Cather's *My Ántonia* (1918) ("There was nothing but land: not a country at all, but the material out of which countries are made" [7]), the emphasis in Faulkner's *Intruder in the Dust* is not on land and earth as a geographic, physiographic fact but as a mythic entity with plows ("the beast the plow and the man" [395]; "the man and the mule and the wooden plow" [396]) appearing symbolically "staged": "On some upland farm, a plough had been left standing in the field. The sun was sinking just behind it. Magnified across the distance by the horizontal light, it stood out against the sun, was exactly contained within the circle of the disk; the handles, the tongue, the share—black against the molten red. There it was, heroic in size, a picture writing on the sun" (Cather, *My Ántonia* 245). Where Faulkner employs the imagery of sculpture, Cather uses lighting effects and magnifying, but the western and the southern regionalists both transform the plow and other realistic details into transregional, universal symbols. Neither Cather nor Faulkner could foresee how short-lived the rural values, set forth as lasting safeguards in the shaken world of post–World War I America, would be, because they could not anticipate the extent and speed of spreading agribusiness, industrialization, and urbanization.

In contrast to the somewhat obtrusive regionalist plows, more ambiguous images such as the equally monumentalized ruinous plantation house continue to fascinate present-day readers. The mansion in which Lee Goodwin and Ruby Lamar have made their home is in dilapidated condition and is a reminder of the fatal southern past; Lee's entanglement, as the operator of a still, with Memphis organized crime illustrates the socioeconomic dilemma of the contemporary South. Ruby's baby, growing up in this house, is sickly, and Ruby's own life as wife and mother, in contrast to that of Lena Grove in *Light in August*, is overshadowed by the invasion of evil.

> The house was a gutted ruin rising gaunt and stark out of a grove of unpruned cedar trees. It was a landmark, known as the Old Frenchman place, built before the Civil War . . . (18)

> The gaunt ruin of the house rose against the sky, above the massed and matted cedars, lightless, desolate, and profound. (25)

> The house came into sight, . . . It was set in a ruined lawn, surrounded by abandoned grounds and fallen outbuildings. (39)

> . . . [Ruby's baby], lying in a wooden box behind the stove in that ruined house twenty miles from town; of Popeye's black presence lying upon the house . . . (92)

The fact that readers are made to encounter the house four times forcefully impresses upon them its importance as a regional and historic landmark. Ruins of great plantation houses in southern landscape and literature have a special iconic quality, indicating the historic dimension characteristic of southern regionalism. Readers, visualizing the house from the viewpoint of Horace Benbow and Temple Drake, the weak and depraved heirs of the southern aristocratic tradition, become more acutely aware of how fallen feudal grandeur is supplanted by the lifestyle of the rednecks ("the people of the neighborhood had been pulling down piecemeal for firewood for fifty years or digging with secret and sporadic optimism for the gold"), a theme that Faulkner will later explore fully in *The Hamlet*.

While the first three passages above are marked by the tension between past greatness and the marks of present rural depression, in the last text Ruby's sickly baby is exposed to the sinister influence of Popeye's silhouette as it overshadows the house, the criminalized present implicating the southern past. Faulkner's intense, not to say obsessive, endeavors to come to terms with the guilty regional past (in so many ways and in so many of his works) seem to be, as it were, encapsulated in the iconic leitmotif of the ruinous plantation house. The recurring traits of its metaphoric realization—it is gaunt, gutted, stark, lightless, darkened by unpruned cedar trees, overgrown by jungle vegetation, and, above all, its silhouette is drawn against a "failing sky"—produce the kind of apocalyptic air surrounding Poe's "The Fall of the House of Usher."

As Poe found himself unable to share the optimistic spirit of Jacksonian Democracy and the ideology of Manifest Destiny, Faulkner was reluctant to herald the New Deal South which some of his countrymen were promoting. The symbolist quality of his prose style would indicate, however, that his concern in creating the dark icon of the plantation house went far beyond the history and sociology of any particular region. Aided by the Swinburnean music of elaborate sound patterns ("gutted ruin rising gaunt"; "massed and matted cedar"), the metaphoric suggestions of the dark, eviscerated house overwhelmed by the chaotic growth of vegetation carry us to the depths of meaning where *social experience* passes into a confrontation with the *collective unconscious*.

The tendency to elevate the regional element by combining the realistic with the monumental marks the transition from the Roaring Twenties to the Depression of the thirties. After the irony and cynicism of the postwar period, with its relativism and parodistic destruction of traditional forms, the era of Roosevelt's New Deal looks for new orientations. As a reaction against the blasé sophistication of the twenties, many artists in the thirties sought to base their new system of values once again, as in the romantic period, on concepts of naturalness, simplicity, the land, and basic human relationships like motherhood or genuine passion such as that felt by Ruby Lamar for Lee Goodwin (which stands in contrast to the empty flirtatiousness of the spoilt aristocrat Temple Drake or the decadent titillation of Horace's desire for his stepdaughter).

The motif of mother and child in *Sanctuary* and in *Light in August* also has an archetypal quality, in addition to its function as a means of social criticism.[16] The presence of the child heightens the contrast between Temple Drake, the spoilt and egoistic flapper from a so-called "good" family, and Ruby Lamar. Impoverished and victimized yet genuinely loving and bravely enduring, Ruby embodies Faulkner's ideal of heroic womanhood ("Across the child Temple gazed at the woman's back, her face like a small pale mask beneath the precarious hat" [51]). However, what keeps Faulkner's handling of the madonna motif from becoming too obtrusively symbolic is the restrained form of stylization in the first part of the sentence (Ruby Lamar is referred to as "she" and the "woman") and the quick return to a concrete rendering of the situation ("discovered that she had forgotten its bottle" [81]). Nevertheless, the element of stylization is sufficient to raise the contrast between Ruby's and Temple's final exchange of views to the level of a fundamental moral opposition. Ruby, who in her unshaken devotion to Lee Goodwin has prostituted herself to save him, is one of the victimized but idealized low-class heroines of the thirties. Stylized throughout as "the woman and the child," she is set against Temple, the spoilt aristocrat and empty flirt. In the scene at the spring, the heroine, whose description in the novel is consistently grounded in the reality of the depressed South and whose very name, Lamar, is a parodic reminder of the southern tradition, assumes a universal and timeless quality. In the context of the thirties, the mother and her child, sitting at a spring in the country,[17] appear as icon of the continuing power of human rightness, representing the counterpoint to the forces of evil (Temple, the flapper, with Popeye, the gangster, on their way to the metropolis) conveyed in modernist metaphors: "to the woman beside the road it was like a small, dead-colored mask drawn past her on string and then away" (81).

In *Light in August*, too, Faulkner manages to keep the scenes with Lena and her baby from becoming a too openly affirmative, regionalist madonna tableau, presenting, for instance, the final resumé from the humorous perspective of the furniture dealer in bed with his wife. Furthermore, as in *Sanctuary*, the scene with mother and child in *Light in August* develops against the sinister backdrop of a "dark house" where Joe has murdered Joanna, whom Hightower contrastively refers to as a "Poor, barren woman . . . barren and ruined acres" (699). Above all, the regionalist quality of the madonna scene is not communicated authoritatively and directly by the narrator. Instead, it arises from Hightower's interpretation of the scene, which, in its regionalist "healthiness," is as outré as are his decadent visions before his redemption through his "midwifery":

> *More of them. Many more. That will be **her life, her destiny. The good stock peopling in tranquil obedience to it the good earth; from these hearty loins** without hurry or haste descending mother and daughter . . .* "I must do this more often," he thinks, feeling the intermittent sun, the heat, **smelling the savage and fecund odor of the earth, the woods,** *the loud silence . . . It seems to him that he can see, feel, about him the ghosts of **rich fields,** and of the **rich fecund black life of the quarters,** the mellow shouts, the presence of **fecund women, the prolific naked children** in the dust before the doors; . . . The cabin is empty save for the mother and child. She is propped up on the cot, **the child at breast.** (699, my emphasis)*

Nevertheless, readers will register this vitalistic quality of Hightower's regionalism as well as the fusing of regionalism with primitivism. The white madonna, because of her vitalistic connotations, is associated with black life, which, in *Light in August,* as in Sherwood Anderson's novel *Dark Laughter* (1925), is associated with fertility and primitivism. As we shall see, the white woman Lena and the black woman Dilsey have as regionalist icons similar symbolic implications, both playing similar roles as redemptive fantasies of a white male.

Strategies such as time shifts and leitmotifs, word and sound repetitions in Faulkner's open novels provide a kind of metaphoric deep structure or extended imaginative space for the "regionalist madonna" in which readers engage more fully in processes of metaphorization than in the traditional novel: "backrolling now behind her a long monotonous succession of peaceful and undeviating changes from day to dark and dark to day again, through which she advanced in identical and anonymous and deliberate wagons as though through a succession of creakwheeled and limpeared avatars, like something moving forever and without progress across an urn" (*LA* 403). The repeated segments of the narrative affect readers in the same way as the many repetitions of formulaic phrases and individual words ("from day to dark and dark to day"; "between darkness and day"; "slow and terrific"), and these rhetorical effects provide a frame in which the metaphoric gist of the passage evolves. The image of the mule wagons appears in a modulation of Faulkner's favorite passage from Keats, "like something moving forever and without progress across an urn."

What is obvious to sensitive readers is that Lena's metaphoric contemplation of movement without progress in the "still pinewiney silence of the August afternoon" elevates her far beyond the realistic context. Throughout, the story, seemingly proceeding as realistic narrative, takes on a poetic dimension, as when Lena's four-week journey appears allegorized and reinforced by acoustic effects: "Behind her the four weeks, the evocation of *far,* is a peaceful corridor paved with unflagging and tranquil faith and peopled with kind and nameless faces and voices: ***Lucas Burch? I dont know . . . This road? It goes to Pocahontas***" (403, my emphasis). This effect is enhanced by the chorus of "kind voices" continuing the responsory: *"Lucas Burch? You say you tried in Pocahontas? This road? It goes to Springvale"* (405). The romantic name of the true Indian maid, Pocahontas, for some out-of-the-way place in the deep South functions like the metaphoric refrain of a ballad, endowing Lena's shabby fate with irony and pathos. Clearly, the new ways in which Faulkner uses metaphor in his fiction

215

substantially alter our reading experience. What Lena's portrait has in common with Dilsey's—and, as we shall see, also with Mrs. Armstid's in *The Hamlet*—is that the rich concreteness of their regional characteristics are realistically captured, but, through Faulkner's metaphorizing, readers experience them as icons of universally relevant values.

In a similar way, the setting at the beginning of part 4 of *The Sound and the Fury* prepares for the *monumental features* in Dilsey's portrait as in the solemn opening phrase, "The day dawned bleak and chill, a moving wall of grey light out of the northeast" (330). Against the contrastive but also congenial background, "wall of grey light," the narrator carefully *sculpts the statue* of the black matron who keeps the moribund household of the aristocratic Compsons from collapsing totally. The tenor of Dilsey's description is the tension between her aged but still impressive figure, between her shabby and grotesque but in regard to their symbolic suggestiveness also impressive clothes, "a maroon velvet cape . . . above a dress of purple silk."[18] What above all gives Dilsey's appearance a monumental quality are similes establishing a rapport between her physical features and moral qualities ("as though muscle and tissue had been courage or fortitude") and between her stature and the southern landscape. The feature in Dilsey's appearance suggesting the very regional simile of "a ruin or a landmark," such as the plantation houses in *Sanctuary* and *The Hamlet*, is the prominence of her bone structure: "She had been a big woman once but now *her skeleton rose*, draped loosely in unpadded skin that tightened again upon a paunch almost dropsical, *as though muscle and tissue had been courage or fortitude which the days or the years had consumed* until only the *indomitable* skeleton was left rising *like a ruin or a landmark* above the somnolent and impervious guts, and above that the collapsed face that gave the impression of *the bones themselves being outside the flesh*, lifted into the driving day with an expression at once *fatalistic and of a child's astonished disappointment*, until she turned and entered the house again and closed the door" (331, my emphasis). The monumentalizing traits achieved through daring metaphors in Dilsey arise from an urge to affirm values, in particular the moral stamina and heroism of the underprivileged against the odds. The portraits of Lena and Dilsey are prominent examples of how realist description and mannered metaphors, affirmation of moral qualities and distortive monumentalizing together contribute to the symbolist effect of Faulkner's regional inspiration.

Albert C. Barnes, in "Negro Art and America," calls the "Negro a poet by birth" (20) and, with a vocabulary reflecting an unexpected affinity between the Harlem Renaissance and Herder, Wordsworth, and the romantic worship of unspoiled folk art, stresses the poetic nature of black religion: "Poetry is religion brought down to earth and it is of the essence of the Negro soul . . . The Negro has kept nearer to the ideal of man's harmony with nature" (20). This view of African Americans is significant not because it is based on any political, economic, or social black reality, but because it emerges as a contrast and supplement to the decadence of the white imagination. The distinctive feature of the black image is that of a countermask, black not as fact but as white metaphor.[19]

As far as the metaphoric element in character drawing is concerned, psychoanalytic critics like Irwin and Jenkins have been particularly important because they have examined projection and transformation in addition to mimesis. We should remember, however, that the interest of such critics has been directed more to the psychological content than to the aesthetics of metaphoric transfer (Jenkins 159). Although such psychoanalytic interpretation has an undeniable validity, particularly for Faulkner's self-projection into nonwhite characters such as Joe Christmas in *Light in August* and Charles Bon in *Absalom, Absalom!*, we should not regard it as absolute (61–105).[20] There are other black characters in Faulkner where the metaphoric transfer seems to be more adequately discussed in terms of cultural or intellectual history, and where "black" functions not, as with Charles Bon in an ambiguous image of an unacknowledged side of the white ego, but as a regionalist symbol of life-giving forces.

Faulkner's references to the book as the writer's dark twin (*MOS* 251), on which I have drawn in testing the applicability of the concept of mask and role-playing, show the young author already aware of the metaphoric dimension of character drawing. Quentin Compson's stream of consciousness in *The Sound and the Fury* allows us not only to assess the content psychoanalytically with Jenkins but also to observe a white imagination at work forming black metaphors.[21] The hero, having sat down beside a black person in the only vacant seat in a Cambridge streetcar, under the impact of the regional difference between the northern and southern codes reflects first upon his attempt to adjust to the northern view of blacks: "I just kept thinking you've got to remember to think of them as colored people not niggers." His new awareness of the two different social responses causes him to reflect perceptively on the metaphoric element in racial communication: "That was when I realised that a nigger is not so much a person as a form of behavior: a sort of obverse reflection of the white people he lives among" (106). A black person in this definition, instigated in the young southerner by the experience of the North, appears as "invisible man," a nonperson to the point of being an abstraction. "Nigger," for the intellectually conscious Harvard student, does not represent any positive or negative individual projection but is taken as an indicator of the moral condition of white society.

Faulkner, however, does not let Quentin rest with his generalization. Journeying through Virginia on his way home for the Christmas holidays, Quentin suddenly stops considering how and what northerners might expect him to think about blacks and affectionately remembers Dilsey and Roskus: "I didn't know that I really had missed Roskus and Dilsey and them until that morning in Virginia" (106). This momentary recovery from his alienation and emotional paralysis is initiated by the regional image of "a nigger on a mule": "The car was blocking a road crossing, where two white fences came down a hill and then sprayed outward and downward like part of the skeleton of a horn, and there was a nigger on a mule in the middle of the stiff ruts, waiting for the train to move. How long he had been there I didn't know, but he sat straddle of the mule, his head wrapped in a piece of a blanket, as if they had been built there with the fence and the road, or with the hill, carved out of the hill itself, like a sign put there saying You are home again" (*SF* 106). The scene, closely observed and realistically rendered, at the same time has wider metaphoric implications. For Quentin perceives the landscape as one does the Cézanne-inspired, Cubist landscape in Hemingway's *The Sun Also Rises*, and he experiences the "nigger on the mule" like a sculpture or the figures on Keats's Grecian urn—freed from time and space—as an emblem of home. The realistic snapshot of a black rural southerner, transposed to an imaginative plane, takes on the status of art and, as a consequence of this selection and metaphoric transfer, becomes charged with value, assuming a mythic and timeless quality.

218

But this piece of black sculpture has a white theme: it suggests to Quentin's homesick, split personality a vision of the South as his home region, as a social and psychological context in which he can sooner preserve his identity than in the North at Harvard. If the associations and reflections evoked by the image seem to derive more from the author using Quentin as a persona, this does not affect their relevance regarding the use of black as white metaphor.

The cultural environment that the formula "black as white mask and metaphor" seeks to address is recognizable in the following sentences from Carl Van Vechten's novel on the Harlem Renaissance, *Nigger Heaven*, which appeared alongside *Soldiers' Pay* in 1926: "And now the white editors are beginning to regard Negroes as interesting novelties, like white elephants or black roses. They'll print practically anything our coloured writers send in" (49). Van Vechten's novel of the Jazz Age is written with a great awareness of the effect of the discovery of African culture on the development of twentieth century literature and art, manifest in the references to blues and spirituals and to Gertrude Stein's "Melanctha," another classic example of the white projections of a black mask. The novel is also influenced by African sculpture, the effect of which upon Picasso, Braque, and Matisse is noted by Stein in *The Autobiography of Alice B. Toklas*.

A further illustration of the fascination exercised by the black image on the white imagination is the exhibition of De Zayas's collection of African art, photographed by Charles Sheeler (1926) and so important to the New York avant-gardists around Stieglitz and Arensberg. Main events in this tradition were Gauguin's discovery of native art in Tahiti (1891), such sculptures as Picasso's "Dancer" (1907) and "Bronzehead" (1909), Matisse's "Two Negresses" (1908), and the expressionist paintings by Erich Heckel, "Sleeping Negress" (1911), and Emil Nolde, "The Missionary" (1912). That white artists sought to embody in their black masks values lost in white culture becomes clear from Nolde's nostalgic primitivism that in turn is related to the holistic yearnings of the regionalists: "Primeval man lives within his nature. He is at one with it and a part of the whole universe. Occasionally I feel that he is the only real human being left, while we are more like marionettes, spoilt, artificial and completely in the dark" (qtd. in Kunst 46).

In Faulkner's first novel, *Soldiers' Pay* (1926), as in Van Vechten's

Nigger Heaven (1926) and Anderson's *Dark Laughter* (1925), the descriptions of African Americans act as a positive, vitalistic metaphor associated with "the passion of spring and flesh" and "something pagan" in the sense of something exotic, vigorous, and subconscious (*SP* 312). The darkness of color ("from it welled the crooning submerged passion of the dark race" [319]), also evident in *Light in August* ("dark and inscrutable" [565]) and in Sherwood Anderson's title, tends to become mystified, assuming that Freudian aura to which Faulkner had referred in *Mosquitoes*. His debt to the modernist use of the black image as white metaphor also manifests itself in the structure of his fiction and in the contrapuntal setting of the naturalness and continuity of black life against Donald's paralysis in *Soldiers' Pay* and Bayard Sartoris's war trauma in *Flags in the Dust*. This structural pattern in Faulkner's first two novels is considerably modified in *The Sound and the Fury* but is nevertheless recognizable—despite Dilsey's highly individual character—in the superiority of her black existence, outlasting the Compsons and achieving mythic timelessness: "I seed de beginnin, en now I sees de endin" (371). The tendency to turn the black image into myth is also apparent in numerous minor stylistic features, such as when the blacks and their mule wagon in *Soldiers' Pay* are metamorphosed into "a pagan catafalque . . . carved in Egypt ten thousand years ago" (151). Here, the reality of the rural South's black regional culture assumes a dignity comparable to the classicist stylization of contemporary industrial reality in the paintings of Charles Demuth and Charles Sheeler (*Classic Landscape*, 1931).

The groups of African Americans in *Flags in the Dust*, drawn still more concretely than in *Soldiers' Pay*, authentically represent black southern reality: "young girls in stiff mail-order finery, the young heritage and labor on unaccustomed high heels" (*FD* 127). However, it must be small comfort to modern African Americans that black southerners appear as white projections—even if they constitute a positive counterimage to the cold violence and emotional atrophy of Bayard's split personality—particularly in view of the animalist and primitivist features ("animal odor") of this projection: "He stood for a moment on the sidewalk . . . Negroes slow and aimless as figures of a dark placid dream, with an animal odor, murmuring and laughing among themselves. There was in their consonantless murmuring something ready with mirth, in their laughter something grave and sad" (127). Similarly, in *Light in August* the anonymity of the "summer voices of invisible negroes" (483) conveys by metaphoric contrast Joe's desperate search for identity. However, the theme of the novel is not black as a positive counterimage but the tragedy of its white metaphorical use.

Since psychoanalysis depends upon the binary system of a symbolic relationship between the known and the unknown, the conscious and the unconscious, and since black has symbolized the unknown and the dangerous to the white world view, its frequent appearance as a psychoanalytical image of a white dilemma comes as no great surprise. That it does indeed act as a white metaphor is confirmed by its function in *The Unvanquished*, *Absalom, Absalom!*, and *Go Down, Moses* as a replacement for the twins in the sibling motif of *Flags in the Dust*. A somewhat dubious means of alerting readers to the metaphoric quality of the black characters is Faulkner's tendency to editorialize, as in the debate on black virtues and vices between Ike and McCaslin in "The Bear" of *Go Down, Moses*. The extensive theorizing inevitably draws readers into a search for the embodiment of the black virtues dear to the author's white heart, and consequently overlooks those features which—as Noel Polk has pointed out—may be less flattering, but still make Dilsey come to life (*Children* 219–41).

This moralizing tendency and emphasis on representative aspects to the neglect of the concrete and noticeable in "The Bear" become even stronger in the "Sambo" passages of *Intruder in the Dust*. The Lucas Beauchamp of *Go Down, Moses* has here shrunk to an ideological puppet—the object of Faulkner's affirmation and expiation—yet another example of worthy political intentions leading to inferior literature and an extreme example of black as a white image. What clearly distinguishes *Intruder in the Dust* from *Flags in the Dust* is that, in line with historical developments, the content of the black image is more directly political, whereas in Faulkner's earlier novels, in conjunction with the impact of the Harlem Renaissance, black appears as a cultural metaphor, expressing the modernists' sophisticated yearning for the simple and regionalist, the archaic and unconscious. Among the black images that Faulkner uses as white masks, there are some personae that sooner represent regionalist values and others that rather suggest primitivist qualities. For, despite the overlapping between the terms, there are also some distinctions that can be made: the term "regional" suggests the local, traditional, and emotional, while the term "primitivist" refers more to the preindividual, archaic, and pre-rational. In this sense Quentin's encounter with the black mule rider is more of a regionalist experience accompanying his return from uncongenial New England to his southern homeland, in contrast to Joe Christmas's nightmare of the black pit that embodies his subconscious sexual-racial fears. There is little doubt that in reenacting Faulkner's regionalist and primitivist black role-play, readers have to exercise considerable flexibility.

EIGHT

Regionalism and Beyond

The Hamlet

One of the most bewildering perspectives thrown open by the new *reception* aesthetics is the complexity of the metaphoric experience in reading Faulkner's novels. While this new approach leads to a better understanding of Faulkner's fusion of regionalism and modernism, readers still have to be as flexible in their reactions to the widely varying metaphoric forms as the role-playing author. In addition to identifying with the artist as "countryman" and sharing with him the metaphoric implications of eyes "the color of a new axe blade" (756) and of a "sagging broken-backed cabin" (746), one should be able to catch the literary allusion of his adjective "Rabelaisian" (733). It prepares for the grotesque dimension of *The Hamlet* and suggests a humorously detached view of Will Varner, the linchpin of its socio-economic cosmos. When the metaphoric signal "Rabelaisian" recurs (814), it is supplemented in a complex manner by the rural irony of the proverbial simile "cheerful as a cricket" and its sardonic parallel, "bowel-less as a tax-collector," the latter serving as satiric link to money, the central leitmotif.

The following instance of imagery from the sport of fencing has a similarly distancing effect on readers, particularly through the mannered extension of the metaphoric material: "all levity was gone from his voice, all poste and riposte of humor's light whimsy, tierce quarto and prime" (738). This technical lingo evolves after Will Varner's ironic remark to his equally rapacious but less cunning son, Jody: "Then you can point out to him which house to burn too." The elegant and clever fencing metaphor, when contrasted to Jody Varner's boorish stupor, makes readers register how the would-be exploiter panics when the projected victim of the sharecropping system turns out to be a dangerous arsonist. Both of these examples illustrate the subtle role that metaphorics play in the narrative communication between characters and readers.

However, the needed flexibility in readers' responses to imagery of apparently similar content or reference area can just as easily be demonstrated by the many short comparisons belonging—besides very complicated metaphorized syntax—to the style of Faulkner's "rural" narratives. The following short rural comparisons, which are placed at the beginning of the novel, have the oral quality of metaphor in proverbs and are all characteristic of *The Hamlet* as a regional novel:

> . . . thin as *a fence rail*. (733)

> . . . and one broad black-haired hand motionless and heavy *as a ham* . . . fire seems to follow him around *like dogs follow some folks* . . . druv them out *like a pair of heifers*. (740–41, my emphasis)

Yet within the category of the regional or rural, these short comparisons offer a wide spectrum of stylistic nuances and functional differences. The comparison "thin as a fence rail," for instance, is not an invention of Faulkner's but of the folk imagination. As a consequence of the wear and tear of ordinary language, the imagistic quality of a fence rail is visualized far less in rural speech than it is by readers who encounter it in Faulkner's novelistic context. Here, the narrator mentions Varner's "thinness" after the ironic characterization "He was a farmer, *a usurer*, a veterinarian" and, as the narrator quotes Judge Benbow, no less ironically, "a milder mannered man never bled a mule or stuffed a ballot box," thus taking on additional sociocultural and political implications. The metaphorized context connecting Varner's usury, his veterinary skills, and his political unscrupulousness demands from readers a detached, reflexive response. In the metaphorized description of Jody's hand, they will relate through acoustic aids—"*h*airy, *h*and, *h*eavy, *h*am"—the heaviness of the metaphoric "ham" not just to Jody's uncouth appearance but also to his clumsy exploitativeness as a landlord (his "heavy deliberate sprawling script" on the sharecropper's contract). In the instance of Ab Snopes—the purported arsonist—and the image of "fire following . . . like dogs follow some folk," readers are affected by the simile's narrative function, highlighting both Ratliff's ironic description of Jody Varner (734–35) and its rural dimension.

Here, as in "druv them out like a pair of heifers" (741), the shortness of the simile has the advantage of not holding up the narrative for long and of considerably adding to its regional concreteness. That the latter was indeed Faulkner's ambition can be seen from the narrator's humorously detached qualification: "[a heifer is] just a little too valuable to hit hard with a stick." This detail encapsulates the economic situation as vividly as the patriarchal family and gender relations under the sharecropping system in the depressed rural South. The example illustrates how Faulkner's depiction of the social and political realities of the region, through the metaphoric communication of southern folk culture, becomes aesthetically memorable.

In studying this specific kind of regionalism, attention to the modes and contexts of metaphoricity clearly promises more insights than typologies of metaphoric forms and taxonomies of image contents. That metaphors indeed reveal, as new historicism and cultural studies suggest, an ideological dimension in addition to the narrative content is apparent also in *The Hamlet* in the *collectivist manner* of presenting people. Faulkner's handling of the triumphant final trek of the Snopeses has the same affirmativeness and generalizing quality confronting us in Steinbeck's *The Grapes of Wrath*, in the post office art of the WPA, and, more embarrassingly, in the graffiti of Stalinist and Nazi art: "the weathered and creaking wagons, the plow-galled horses and mules, the men and women and children entering another world, traversing another world, traversing another land, moving in another time, another afternoon without time or name" (1072). The peculiar hovering of the text between an emphasis on the concrete and on generalizing features is characteristic of regionalism. The metaphoric reflection of social experience will receive further attention in our next example, in which native inhabitants of Frenchman's Bend, representing an earlier stage in social history, are characterized through a rural image when they come to look at Flem ("half-wild cattle following word of the advent of a strange beast" [778]). His arrival is so important because it signals a colder and more distant quality than Will Varner's exploitive economic order, based on an individual's ability to seduce and be seduced. It will affect not only Armstid and the pony buyers but also Ratliff, the champion of anti-Snopesism. In contrast to the short rural simile "half-wild cattle," the imagery expressing the peculiarly anonymous and evanescent nonfeatures of the Snopeses and the arrival of a faceless American mass culture in the South laboriously evolves in intensely metaphorized syntax.

> They saw that the clerk was heeled as by a dog by a man a little smaller than himself but shaped exactly like him. It was as though the two of them were merely graded by perspective. At first glance even the two faces were identical, until the two of them mounted the steps. Then they saw that the second face was a Snopes face right enough, differing from the other only by the unpredictable variation within the iron kinship to which they had become accustomed—in this case a face not smaller than the other exactly but closer, the features plucked together at the center of it not by some inner impulse but rather from the outside, as though by a single swift gesture of the fingers of one hand; a face quick and bright and not derisive exactly as profoundly and incorrigibly merry behind the bright, alert, amoral eyes of a squirrel or a chipmunk. (864–65)

Both the optical and the plastic effect ("graded by perspective" and "features plucked together . . . by . . . fingers of") point rather to the distortive modernism of the early T. S. Eliot than to regionalistic pastoralism. A further manneristic effect is caused by the insistence on capturing in detail and with unnatural precision the contraction and transformation of the Snopes face and by the ironic addition of the "amoral squirrel or chipmunk eyes." There is a similar effect in the presentation of the noncharacter I. O. Snopes, whose talkative weasel's face (789, 790) contrasts with the emptiness of his endless stream of dislocated proverbs and the ludicrous vagueness of his clothing. The reader's experience of the clothing is again affected by the grotesque precision in the rendering of the metaphoric material ("of what the body within them might be doing") and above all by its leitmotif-like presentation in several installments:

as though the attitude and position of his garments gave no indication whatever of what *the body within them might be doing*—indeed, if it were still *inside them* at all. (789)

that weasel-like quality of existing *independent of his clothing* . . . (789–90)

the clothes which would still appear *not to belong to him* on the day they finally *fell off his body* . . . (790, my emphasis)

In *The Hamlet*, too, Faulkner makes use of the kind of modernist, distortive, and mechanical imagery that Bleikasten and others have noted in *Sanctuary*. What perhaps needs to be emphasized, however, is that its manneristic effect arises from the stylistic tension between the *modernist metaphorics* and the *regional material*. The difference in this respect between *Sanctuary* and *The Hamlet* consists only in the ratio between modernist and regionalist components.

Flem's "tiny predatory nose like the beak of a small hawk" (777) is among the numerous animal images (see also the use of the chipmunk, weasel, birds, and cows in this section) that, when applied to human beings, produce grotesque effects, while at the same time underlining together with the many other natural images the rural and regional character of *The Hamlet*. What makes this "tiny predatory nose like the beak of a small hawk" relevant to our present discussion is that it serves as departure point for a very manneristic metaphoric extension. Instead of presenting readers with a finished portrait, the metaphors challenge them to match the narrator's ingenuity and to envisage for themselves several caricatures. "It was as though the original nose had been left off by the original designer or craftsman and the unfinished job taken over by someone of a radically different school or perhaps by some viciously maniacal humorist or perhaps by one who had only time to clap into the center of the face a frantic and desperate warning" (777–78). The metaphoric conceit of a portrait "designer or craftsman" is only introduced to note his absence and his unsatisfactory substitution by another, uncongenial artist. These two metaphoric possibilities are then replaced by two equally unattractive artistic alternatives ("maniacal humorist" and "frantic" warner). As a consequence, readers do not receive from this imagery a unified impression but are made to participate in a process—to test, as it were—several imagistic options. In this way, Flem's uncanny indefiniteness or indefinability that does indeed make him such a formidable threat to the community is forcefully impressed on readers. His distorted features appear as a "desperate warning" that the era of Varner's more personal, if cruder, rural system of exploitation will be supplanted by the more far-reaching and more efficient urban-based system of exploitation of Flem Snopes, the banker.

Faulkner's use, in evoking such a caricature, of the kind of distortive modernistic imagery that had impressed him so much in poems like "Rhapsody on a Windy Night" and "The Love Song of J. Alfred Prufrock" by his master T. S. Eliot is very appropriate. But we should note that, before we are exposed to the multiplicity of Flem's cubistic portrait, we see him arrive in an absolutely authentic, regionalist setting. "He rode up on a gaunt mule, on a saddle which was recognised at once as belonging to the Varners, with a tin pail tied to it. He hitched the mule to a tree behind the store and untied the pail and came and mounted to the gallery, where already a dozen men, Ratliff among them, lounged" (777).

The following examples are to demonstrate Faulkner's inventiveness in inserting modernistic metaphorics into regional contexts. In the trivial incident of Jody Varner observing his tenant's daughters at the well pulley, the modernistic imagery opens up a new dimension of meaning. "This time it did not cease when he passed, the two broad faces, the one motionless, the other pumping up and down with metronome-like regularity to the wheel's not-quite-musical complaint, turning slowly again as though riveted and synchronised to one another by a mechanical arm . . . when he saw suddenly, . . .the man whose face he had seen in the window of the house. One moment the road had been empty, the next moment the man stood there beside it, at the edge of a small copse—the same cloth cap, the same rhythmically chewing jaw materialised apparently out of nothing" (749). Readers cannot be sure what the meaning is, but they register the pronounced mechanical quality of the imagery and the fact that the two young women, who are never individualized in the novel, appear as parts of a rural mechanics and are dehumanized as later on Henry Armstid will be. Furthermore, readers know about the sharecropping contract and Jody's fear of Ab Snopes as a suspected arsonist. Finally, they are as startled as Jody is by the uncanny appearance of Flem. This then is the visual and sociopolitical material

228

for the readers' imaginations to work on; in the metaphorizing process, the mechanical quality of the characters comes to be associated with their economic and cultural deprivation.

There is no doubt that what is most sinister about the Snopes family is that nearly all of them—whatever their particular features—are essentially conceived as caricatures and as not fully human. Consideration of this trait is perhaps not superfluous at a time when critics tend to treat the characters in the novel as realistic figures and emphasize their good or bad sociopolitical points. Close study of the kind of metaphors which characterize the figures in *The Hamlet* sensitizes readers to their allegorical dimensions and to their function as embodiments of contemporary—and in particular Faulkner's—fears. The use of the image of the metronome both for Armstid, who is the victim of his individual greed as much as of the socioeconomic system, and for Ab Snopes's daughters, who are just caught in it, demonstrates that Faulkner's regionalist pastoral is of the problematic kind and not an idyl, protected from the intrusion of the mechanical spirit of modern economics:

> waist-deep in the ground as if he had been cut in two at the hips, the dead torso . . . like a *metronome*. (1068–69)

> his *metronome*-like labor . . . with the regularity of a *mechanical* toy and with something *monstrous* in his unflagging effort. (1073–74)

> the two broad faces, the one motionless, the other pumping up and down with *metronome*-like regularity . . . as though rivetted and synchronized to one another by a mechanical arm. (748, my emphasis)

The interrelationship between narration and metaphor shown in the above texts is once more demonstrated when, twenty-five pages later, Ratliff likewise meets the Snopes daughters and also subjects them to an intense metaphorizing process. They appear first as birds and then as cows, and these grotesque metamorphoses accompany the vision of an apocalyptic landscape: "as if the sound had been emitted by two enormous birds; as if the aghast and amazed solitude of some inaccessible and empty marsh or desert were being invaded and steadily violated by the constant bickering of the two last survivors of a lost species which had established residence in it . . . A moment later the two girls came to the door and stood, big, identical,

229

like two young tremendous cows, looking at him . . . bodies of that displacement and that apparently monstrous, that almost oppressive, wellness . . . He had a fleeting vision of them as the two cows, heifers, standing knee-deep in air as in a stream, a pond, nuzzling into it . . ." (773–74). As in the case of the imagery presented from Jody's point of view, Ratliff's metaphorizing vision also serves to reflect aspects of the viewing and viewed characters. However, its major effect is to provide the narration of sociocultural changes, which worried Faulkner, with a more universal appeal and a Beckett-like dimension ("empty marsh or desert . . . the two last survivors of a lost species"). In regard to the interrelationship of narration and metaphor in this humorous novel, it is important to note the comic contrast between these far-ranging metaphoric excursions, functioning like epic similes, and the matter-of-factness of the laconic dialogue: " 'Morning, ladies,' he said. 'Where's your paw?' . . . 'Down to the field' " (774).

In view of Faulkner's regionalist affinities, it is not surprising that in his tragicomic novel about a hamlet in Yoknapatawpha he would draw on the rich southern tall tale and humorist tradition and its respective influences (for example, Augustus Baldwin Longstreet's "The Horse Swap," George Washington Harris's "Sut Lovingood's Daddy, Acting Horse"), which have been duly considered elsewhere.[1] Moreover, the structural parallels and thematic connections between the duelling horse-swapping episode, pitting Ab Snopes against Pat Stamper, and the other money and barter scenes in the novel, contributing to the thematics of economic power, are well known among Faulknerians.[2] However, the role of metaphor in convincingly integrating the tall tale material into this regionalist-*cum*-modernist novel of the late thirties has received less attention.

A great part of the enjoyment in reading the horse-swapping episode derives from Faulkner's ingenious tall tale metaphorics, of which some gain additional effectiveness from being presented in the casual way of oral images in rural speech and proverbs. The narration of Ab's attempt to go easy on the impossible jade, which he aims to barter away, contains good examples of this: ". . . Ab walking up every hill that tilted *enough to run water offen it*, . . . with Beasley's horse kind of half walking and half riding on the double tree . . . with that horse of Beasley's eyes rolling *white as darning eggs* and its mane and tail swirling *like a grass fire*" (760, my emphasis). But there are

230

also tall tale exaggerations reminding readers of the grotesque distortion of modernist metaphors: "we went down the hills with Ab holding the wagon braked with a sapling pole so it wouldn't shove Beasley's *horse through the collar and turn it wrong-side-out like a sock . . .*" (761–62, my emphasis). In fact, Faulkner, indefatigable experimenter that he was, deliberately used modernist strategies in handling tall tale material. In the grotesque instance of Ab's own broken-down horse, which Pat Stamper's "nigger artist"—with the help of a bicycle pump—has so "transformed" that Ab himself does not recognize it anymore, the comic effect of the short similes ("like a hog," " 'tight as a drum," "like they didn't have no weight") is considerably enhanced by the modernist repetition strategies of Gertrude Stein and Hemingway—or of Faulkner's own "Dry September":

> how that horse shined—a horse a little bigger than the one we had traded Stamper, and *hog fat*. That's just exactly *how it was fat*: *not like* a horse is *fat* but like *a hog*: *fat* right up to its ears and looking tight as a drum; it *was so fat* it couldn't hardly walk, putting its feet down like they didn't have no weight nor feeling in them at all. *"It's too fat* to last," Ab says. "It wont even get me home."
> "That's what I think myself," Stamper says. (767, my emphasis)

However, what most clearly distinguishes Faulkner's tall tale from those of the old southwestern humorists is its tragicomic dimension. The horse-swapping episode remains comic to the very end (the black horse loses its color in the rain and the pumped-in air escapes with "a sound like a nail jabbed into a big bicycle tire" [770]), but Ab Snopes appears finally prostrated ("was laying out [dead drunk] in the wagon bed by then, flat on his back with the rain popping him in the face"). There is no character in all the southwestern humorist writings who is so down and out. In fact, Ratliff tells this tall tale not just to entertain but to explain how Ab became "soured" (755). Ab, like Armstid, that other "fool about a horse" (770), has not only ruined himself but has also harmed his wife—in this humorous tale—by losing the money she had saved for the milk separator on which her heart is set. Miz Snopes's comic and, at the same time, very moving agricultural progressiveness transfers readers abruptly from grotesque frontier comedy into the depressed rural South of the regionalist thirties. This return to the narrative frame makes clear

231

that the horse-swapping yarn is contextualized by the separator story, which, notwithstanding Miz Snopes's triumph and the burlesque tall tale solution of selling the cow to buy a milk separator, is a regionalist satire and a potentially tragic story. As in the case of the Armstids— and in a biographically revealing way[3]—Faulkner makes the suffering woman dominate the scene: "She looked like the kind of somebody that never had done much crying to speak of nohow, because she cried hard, like she didn't know just how to do it, like even the tears never knowed just exactly what they was expected to do, standing there in an old wrapper, not even hiding her face, saying, 'Fool about a horse, yes! But why the horse? why the horse?' " (770)

Miz Snopes's dominance in this tragicomedy is largely expressed through the structure and narrative setting of the imagery. Ratliff, sympathizing with Ab and his wife, makes three attempts to communicate his impression of Miz Snopes's sadness at the betrayal of her vision. Readers note that, in the instance quoted above, Ratliff— belying Faulkner's brilliance in devising this conceit—is groping for a metaphoric expression but has apparently no glib or colorful comparison ready. Ratliff's metaphorizing effort has such a moving effect on readers because he remains tied to his regional speech, and, in his search for a reference point for his comparisons, cannot get beyond the heroine herself ("like she didn't know just how to do it"), her tears, and the fact that she is "somebody that never had done much crying to speak of nohow." But this is far enough to endow hard-crying Miz Snopes of Frenchman's Bend and her tragicomic yearning for a separator with universal appeal.

The figure of Mrs. Armstid allows us to study more closely how Faulkner employs metaphor to achieve the fusion of the regional with the universal. Mrs. Armstid plays a major role in the Spotted Horses section of part 4, "The Peasants," attempting first to persuade her husband not to buy one of Flem's useless and violent ponies with the little money she has saved for the children. After this attempt has proved impossible, the Texan, playing the stereotypical role of the gallant cowboy, returns it to her. However, she loses it again because her husband throws it back, and she fails to recover it from Flem, who has picked it up. The two episodes constitute major communal events with Mrs. Armstid's victimization functioning in both as a moral center.[4] While the pony scene presents the seductiveness of

Flem's Vanity Fair—or the gullibility of the rural society—the scene of his rejection of Mrs. Armstid's plea demonstrates the ruthlessness and cynical hypocrisy of Flem's real regime.

Readers experience the two episodes as strong narrative scenes, but are equally under the sway of the no less powerful metaphoric element providing the narration with its symbolist dimension. The most striking metaphoric mode in both scenes is that of imagistic leitmotifs. In the pony scene, with the circus motif dominant and "gaudy" the key word, readers are challenged to register a multitude of impressions but also to synaesthetically relate and thematically functionalize them:

> circus . . . gaudy as parrots. (983)
> the harlequin rumps . . . a kaleidoscopic maelstrom of long teeth and wild eyes . . . (986)
> [the moonlight's] treacherous and silver receptivity. (988)
> gaudy units . . . gaudy phantoms in the gloom. (993–94)
> the towering parti-colored wave full of feet and glaring eyes and wild teeth. (995)
>
> The bright cloudless early sun gleamed upon the pearl butt of the pistol in his hip pocket and upon the bell which Mrs. Littlejohn still rang . . . the butt of the pistol catching and losing the sun in pearly gleams. (996–97)
> a kaleidoscope of inextricable and incredible violence on the periphery. (1000)

It is against this bewildering and dubious play of impressionistic colors, or rather kaleidoscopic color changes, light effects, movements, and suddenly appearing details, that we note Mrs. Armstid's "gray" as counterpoint. The color, or noncolor, *gray*, aided by alliteration, appears first as part of the introduction of the heroine, characteristically behind her husband: "She came up among them behind the man, *g*aunt in the *g*ray shapeless *g*arment and the sunbonnet, wearing stained canvas gymnasium shoes" (1001, my emphasis). But a symbolist setting in the next instant of the leitmotif makes us soon realize that gray is more than a color adjective: "The wife had gone back to the wagon, *where she sat gray in the gray garment*, motionless, looking at nothing still; she might have been *something inanimate which he had loaded into the wagon to move it somewhere*, waiting now in the wagon until he should be ready to go on again, *patient, insensate, timeless*" (1004, my emphasis).

The leitmotif "gray," emphasized through repetition, reaches readers as part of a complex context in which several aspects, variants, or nuances of one basic state of being or quality, "motionless-looking at nothing-inanimate-waiting-patient-insensate-timeless," are offered to the readers' meditative attention. What gradually impresses itself on sensitive readers is a polarity or tension. On the one hand, Mrs. Armstid is degraded into a thing ("to be loaded in her husband's wagon"); on the other, she is elevated into something timeless like a piece of art. If the one status reflects Faulkner's view of the regional realities of the depressed South, the other was that of his idealistic art, universalizing a Mississippi peasant woman into an icon of human misery and dignity.

In the process of integrating the regional and the universal, the swallows in the soft, vague blue over Mrs. Littlejohn's regional chinaberry tree issue very modernistic cries "like strings plucked at random" (1005), and Mrs. Armstid's gray and shapeless garment is made to give her movements the stylized appearance of a statue on a float in a procession ("the gray and shapeless garment within which she moved without inference of locomotion, like something on a moving platform, a float" [1006]). This leitmotif recurs, slightly modified, at the conclusion of the breathtaking scene in which Flem, after refusing to return to her the money for the horse, gives her five cents' worth of candy, "A little sweetening for the chaps" (1027). At the end of her desperate and degrading quest ("Snopes . . . spat neatly past the woman, across the gallery and into the road" [1026]), the intensity of which is emphasized by the scene being watched with absorption by several characters (*HAM* 1025–26), Mrs. Armstid again "seemed to progress without motion like a figure on a retreating and diminishing float; a gray and blasted tree trunk moving, somehow intact and upright, upon an unhurried flood" (1027–28).

The structuring of the imagery, a very purposeful parallelization of the cult-figure image and the realistic metaphor of the floating tree trunk (as seen by Faulkner in the Mississippi River flood of 1927) is to impress on readers the elevated status of the heroine. The most striking attempt to stylize this regional character, in "stained canvas gymnasium shoes, sunbonnet, and gray shapeless garment" and obviously close to the regionalist photos and verbal portraits of deprived peasants in Walker Evans's and James Agee's *Let Us Now Praise Fa-*

mous Men (1941), is through the metaphoric suggestion of a bronze sculpture: "Motionless, the gray garment hanging in rigid, almost formal folds like drapery in bronze" (1026). But, then again, Faulkner had behind him a thorough training in the art of stylization, and the sculptor, as we have seen in chapter 3, was one of his favorite personae.

The question of artistic stylization as a means of negotiating the tension between the regional and the universal refers us to the more comprehensive problem of the philosophical underpinnings of the regionalist preoccupation of Faulkner and his contemporaries. Again, metaphor, so often revealing the deep structure and basic values underlying grotesque or realistic surface descriptions, provides us with interesting insights. There are in *The Hamlet*, in contrast to the works of other regionalists such as Willa Cather or Knut Hamsun and also in contrast to Faulkner's own *Go Down, Moses* and *Intruder in the Dust*, very few references to the reassuring regionalist value system and southern world picture that Cleanth Brooks maintained he had found and that his successors have since so thoroughly dismantled. However, we do find in the imagery occasional universalizing gestures, marking moments of reflection in which the characters gain distance from their struggles and miseries, as when Eula's suitors, after their savage fistfights, appear "freed even of rage and frustration and desire, beneath the cold moon, across the planted land" (852), or when, after the Texan has returned Mrs. Armstid's money for her children, there is a sobering lull in the mad turmoil of the ponies and the virulence of the peasants' greed: "They leaned along the fence, grave and quiet, as though the fence were in another land, another time" (1008).

Apparently, there is no sustenance to be drawn from the land nor from "the summer constellations march[ing] overhead" (1065; see also 1067) or "the ordered stars [that] seemed to glare down in cold and lidless amazement at an earth being drowned in dust" (974). Rather, readers, when confronted with the ordered stars shortly before observing—with Ratliff's eyes—the "two small grimed hands" of the imprisoned Mink Snopes or the foolish and greedy treasure hunters, will experience these juxtapositions as ironic metaphors. The companion piece of the thirties tableau, depicting the departure of the Snopes family into town, is the picture at both the beginning and the end of the novel of the "shell of the tremendous house" (1047). In its ruins the dust of the feudal owner commingles with that of the exploited architect and the abused slaves ("the progenitors of saxophone players in Harlem honkytonks" [1048]). In the great scene of the region in winter, the image of the trains and the sheet-iron stove in Mink's prison cell seem to encapsulate Ratliff's feelings about the region and world. Clearly, the regionalism of *The Hamlet* is not of an affirmative but of a problematic kind, and what Faulkner, by metaphorically integrating the regional and the universal,[5] communicates to readers is not any edifying message but the human dilemma and the experience of art: "[the daily trains] black, without dimension and un*peopl*ed and *pl*umed with fading va*p*or, *r*ushing without *purpose* through the white and *r*igid solitude. . . . and he would think of the four of them sitting, huddled still in the coats, about the small ineffective sheet-iron stove which did not warm the cell but merely drew form the walls *like tears* the *old sweat* of *the old agonies* and despairs which had harbored there" (977, my emphasis).

Since we know from several competent thematic analyses that the complex "property-barter-money" is one of the central concerns of *The Hamlet* (Vickery 167),[6] it seems questionable whether the readers' metaphoric experiences of its socioeconomic dimension can tell us anything new about the book. However, the interesting results of new historicist rereadings of old texts encourage us to find by "indirections directions out." In this respect, it is of interest to discover in descriptions of Ratliff's and Flem's business activities very similar imagery, although we know from the discussion of the novel's thematic and structural level that the honest trading of the sewing machine agent is contrasted with Flem's exploitive business practices:

> he looked about him with something of the happy surmise of the first white hunter blundering into the idyllic solitude of a virgin African vale teeming with ivory, his for the mere shooting and fetching out. (781)

> In the tunnel-like room lined with canned food and cluttered with farming implements and now crowded with patient earth-reeking men waiting to accept almost without question whatever Varner should compute he owed them for their year's work, Varner and Snopes resembled the white trader and his native parrot-taught headman in an African outpost. That headman was acquiring the virtues of civilization very fast. (786)

In each case, the syntax of the passage gives readers ample opportunity to catch the irony of the leisurely unfolding colonial imagery from the world of Joseph Conrad or Edgar Rice Burroughs, illustrating the dilemma of southern economics. Varner and Snopes appear as colonial traders because—using the commissary as a key institution of the sharecropping system—they exploit their tenants. Ratliff is, of course, not an exploiter in that sense, but he is a party to the unhealthy economic system, finding himself one day in this summer temporarily alienated from the rural society of his Mississippi home as the ironic metaphor reveals (". . . not only on foreign soil and shut away from his native state by a golden barrier, a wall of neatly accumulating minted coins" [781]). As one of those flourishing under the overheated economic system ("he had done a little too well. He had oversold himself, selling and delivering the [sewing] machines against the coming harvest" [781]), he is, as we can deduce from the metaphors, in a manner implicated in the crash of 1929 that aggravated the misery of peasants like the Armstids and those in Evans's and Agee's *Let Us Now Praise Famous Men*.[7] The undergirding for such a reading derives from scenes like the very funny episode of tall tale humor and thirties satire in which Eck Snopes, with breathtaking innocence, tells Ratliff how his kinsman I.O. suggested that they name the son whom Eck fathered at sixteen, and who "never had no name to speak of until last year" (981), Wallstreet Panic: "I.O. read about that one in the paper. He figured if we named him Wallstreet Panic it might make him get rich like the folks that run that Wallstreet Panic" (981).

That someone of Ratliff's probity appears as part of the fatal economic nexus of boom and crash is the deeper reason why in the end, even he, the champion of anti-Snopesism, falls victim to Flem's temptation of the hidden treasure in the old plantation house. What the colonial imagery impresses on readers is that the situation of the "patient and earth-reeking" tenants in *The Hamlet* is anything but that of the Jeffersonian yeoman tillers of the soil, and that *The Hamlet* is a regionalist novel not in affirming regionalist values but in critically exposing the impact of their absence.

Another example of the uncanny similarity between the strategies of the representatives of good and evil characteristic of this humorous novel is Ratliff's attempt to entrap Flem through his goat ranching project. Following the suggestions of the imagery, we recognize in the skit about the North's superior business style the bitter southern resentment of the doubtful practices of that northern colonialism[8] which the regionalist Walter Prescott Webb, in *Divided We Stand: The Crisis of a Frontierless Society* (1937), had attacked shortly before the publication of *The Hamlet* in 1940:

> Because the Northerners were "the masters of the Industrial Revolution," Webb argued, the "story of the sections since the Civil War" was the story of "how the North has extended its economic conquest over the other two sections, how it has drawn the bonds constantly tighter until it owns not only its own section but a controlling interest in the South and the west." (qtd. in Dorman 160)

> When [a Northerner] does something, he does it with a organized syndicate and a book of printed rules and a gold-filled diploma . . . for all men to know by these presents, greeting, that them twenty thousand goats or whatever it is, is goats. He dont start off with goats or a piece of land either. He starts with a paper and a pencil and measure it all down . . . (79)

The metaphorics deepening the readers' understanding of the exploited is no less striking than that satirically exposing the exploiters (white trader and "gold-filled diploma"). There are metaphors that are such integral parts of Ratliff's narrative voice that they reach readers as naturally as the images in folk speech and proverbs. They just as unobtrusively identify the miserable hill farm of Mink Snopes as a representative example of the social situation. "Ratliff turned in beside it—a rutted lane now, at the end of it a *broken-backed* cabin of the *same two rooms which were scattered without number* through these remote hill sections which he travelled. It was built on a hill; below it was a foul muck-trodden lot and a barn leaning away downhill *as though a human breath might flatten it*" (798, my emphasis).

This insistence on catching the fate of the common man, "the people" (see chapter 7), was so important in the thirties that it informed societal visions otherwise as different as the novels of Caldwell and Faulkner and the scholarly publications of the social scientists at Chapel Hill (Singal 115–52). However, equally strong and intimately related to the tendency of what in aesthetics is referred to as "generalizing" is the urge to capture in the collective the individual. The photos, contemporary with *The Hamlet*, of Eudora Welty, Walker Evans and Arthur Rothstein attest to this.[9] We find the same insistence on the individuality of a common peasant in Faulkner's rendering of Mink Snopes's battered mailbox and the singular lettering of his name. "[The mailbox] was battered and scarred; at one time it had apparently been crushed flat as though by a wagon wheel and straightened again, but the crude lettering of the name might have been painted on it yesterday. It seemed to shout at him, all capitals, MINK SNOPES, sprawling, without any spacing between the two words, trailing off and uphill and over the curve of the top to include the final letters" (798). After the text's low degree of transformative energy and its smooth transition between detailed description and equally photographic metaphor, readers are exposed to the startling iconic experience of MINK SNOPES and its synaesthetically metaphorizing anticipation ("seemed to shout at him" [798]). This strong effect confirms the overall impression of Faulkner's peculiar preoccupation with this unprepossessing character, who, in his smallness and through his ruthless sense of honor and unlimited toughness, might be another of his personae and certainly was close to his heart. The iconic image of MINK SNOPES does not just prove once more Faulkner's well-known sense of graphic effects. It is characteristic of "the artist's way of scribbling 'Kilroy was here' " (*LiG* 253) and of his moral insistence that "the puny inexhaustible voice . . . will prevail" (qtd. in Fant and Ashley 131).

What makes this "prevailing" difficult for everybody in Frenchman's Bend is the alliance between Will Varner and his son-in-law, Flem Snopes, which is demonstrated by their riding together in Varner's new buggy. Faulkner succeeds in making these buggy trips metaphorically suggestive of the "speeding aura of constant and invincible excursion" of the twenties, while, at the same time, they communicate to readers the kind of sinister gaudiness characterizing the pony auction in part 4 ("It's a circus . . . It's Flem Snopes" [983]). "A month after that Varner bought a new runabout buggy with bright red wheels and a fringed parasol top, which, the fat white horse and the big roan in new brass-studded harness and the wheels glinting in vermilion and spokeless blurs, swept all day long along back country roads and lanes while Varner and Snopes sat side by side in outrageous paradox above a spurting cloud of light dust, in a speeding aura of constant and invincible excursion" (814). The "outrageous paradox" that this brilliant impressionist image of the buggy with the ill-matched team encapsulates is the uneasy truce between the representatives of the old and of the new, more efficient, method of exploitation of the hamlet.[10]

As there has been a tendency in the criticism of this novel to reduce its main concern to the battle against Snopesism, some supplementary study of its metaphoric level to redress the balance may be welcome and should make us realize that Faulkner's motive was not so much a sociopolitical antagonism as an artistic fascination with the very complex sociocultural consequences of the rise of the rednecks.[11] One of the many manifestations of this is the portrait of Labove, who will receive further attention in connection with the love theme. What concerns us here are the sociological and anthropological aspects and their metaphoric expression in such instances as the football episode, in which the setting is as hilariously funny as it is socially revealing.

Will Varner, looking for a schoolteacher for his hamlet, is astonished to find on a remote hill farm "an incredibly old clay pipe smoking woman" wearing football shoes, and, more amazing still, a letter sweater from the University of Mississippi's football team. As it turns out, her great-grandson, Labove, whom Varner subsequently hires, has recently been discovered at the university as football talent and has sent home the sweater and seven pairs of football shoes to support his impoverished redneck family. In its comic incongruence, the appearance of the old hillbilly woman in football shoes and a "dark blue man's sweater with a big red M on the front of it" humorously epitomizes the response of the redneck population to the challenges of sociocultural changes and sophistication. "She would wear it on Sundays, winter and summer, sitting beside him on the seat of the churchward wagon on the bright days, the *crimson accolade of the color of courage and fortitude gallant in sun*, or on the bad days, sprawled and quiet *but still crimson, still brave, across her shrunken chest and stomach* as she sat in her chair and rocked and sucked the dead little pipe" (826, my emphasis).

The imagistic unit, fusing comedy with accolade (courage, fortitude, gallant, brave) and enhancing its affective power by word repetition and alliteration, rises momentarily from a normal descriptive sentence. It provides readers, as a direct statement could not, with a concrete sense of redneck toughness and a fitting background for Labove's portrait. What makes this portrait so important in the novel, and also, one should add, in the history of American civilization, is the fact that it represents a new type of leader—boss Willie Stark in Robert Penn Warren's *All the King's Men* in fiction and Lee Russell, Bilbo, Vardaman, Huey Long in fact—who, emerging with the rise of the rednecks, lives on, in a modified form, in their fundamentalist successors: "a man who was not thin so much as actually gaunt, with straight black *hair coarse as a horse's tail* and *high Indian cheekbones* and quiet pale hard eyes and *the long nose of thought* but with *the slightly curved nostrils* of pride and *the thin lips of secret and ruthless ambition*. It was a *forensic face*, the face of invincible conviction in the power of words as a principle worth dying for if necessary. *A thousand years ago it would have been a monk's, a militant fanatic . . .*" (827, my emphasis)."

In gauging the metaphoric impact of the passage, we should note that it derives above all from the symmetrical allegorization of the three physiognomic features ("nose of . . . nostrils of . . . lips of") and the invocation of a historic prototype (monk, militant). The imagistic supplement of the description "*h*air coarse as a *h*orse's tail and *h*igh Indian cheekbones and quiet pale *h*ard eyes" catches the reader's attention not through any great metaphoric transformation but through its effect as an acoustic unit. In view of the many indiscriminate references to "the endless and formless Faulkner sentence," one should perhaps mention that the present example is fairly representative in illustrating the degree of careful—not to say formalist—rhetorical patterning that, as his early études document,[12] had been long in coming.

In this novel, set at the turn of the century, Faulkner, with as much sociocultural perspicuity as artistic inventiveness, chose the example of college football at the University of Mississippi to illustrate Labove's acculturation difficulties. Upon entering the university, the hero's economic and religious background makes it difficult for him to understand that there should be in addition to life as he knows it—as all-out fight for subsistence—a sphere of cultural play, that sports matter, and, most impressive to his hillbilly sense of value, that people should be actually prepared to spend money on sports. In anthropological terms, Labove's most important experience is that of

241

sport as a form of cultural play, entailing not only a dress code (that one does not play in overalls [830]) but also a civilizing ethics: "how there were rules for violence" (830). This complex experience informs Labove's stream of consciousness in which perceptions distanced through the reflecting process affect readers as metonymic images: ". . . when he carried a trivial contemptible obloid across fleeing and meaningless white lines. Yet during these seconds, despite his contempt, his ingrained conviction, his hard and spartan heritage, he lived, fiercely free—the spurning earth, the shocks, the hard breathing and the grasping hands, the speed, the rocking roar of massed stands, his face even then still wearing the expression of sardonic not-quite-belief" (831).

One of the achievements Faulkner is not so often given credit for is his art of making, through metaphor, complex political and socioeconomic situations of southern history universally relevant. The last sentence of the first part of *The Hamlet* is a good illustration of this: "Then he added, as if in trivial afterthought: 'It was Flem Snopes that was setting in the flour barrel' " (816). The reference here, in this prominent place, parodically called a "trivial afterthought," is to nothing less than Flem's economic takeover. The flour barrel as a symbol of power was introduced in the first pages of the novel, where Will Varner sits in it "on the jungle-choked lawn of the Old Frenchman's homesite . . . planning," as the people who know him believed, "his next mortgage foreclosure in private." The sociocultural implications of this Yoknapatawpha coronation chair and cathedra are even more interesting than its obvious economic and political ones: "His blacksmith had made the chair for him by sawing an empty flour barrel half through the middle and trimming out the sides and nailing a seat into it, and Varner would sit there chewing his tobacco or smoking his cob pipe, with a brusque word for passers cheerful enough but inviting no company, against his background of fallen baronial splendor" (734).

The image illustrates Varner's authority as much as the improvised, homemade quality of its cultural symbol. Varner's total lack of understanding for the aristocratic ambitions of a Sutpen in *Absalom, Absalom!*, the novel to which in a deeper sense *The Hamlet* is a sequel, seems characteristic. In this respect, Varner's key sentence is "I like to sit here. I'm trying to find out what it must have felt like to be the fool that would need all this" (734). "All this" refers, of course, primarily to the stately mansion built by a French architect, with its brick terraces and formal gardens, exquisite cabinets ("highboys," from the French word *boit*) by Thomas Chippendale (1718–1779) and his British-born American "successor," Duncan Phyfe (1768–1854), and elegant stairs with "walnut newel posts" that have meanwhile been barbarously chopped up for firewood by Varner's rednecks. Indirectly, "all this" in the description reminds one of Faulkner's loving care in restoring Rowan Oak and its garden, implying his regret at the dearth of his own north Mississippi culture and his appreciation of New Orleans, his assimilation of sophisticated European fin de siecle literature and art, and even his snobbish flirtation with British RAF postures. If some of his American compatriots, resenting this, argue away the role of this European influence, they should perhaps consider that, like many of us, Faulkner apparently could only come into his own through the detour of assuming the roles of an alien culture. The study of the socioeconomic metaphors in *The Hamlet* shows that Faulkner had no doubt of and did full justice to the final takeover of the aristocratic regime by the emerging (Varner, Flem) redneck class. However, the context of the flour barrel makes it equally clear that the author felt closer to Sutpen in his moving strife for cultural articulation of economic power than to Will Varner, for whom the aristocratic mansion was "the only thing I ever bought in my life I couldn't sell to nobody" (734).

One of the central areas in which Faulkner, through his conception, plotting, and, above all, his metaphorical projections, captures and transcends the regional is the thematic complex of money and love.[13] Olga Vickery writes, "Faulkner's choice of the love story and the tale of barter as frames for the actions of his characters is directed by the fact that sex and economics involve the two primary modes of human survival, the one natural and the other social" (167). The case of Lump Snopes presents a startlingly, if bitterly, burlesque example of Faulkner's blending of the regional and the universal through erotic metaphor. After readers know that Lump Snopes has arranged a peep show of the idiot Ike with his beloved cow, they are to share Ratliff's fascination with the inarticulate love instinct of the idiot and the narrator's utter disgust at the voyeurism and exploitiveness by articulate humankind. "He knew not only what he was going to see but that, like Bookwright, he did not want to see it, yet, unlike Book-wright, he was going to look. He did look, leaning his face in between two other heads; and it was as though it were himself inside the stall with the cow, himself looking out of the blasted tongueless face at the row of faces watching him who had been given the wordless passions but not the specious words" (913).

Faulkner, "always testing the margins" (262) as Richard Gray has put it, shares with the expressionists and other modernists the artistic interest in *ur*-instincts. However, the contrast between the primitivist sexuality of the idiot and Lump's perverted and exploitive sexuality is brought to a head when readers shortly afterwards learn from Ratliff that "Lump" is Mississippian for "Launcelot." Lump's mother—"a thin, eager, plain country school teacher who never had quite enough to eat and showed it"—in an equally comic and touching protest against her social and cultural handicaps, has given her son the name of the famous lover of Arthur's Queen Guinevere in Chrétien de Troyes's twelfth-century *Erec*: "And who brought with her into that marriage, as sole equipment and armament, the ability to wash and feed . . . and a belief that there was honor and pride and salvation and hope too to be found for man's example between the pages of books, and who bore one child and named it Launcelot, flinging this quenchless defiance into the very jaws of the closing trap, and died. 'Launcelot!' Ratliff cried. He did not even curse" (914).

Ratliff's tragicomic outcry expresses no complacent disgust at Lump's depravity—he even points out to Mrs. Littlejohn the boy's "shame and horror when he got big enough to realise what his ma had done to his family's name and pride" (914). Rather, it has the quality of the concluding words of Melville's great story: "Ah, Bartleby! Ah, humanity." Rhetorically, the peak of Ratliff's necrology on the piteous Mississippi school teacher approaches the pathos of the Nobel Prize speech: "honor and pride and salvation and hope . . . man's example . . . books." There is no doubt that Faulkner felt that specific urge of the "revolutionary" thirties to eulogize the courage of the "common man," or rather, of the "common woman": Dilsey, Ruby Lamar, and Mrs. Armstid.

The bitterly burlesque quality of the "Lump-Launcelot" parody is in line with the cynical treatment of Varner's tryst with the wife of one of his tenants "in a thicket beside the creek near her house, in which sylvan Pan-hallowed retreat, the fourteen-year-old boy whose habit it was to spy on them told, Varner would not even remove his hat" (861). There is a similar note of disgust—"a leashed turmoil of lust like so many lowering dogs after a scarce-fledged and apparently unawares bitch" (851)—in the metaphoric deep structure of the courtship episode in which rural decorum, sexual violence, and, eventually, the regionalist redemption of Eula's suitors is captured with minute precision: "the half dozen or so bright Sunday shirts with pink or lavender sleeve-garters, the pomaded hair above the shaved sun-burned necks, . . .and with bare fists fight silently and savagely and wash the blood off in the water . . . and for the time being freed even of rage and frustration and desire, beneath the cold moon, across the planted land" (851–52).

The following analysis of metaphor in the Labove, Houston, and Mink plots is to determine to what extent the impression conveyed by the parody and inversion of the Lancelot motif is characteristic of the treatment of love in other main parts of the novel. From a first reading of *The Hamlet*, one might not expect this, because, on the level of plot and characterization, the three figures and the three love relations—Labove and Eula, Jack Houston and Lucy Pate, Mink Snopes and Yettie—could not be more different. But on the metaphoric level, psychoanalytical affinities in Labove's, Houston's, and also Mink's basic sexual disposition reveal themselves. The emerging structural pattern is that of a strong but frustrated sexual attraction producing antagonism instead of union, pain instead of joy.

In an interesting remark and a telling metaphoric supplement of the Houston plot, the narrator connects the hero's negative form of sexuality with an "inherited southern-provincial-protestant fanaticism regarding marriage and female purity" (928). While similar imagery in the Labove plot confirms this impact of southern religion, the resulting disturbed sexuality is, to all appearances, independent of the social status within the spectrum of redneck culture. In fact, as a comparative structural analysis shows, the love-hatred between the sharecropping couple, Mink and Yettie, corresponds with the student Labove's sadistic vision and with the negative feelings of "yeoman farmer" Jack Houston, who experiences as oppressive and continuously antagonistic Lucy's unflagging support at school and later her Solveig-like devotion.

245

". . . when they come to hang you, I'm going to be where I can see it!" . . .
He struck her across the mouth . . . beyond both hatred and desire . . .
[thinking] It's like drink. It's like dope to me. (937 [Mink and Yettie])

There would be times now when he did not even want to make love to her
but wanted to hurt her, see blood spring . . . "a man and a woman fighting
each other. The hating." . . . her other hand struck him a full-armed blow
in the face. (841–31 [Labove and Eula])

. . . female ruthlessness . . . But now it had become a contest between
adults. (925 [Jack Houston and Lucy])

In all three cases this psychological pattern appears as conceived
from the male perspective. As we shall see, no less male-oriented are
the two redemptive projections that are to overcome the dilemma:
the Eula and Ike stories. Karen R. Sass, drawing on Nancy Chodorow's *The Reproduction of Mothering*, explains "the male tendency to my-
thologize women in terms of their spiritual and emotional ties to their
mothers," and on that basis very plausibly links the Eula and Ike
Snopes plots: "Just as Ike projected desired qualities onto the cow to
fill his needs, the males in the village project onto Eula the attributes
deriving from their primal longing for the feminine."[14] However, in
the present study, this thematic concern and also the reflections of
the author's sexual difficulties, which Joel Williamson has recently
explored (365–98), serve only as a departure point for an investigation of how Faulkner—not least through different metaphoric strategies—developed from the same basic psychological experience totally
different characters.

In line with Labove's "forensic face, the face of invincible conviction in the power of words" (827), his erotic self-torture is expressed
through culturally well-established roles ("out of the books again"
[840]), each illustrating specific aspects in this metaphoric masquerade. Christ ("his Gethsemane . . . his Golgotha" [839]) is prototypical
for Labove's suffering, and "the virile anchorite of old time" suggests
antifeminine ascesis, while "the crippled Vulcan to that Venus" (840)
and the "old headless horseman Ichabod Crane" (843), as Eula addresses him in comic abuse, point to erotic failure. That "his legs [are]
haired-over like those of a faun" (839) calls up Faulkner's toying, in
his early phase, with the faun persona and hints at his intense but
unfulfilled and ambiguous sexuality stressed in recent biographical

studies (Williamson 375–77; 388–89; 393–98). There is no doubt about the strong antifeminine impulse speaking from the metaphorically laced sentence: "And he did not want her as a wife, he just wanted her one time as a man with a gangrened hand or foot thirsts after the axe-stroke that will leave him comparatively whole again" (839). The repetition of the same image as local leitmotif and its ingenious if horrid metaphoric extension—"Then one afternoon he found his axe. He continued to hack in almost an orgasm of joy at the dangling nerves and tendons of the gangrened member long after the first bungling blow" (841)—will probably remind sensitive readers more of Quentin's self-destructive urge, but then Faulkner's antifeminism and his suicidal temptations are obviously interrelated, and the concept of his role-play accommodates a wide range of psychological phenomena.

While the narrative commentary in our next example identifies Labove as representative of redneck culture ("his hill-man's purely emotional and foundationless faith in education"), the medievalizing imagery ("the white magic of Latin degrees, which was an actual counterpart of the old monk's faith in his wooden cross" [838]), and, above all, Labove's metaphoric masks (Christ, Vulcan, faun, Ichabod Crane) widen the regional frame of reference. In this way the redneck student Labove becomes a universally relevant literary character in whom the powerful motives of frustrated sexuality and fanatic sociocultural ambition convincingly blend.

In the case of Jack Houston's relation to Lucy Pate ("the two of them chained irrevocably from that hour and onward forever, not by love but by implacable constancy and invincible repudiation" [923]), the pain of a warped sexuality expresses itself through images such as slavery (923), trapping (931), and, above all, through the "bitless" and the "bitted" stallion. The latter image is particularly prominent because the stallion also plays an important role in the action. As in *Flags in the Dust*, the horse in *The Hamlet* does not quite have the usual connotations of sexual power but does represent deadly violence. However, in contrast to the stallion in *Flags in the Dust* and Bayard's drunken irresponsible ride, the stallion in *The Hamlet* appears under control, "bitted," signifying that Houston has relinquished "that polygamous and bitless masculinity" (931) that had torn him away from Lucy for many years for a life of wandering and sexual relationships with various women. As it turns out, Houston's attempt to force himself into a married life with Lucy fails. The stallion, proving to be "a man's horse" as the black stablehand had warned her, kills Lucy when "she was hunting a missing hen-nest in the stable" (932).

This episode constitutes a good example of Faulkner's "thinking" in metaphors, respectively, of an essential mode of metaphoric communication between the narrator and readers of this novel.

> He was *bitted* now, even if it did not show so much yet. There was still the mark of *space and solitude* in his face, but fading a little, *rationalised and corrupted* even into something consciously alert even if it was not fearful; *the beast, prime solitary and sufficient* out of the wild fields, drawn to the trap and knowing it to be the trap, not comprehending why it was doomed but knowing it was, and not afraid now—and not quite wild.
>
> They were married in January . . . He bought the stallion too then, *as if for a wedding present* to her, though he never said so. Or *if that blood and bone and muscles represented that polygamous and bitless masculinity which he had relinquished*, he never said that. And if there were any among his neighbors and acquaintances—Will Varner or Ratliff perhaps—who discerned that *this was the actual transference, the deliberate filling of the vacancy of his abdication*, they did not say it either. (931, my emphasis)

The metaphor "bitted" is not unusual in this rural novel, in which we have seen Houston several times on horseback, but in its application to Houston and in its unprepared occurrence, it is a bit startling, having that slightly mannered effect characteristic of much of Faulkner's imagery. Readers come to realize that "bitted" is set in contrast to "space and solitude" but may hesitate at the daring phrasing "rationalized and corrupted" before fully grasping that these value-charged words are to make them see Houston's domestication process as ambiguous—"rationalized: making sense, being appropriate"—but also negative as "corrupting: limiting."[15]

The image of the "beast" arises, transitionless, from the preceding reflection and remains reflective in its gist, its function being not to call up the concrete impression of any specific animal but to suggest an attitude, a kind of behavior. The qualification ("prime solitary and sufficient out of the wild fields") of the beast as "essentially not tameable" is characteristic of Faulkner's *metaphoric thinking*, his special stylistic blending of the abstract and concrete. The stallion appears as part of the fictional reality but is then consciously transferred to the metaphoric level, functioning as an image of Houston's former "polygamous and bitless masculinity." This metamorphosis, or reflective transformation into a symbol, is facilitated by the "vivisection" of the animal into "blood and bone and muscles." The symbolism ("as if for a wedding present") is understood by both Houston and his acquaintances but not directly stated or referred to. This fact and the awareness of it are appropriately transmitted through a peculiar abstract imagery ("actual transference, the deliberate filling of the vacancy of his abdication"), signaling to readers the intense consciousness of the metaphoric communication in which they are to participate.

Among the three representatives of disturbed male sexuality, Mink Snopes shares Labove's reductive feeling of appearing as a child to their sexual counterparts and Houston's obsession in his partnership "with a once-public woman," with numberless predecessors:

> . . . not only as a child but as a child of another race and species. (953 [Mink])

> He would be as a child before that knowledge. (840 [Labove])

> . . . [she] was surrounded by the loud soundless invisible shades of the nameless and numberless men . . . the cuckolding shades which had become a part of his past too (938); he would have to tear aside not garments alone but the ghostly embraces of thirty or forty men. (953 [Mink])

> . . . the blight of those nameless and faceless men, the scorched scars of merchandised lust. (929 [Houston])

The knowledge that Labove attributes to the mythical fourteen-year-old Eula is of the fin de siècle kind ("a weary knowledge which he would never attain, a surfeit, a glut of all perverse experience" [840]) which Walter Pater and, after him, W. B. Yeats, had invoked in their late romantic rewriting of Leonardo's *Mona Lisa* and which, in turn, the young Faulkner had found so important as a *chiffre* for respective feelings of his own that he continued to return to it, from his early Beardsley-like drawings through his carefully crafted allusions in *Absalom, Absalom!*[16] What needs stressing here, however, is the interdependence of the two images (child, rivalling predecessors) and their gist, male sexual fear turning woman into the mythic femme fatale.

Again, attention to the metaphoric level of *The Hamlet* proves illuminating, providing evidence of Faulkner's cultic distortion of male-female relationships: "saw her [Yettie] framed in the open door, immobile, upright and unlistening, while those harsh loud manshouts and cries seemed to *rise toward her like a roaring incense*" (952, my emphasis). The framing of the heroine and her immobility and remoteness function as a local leitmotif in the context, and, together with the "rising incense," belong with the stylizing devices producing the mythic dimension which shall be discussed later. Further characteristics of the femme fatale tradition are prominent in the sensationalist flashback of Yettie Snopes's prehistory, with the future sharecropper's wife appearing, somewhat surprisingly, as "the confident lord of a harem" (953), who, after looking at Mink "as a bold and successful *man* would," summons him, like so many other inmates of her father's prison camp, to her bed ("the constant stallion-ramp" [953]; "the fierce simple cave of a lioness" [954]). Undoubtedly, Faulkner's masculinization of woman in this instance corresponds to his several feminizations of men that Frann Michel and other feminist critics have observed.

What is relevant in connection with our investigation of the metaphoric layer of the narrative is the image clusters leading up to Mink's arrival at "the cave of the lioness": "He was seeking the sea; he was twenty-three then, that young. He had never seen it; . . .Perhaps he was seeking only the proffer of this illimitable space and irremediable forgetting along the edge of which the contemptible teeming of his own earth-kind timidly seethed and recoiled, not to accept the proffer but merely to bury himself in this myriad anonymity beside the impregnable haven of all the drowned intact golden galleons and the unattainable deathless seamaids" (951–52). The "unattainable deathless seamaids" that are here attracting the Mississippi sharecropper Mink Snopes had been exercising their fascination on Faulkner ever since he had heard their parodic singing in T. S. Eliot's "The Love Song of J. Alfred Prufrock":

> I shall wear white flannel trousers, and walk upon the beach.
> I have heard the mermaids singing, each to each.
>
> I do not think that they will sing to me. (15)

What may help us catch more fully the implications of the motifs of the sea and seamaids is a reminder that, while Faulkner had only heard their echo, one of the personae particularly close to him, Quentin Compson in *The Sound and the Fury*, had actually followed their call.

The account of Mink's quest for the sea is given in fairly clear narrative prose, mostly as the hero's interior monologue. This makes sense because the journey to the sea is obviously as much mental as factual. However, while the main outlines and the thematic gist, the regressive movement from "the land, the earth," the life-giving force towards the deadly but liberating sea, are fairly clear, several of the syntactical and logical connections and the precise meaning in all its aspects are not. But a closer look reveals that the resulting structural ambiguities are strictly functional, reflecting the hero's uncertainties. However, readers are not to resolve the indeterminate and substitute the open-ended structure by closure and singleness of meaning. Rather, they are to ponder possibilities and capture the emotional ambivalence. If Mink "could not have said why he wanted to go to it" (951), readers should not try to give pat answers. They need not decide "where his body or intellect had faulted" (951), whether the "repudiation of the land" (951) was due to some fault of his, or what the "coldness of the undeviation of his will to do" (951) implies. Instead, they should note that there is a masochistic urge for self-punishment ("to punish that body and intellect which had failed him" [952], cf. the axe and the gangrened limb in the Labove story and its suggestion of self-castration), that there are apparently guilty feelings about the departure from the land, and, furthermore, that the land, particularly, if its repudiation is a fault, continues to have its positive regionalist connotations.

A major stumbling block in the metaphorized syntax of this passage is the contradiction of seeking and not availing himself of the offer of "limitless space" (952), the "proffer of space and oblivion" (951) being twice made and twice rejected ("seeking what of that iodinic proffer of space and oblivion of which he had no intention of availing himself, would never avail himself" [951]). The outcome seems to be a kind of compromise between the will to live and the death instinct, the existence at the edge of the suicidal sentimentalist, whose urge to live is weak, as the ironic alliteration indicates ("con*t*emplible-*t*eeming-*t*imidly"), but who clings to life while flirting with death. The self-disgust of the writer seems to shine through the metaphoric presentation of his Mink persona: "Perhaps he was seeking only the proffer of this illimitable space and irremediable forgetting along the edge of which the contemptible teeming of his own earth-kind timidly seethed and recoiled" (952).

However, the position of the sentimentalist is also that of the artist as survivor, who, in imaginatively flirting with the suicidal role, demonstrates once more the existential and creative function of masks and role-playing. There are more features in Mink than just his small physique which suggest that he, too, was one of the author's personae. Indeed, not only the psychological aspects of Mink's metaphorics but also their aesthetic dimension point in that direction: "to bury himself in this myriad anonymity beside the impregnable haven of all the drowned intact golden galleons and the unattainable deathless seamaids." That the "haven should be impregnable," "the golden galleons be drowned intact," and "the seamaids deathless but unattainable" correlates with the unfulfillment of Faulkner's aesthetic idealism embodied in Horace Benbow and Gavin Stevens, in turn recalling the blend of sexual and aesthetic connotations in his favorite Keats poem, "Ode on a Grecian Urn," with its polarity of the unlived potential of permanent art and the transience of actualized life.[17]

What follows on the narrative level of the novel, the realistically told sexual encounter with Yettie, seems hardly in line with the preceding symbolist imagery and the deadly flirtation with the deathless seamaids of art and death. However, the metaphors, turning Yettie into a femme fatale and suggesting the masochistic quality of Mink's sexual vision (the threatening shades of the predecessors, his subjugation under Yettie as "the confident lord of a harem" [953]), prove that the suicidal urge has been taken along into the "cave of the lioness." The use in *The Hamlet* of "the cave of the lioness" as an image of sexual anxiety had been anticipated in a very similar metaphoric projection of similar sexual fears in the Horace Benbow persona in *Flags in the Dust* (1926), thereby once more documenting the close relationship between metaphors and masks. In addition to the resemblance between "the dark warm cave of Belle's rich discontent and the tiger reek of it" (*FD* 223) and Yettie's "cave of a lioness," we find a further affinity in the psychoanalytic contextualization of these images. There is, in an analogy to Mink's regressive movement towards the sea, in *Flags in the Dust* a "road stretching on through

252

darkness, into nothingness and so away" (223). What the metaphoric realizations of the otherwise totally different personae of Horace Benbow and Mink Snopes reveal to readers is that for these heroes the experience of sex is close to and overshadowed by death. "It was like a road stretching on through darkness, into nothingness and so away; a road lined with black motionless trees O thou grave myrtle shapes amid which Death. A road along which he and Narcissa walked like two children drawn apart . . . And somewhere, everywhere, behind and before and about them pervading, the dark warm cave of Belle's rich discontent and the tiger reek of it" (*FD* 223).

Faulkner has long ceased to be the naive genius from the rural South. Instead, critics have turned him into an international modernist, inspired by T.S. Eliot and James Joyce and by cubism and vorticism. However, what has perhaps not been fully understood is that it is as a modernist that Faulkner becomes preoccupied with myth. His mythmaking, in instances such as the Eula and Ike Snopes episodes in *The Hamlet*, should be seen in the context of the mythmaking by modernists such as Eliot, Joyce, Stravinsky, and Picasso. The inverted and grotesque myths of the modernists appear as attempts to affirm certain values in the face of the international and regional dilemmas captured in works such as *The Waste Land* and *The Sound and the Fury*.

Most readers of *The Hamlet* have been bewildered and put off by the daring thematics as well as the difficult language of the improbable story of a fourteen-year-old Mississippi girl featured as a fertility goddess and the embarrassing case of the sodomitic relationship of an idiot with a cow. However, appreciation of the Eula and Ike stories is facilitated when readers conceive of these unlikely stories, or *unerhörte Begebenheiten*, as thematic counterpoints to the stories of sexual anxieties projected into the Labove, Houston, and Mink Snopes plots. Moreover, the points of similarity in content and structure of Labove's, Houston's, and Mink's frustrated love relations suggest that they may be regarded as so many fictionalizations of the same autobiographical trauma. In line with the concept of role-play, the Eula and Ike Snopes stories might then be read as redemptive myths. However, few readers seem to have been able to understand that very well. In fact, from Faulkner's parodic skit, "Afternoon of a Cow," which toys with some of the material that went into the Ike Snopes story, some critics have derived the suggestion to dismiss the whole

Ike Snopes plot either as parody, travesty, or as outright failure: "his sense of balance, his control fails him" (Reed Whittemore qtd. in Grimwood 10–11, 3–17). Michel Gresset (*Fascination* 104–11) and Richard Gray (*Life* 262–63) are among the few critics who have appreciated and traced the subtle verbal symphony of Ike's love story and "Faulkner's orchestration of this perverse parody of a pastoral idyll" (Gresset 109).

The intellectually and emotionally demanding style of the Eula and Ike Snopes plots is meant to involve readers in transfer operations, and, ultimately, in liminal or mythic experiences. At the same time, the intensely metaphorized style alerts them through ironic signals to the tension between the epiphany of the divine and its mundane, grotesque, and even sordid circumstances. The resulting difficulties are unavoidable and aesthetically justified. Indeed, perceptive readers recognize that the mannerisms and tortured abstractness of the language in the Eula and Ike Snopes episodes are not caused by caprice or a fatal decay of style, but by that specific courage which Faulkner had missed in Hemingway: "to get out on a limb, to risk bad taste, overwriting, dullness etc." (*SL* 251). It is the courage to tackle such ultimate and impossible subjects as the incarnation of Venus and the Madonna in the very earthy body of Eula Snopes, and to represent in the sodomite idiot Ike Snopes the only true lover in *The Hamlet*.

At the beginning of book 2, "Eula," Faulkner associates his heroine expressly with the "old Dionysic times" and the traditional Dionysian imagery (honey, grapes, vines, goats). Such an experience he had already sought to convey in the short story "Black Music," which has been discussed above in connection with the reenactment of the role of a faun. However, in *The Hamlet* he effects a new sensuous experience of the venerable contents by overwhelming readers with a crammed pattern of sensuous adjectives and nouns: "honey in sunlight and bursting grapes, the writhen bleeding of the crushed fecundated vine beneath the hard rapacious trampling goat-hoof." This effect is enhanced by syntactical units affecting readers as much through their blend of the metaphoric with the acoustic and the iconic ("listen in sullen bemusement, with a weary wisdom heired of all mammalian maturity") as through their rational content. Although the stylistic devices comprise synaesthetic units and mythological allusion, remote vocabulary ("integer"), and scientific imagery or observation ("teeming vacuum," "soundproof glass," and "enlarging organs"), their aggregate effect is clearly focussed and serves to suggest the universal and, in that sense, the transcendental dimension of regional reality.

In this context, Eula's curious unwillingness to move appears not as a trivial idiosyncrasy but as a kind of mythic immobility ("she already knew there was nowhere she wanted to go, nothing new or novel at the end of progression, only place like another anywhere and everywhere" [817]). That this is indeed the author's aim is confirmed by the direct use of the term "symbol" in such phrases as "suggested some symbology out of the old Dionysic times" (817) and "the drowsing maidenhead symbol's self" (836): ". . . her entire appearance suggested some symbology out of the old Dionysic times— honey in sunlight and bursting grapes, the writhen bleeding of the crushed fecundated vine beneath the hard rapacious trampling goat-hoof. She seemed to be not a living integer of her contemporary scene, but rather to exist in a teeming vacuum in which her days followed one another as though behind sound-proof glass, where she seemed to listen in sullen bemusement, with a weary wisdom heired of all mammalian maturity, to the enlarging of her own organs" (817). Faulkner's continuing fascination with the Dionysian motif and image clusters indicates his Puritan urge to project a pagan countervision. It is therefore not surprising that the Eula-Labove plot is marked by rich metaphoric variations of a central tension between a regressive but culturally productive male principle and an unconscious but vitalistically superior female principle. To embody this polarity parodically in the frustrated infatuation of a redneck student and schoolmaster with a phlegmatic Mississippi schoolgirl was one of Faulkner's great ironic inventions.

> . . . he had not only extricated [the school] from the chaos in which his predecessor had left it, he had even coerced the *curric*ulum itself into something resembling *order*, . . . he was satisfied that it was *motion, progress*, if not *toward increasing knowledge* to any great extent, at least *toward teaching order and discipline*. Then one morning he turned from the crude blackboard and saw a face eight years old and a body of fourteen with the female shape of twenty, which on the instant of crossing the threshold brought into the bleak, ill-lighted, *poorly*-heated room dedicated to the harsh functioning of Protestant *primary education* a moist blast of *spring's liquorish*

corruption, a *pagan* triumphal *p*rostration before the supreme *p*rimal uterus. (835, my emphasis)

Since Faulkner invokes Rabelais in the Varner plot, it comes as no surprise that "buttocks" and "mammalian," with its alliterative echoes, are dominant verbal leitmotifs, as instanced in the humorous juxtaposition of Eula's overwhelming feminity and her brother Jody's frustrated efforts to contain it: "... the roan horse bearing the *seething and angry* man and the girl of whom, even at nine and ten and eleven, there was *too much—too much* of leg, *too much* of *b*reast, *too much* of *b*uttock; *too much* of *m*ammalian fe*m*ale *m*eat . . .'" (821–22, my emphasis). However, Eula's "mammalian" superiority, making "a travesty and paradox on the whole idea of education" (822), is also, as her metaphors show, of a monstrous and grotesque kind:

> ... an invincible abhorrence of straight lines, jigging its component boneless curves against his back. (822)

> ... the bare section of thigh between dress and stocking-top looking as gigantically and profoundly naked as the dome of an observatory. (823)

These grotesque effects, deriving in the example of the observatory dome or the following metaphor of the house from the great distance between imagistic tenor and vehicle, mirror Eula's peculiarly divided nature:

> Even while sitting behind her brother on the horse, the inhabitant of that meat seemed to lead *two separate and distinct lives* as infants in the act of nursing do. There was *one Eula Varner* who supplied blood and nourishment to the buttocks and legs and breasts; there was *the other Eula Varner* who merely inhabited them,

> ... as you are *in a house which you did not design but where the furniture is all settled and the rent paid up.* (822, my emphasis)

Labove, too, forces together very heterogeneous images in associating the eleven-year-old girl "eating a cold potato," on the one hand, with a cat in the sun, and on the other, "with the goddesses in his Homer and Thucydides" (834). Moreover, he allows readers to recognize the philosophical purpose of these grotesque metaphors by making the schoolgirl Eula the *coincidentia oppositorum* of myth and religion: "of being at once corrupt and immaculate, at once virgins and the mothers of warriors and of grown men" (834). The same tendency to mythicize the heroine through unorthodox religious metaphor speaks from the metamorphosis of Jody Varner into "a seething eunuch priest" and the "wooden desks and benches" of the Mississippi schoolhouse "into a grove of Venus" (836).

As Eula appears from both the narrator's and Labove's viewpoints metaphorically elevated, it is not surprising to find Ratliff, too, envisioning her as "the unscalable sierra, the rosy virginal mother of barricades for no man to conquer scot-free" (877). Apparently, there were, in addition to Faulkner's thematic impulse to embody in Eula the paradox of "the virginal mother," more personal reasons—above all, his relation to Maud Falkner—as to why he would be fascinated with such an avatar of sexual taboo (Williamson 393–98). In regard to the stylistic challenge of blending the universal with the regional, Ratliff's outburst at seeing his rural Venus wasted on the impotent moneymaker Flem is of interest because in it rural images such as heifer and rat commingle with gods and creation: "a situation intrinsically and inherently wrong by any economy, like building a log dead-fall and baiting it with a freshened heifer to catch a rat; or no, worse: as though the gods themselves had funnelled all the concentrated bright wet-slanted unparadised June onto a dung-heap, breeding pismires" (877–78).

It seems characteristic of Faulkner's involvement with regionalist ideals that Labove, in defining his relationship with Eula, comes eventually to envision her as "the fine land rich and fecund and foul and eternal and impervious to him who claimed title to it" (840). What is striking here is Faulkner's reapplication of the mythic *coincidentia oppositorum* and his implication of the tenuous hold that humans have on land (cf. "their hold upon it actually was . . . trivial and without reality" ["The Old People," *GDM* 127]). From this perspective, Varner's sale of his daughter to Flem is a particularly sinister aspect of the property theme, and most readers are inclined to accept that this marriage has an enslaving effect on Eula. However, the overall implication of Faulkner's metaphoric rendering of this theme is that Eula is superior to any such enslaving, which is a typical consequence of Faulkner's belief in a vitalistic myth instead of a socio-economic-political model.

There are instances, like the final tableau, in which Eula is repre-

257

sented with pathos, where she appears "Olympus-tall" and her "gesture immemorial and female and troubling" (1071), but more typical are Faulkner's intense efforts to curtail the pathos of mythicizing Eula by comedy. Against "the moon-blanched dust in the tremulous April night" with its connotations of moon and spring rituals, Eula appears in a white garment and is blank-eyed like a Greek sculpture, "the heavy gold hair, the mask not tragic and perhaps not even doomed: just damned," but this pathos is then counterbalanced, not devalued, by a parodic allusion to opera settings: "the strong faint lift of breasts beneath marblelike fall of the garment; to those below what Brunhilde, what Rhinemaiden on what spurious river-rock of papier-maché, what Helen returned to what topless and shoddy Argos, waiting for no one" (1017). The romantic theatricality vanishes straightaway when Ratliff confronts us with regional reality, asking Mrs. Snopes to call her father: "We want Uncle Will. Henry Armstid is hurt at Mrs Littlejohn's" (1017).

In the Ike Snopes episode, too, Faulkner's principle mode of combining myth and reality is through the grotesque. However, there are considerable differences in both the thematic and the stylistic aspects of the Ike and Eula stories. While the Eula plot, through grotesque imagery, establishes an icon of a male ideal of womanhood, the Ike Snopes plot, blending elaborate rhetoric with travesty, transmits a mythic love story. But the story, in *The Hamlet*, of the love between a human being and an animal is not told in the acceptable style of the love stories of Zeus as bull or swan, Native American stories of the love between bears and humans,[18] or that of fairy tales like "Schneeweißchen and Rosenrot." Instead, Faulkner provokes readers by a diction in which the poetic and thirties realism are manneristically forced together. However, this grotesque combination of the rarified with the rural, and even with the scatological, corresponds with the equally grotesque fact that the love of the mentally handicapped sodomite is the only true love in Frenchman's Bend.

Apparently Faulkner, like other artists experiencing the collapse of traditional values (see also John Steinbeck, Djuna Barnes, D. H. Lawrence, and the German expressionists) felt an urge to *radically* reassess human essence by exploring the liminal, by expressing the views of the primitive, the simple-minded and marginalized. This seems to be the true motive for his groundbreaking creation of Benjy's "restricted code," for his portrait of the socially disturbing "mad artist" Darl, and for Ike Snopes's representation as

> the Gorgon-face of that primal injustice which man was not intended to look at face to face and had been blasted empty and clean forever of any thought, the slobbering mouth in its mist of soft gold hair. "Say what your name is," Snopes said. The creature looked at Ratliff, bobbing steadily, drooling. "Say it," Snopes said, quite patiently. "Your name."
>
> "Ike H-mope," the idiot said hoarsely. (810)

As John Steinbeck did through Tularecito ("Tularecito," 1932) and Lennie (*Of Mice and Men*, 1937), Faulkner, through Benjy (1929) and Ike (1940), explored the anthropological and mythic borderlines of humankind ("the creature" [810]; "pointed faun's ears" [811]) as well as of his art. We should perhaps remind ourselves that these literary assessments of humanity took place at about the same time that Hitler had begun to draw his borderline of humankind through his eugenic mass murders, the *Vernichtung unwerten Lebens*. Part of the greatness of *The Sound and the Fury* and of *The Hamlet*—and this is sometimes ignored in scholarly debate—lies in the portrayals of both Benjy and Ike not as clinical cases but as human beings, feeling affection and receiving human attention.[19]

In contrast to the regressive and antagonistic love experience of Labove, Houston and Mink, Ike, the idiot, being outside the rationality and morality of societal codes awaits his beloved "indivisible in joy" (883) and at one with nature. In this opening passage of the episode, Faulkner, through carefully orchestrating acoustic and metaphoric effects, has created a nature setting and a linguistic medium in which realistic features ("smell her," "reeked") and stylizing elements ("malleate hands of mist . . . palped her pearled barrel") are cautiously balanced. The alliterative expression of morning mist, in particular, suggests the harmony of the human being and the animal as integral parts of nature ("the same malleate hands of mist which drew along his prone drenched flanks palped her pearled barrel too and shaped them both somewhere in immediate time, already married" [883]). The miniature drawing of natural details proves an especially effective means of communicating Ike's closeness to nature. "He would lie *am*id the waking instant of earth's teeming *mi*nute life, the *mo*tionless fronds of water-heavy grasses stooping into the *mi*st before his face in black, fixed curves, along each parabola of which the *m*arching drops held in *m*inute *m*agnification the dawn's rosy *m*iniatures, . . ." (883, my emphasis).

In tracing closely the shifts between the realistic and the stylized components in the Ike Snopes episode, one comes to appreciate Faulkner's delicate sense of balance between more harmonious and more dramatically contrastive passages of naturalist description ("the plopping suck of each deliberate cloven mud-spreading hoof" [883]) and symbolist elevation ("invisible still in the mist loud with its hymeneal choristers" [883]). Unfortunately, few readers seem ready to engage in the necessary metaphorizing role-play and to activate sufficient lexical sensitivity to match Faulkner's verbal genius in yoking such heterogeneous elements together. How difficult but also how rewarding such an effort can be is apparent in the experience of the fire scene and the cubist superimposing and blending of Ike and the cow with the horse. Through distortive metaphors, realistic action here assumes a visionary quality: "For an instant they yelled face to face, the wild eyes, the yellow teeth, the long gullet red with ravening gleeful triumph . . . His voice and that of the horse became one voice, . . . he ran into and through the fire and burst into air, sun, visibility again, shedding flames . . . The air was filled with furious wings and the four crescent-glints of shod hooves as, still screaming, the horse vanished beyond the ravine's lip, sucking first the cow and then himself after it as though by the violent vacuum of its passing. Earth became perpendicular and fled upward . . ." (890–91).

How carefully crafted the transitions are that lead readers from realist perception to symbolist insight is evidenced by the use of the metaphor of mirroring, contemplation, vision, and the allusion to the myth of "cow-eyed" Juno: "She stands as he left her, tethered, chewing. Within the mild enormous moist and pupilless globes he sees himself in twin miniature mirrored by the inscrutable abstraction; one with that which Juno might have looked out with he watches himself contemplating what those who looked at Juno saw" (899).

Similarly, through religiously heightened nature imagery ("It is now bald and forthright day . . . but the cries [of the birds] are no longer the mystery's choral strophe and antistrophe rising vertical among the leafed altars" [900]), the times of the day become occasions for metaphorically linking the lovers' progress with cosmic processes: ". . . they will advance only as the day itself advances, no faster. They have the same destination: sunset. They pursue it as the sun itself does and within the compass of one single immutable horizon. They pace the ardent and unheeding sun, themselves unheeding and without ardor among the shadows of the soaring trunks which are the sun-geared ratchet-spokes which wheel the axled earth, powerful and without haste . . ." (900–901). In dramatic contrast to the steady accomplishment of the diurnal cycle is the sudden shower of rain, which, through animal metaphor, turns into a vitalistic symbol and fertility myth: ". . . the shaggy pelt of earth became overblown like that of a receptive mare for the rampant crash, the furious brief fecundation which, still rampant, seeded itself in flash and glare of noise and fury . . . then the actual rain . . . the windy uproar which had begotten and foaled them . . ." (901-2).

The cited instances indicate that it would be a very reductive reading indeed if one were to consider Ike's love story and the cow episode in *The Hamlet* as just a variant of the travesty "Afternoon of a Cow." Although the text contains numerous farcical and grotesque features ("received the violent relaxing of her fear-constricted bowels" [891]; the "violation of [the cow's] maiden's delicacy" [891]), they are only to keep it from empty solemnity and affirmativeness and do not put the dominant symbolist tenor in doubt.

However, after readers have been exposed to the metaphoric presence of "the Lady Helen of Troy" in the symbolist imagery from Synge's *The Playboy of the Western World* ("Helen and the bishops, the kings and the graceless seraphim" [903]), they retain something of this universal perspective even after returning to the regionalist world of Yoknapatawpha, where poor Ike Snopes lies down with his cow "first the forequarters, then the hinder ones, lowering herself in two distinct stages" (903). The goal of the writer's breathtaking tour de force is without a doubt to make the reader experience a mythic love story within the realistic framework of a regionalist novel.

I am not really a writer in the sense you mean—my life was established before I began to write. I'm a countryman. My life is farmland and horses and the raising of grain and feed. I took up writing simply because I liked it—it was something very fine, and so I have no plans—I look after my farm and my horses and then when there is time I write . . . (*LiG* 169)

Conclusion
Pastoral Portrait

As the investigation of Faulkner and the regionalist context has led us to that of his regionalist and modernist metaphors in *The Hamlet*, the study of the *transcendence* within these metaphors refers us to the similar transcendence occurring in his role-play as country gentleman and farmer. What makes the epigraph above relevant to the theme of "masks and metaphors" is not so much that it contains an obvious falsehood but that Faulkner should feel an urge to transcend or move beyond his status as a writer and assume another profession and mode of existence. The regionalist context helps us to understand both why Faulkner would create the peculiar regionalist-*cum*-modernist metaphors of *The Hamlet* and why he would insist on his rural role-play. Moreover, there may also have been individual anxieties and feelings of inferiority which he sought to exorcise through his particular brand of pastoralism. In any case there is little doubt that, among the several masks adopted by Faulkner in the course of his life and his literary career, that of the countryman is of particular importance. While such masks as the dandy or the sculptor only served to help the young man establish himself as artist, the role of countryman deeply rooted in his regional culture remained congenial to Faulkner to his dying day. But it was nevertheless a *role*, and in the *as if* that mask and metaphor share lies one of the Faulkner features that has made him appear as a forefather of the postmodernists.

As the 1952 *Omnibus* television program demonstrates, Faulkner enjoyed the whole register of the role of country gentleman and farmer; however, we critics should distinguish between the different metaphoric implications of horseback riding and farming. Moreover, the range of the thematic functions of either role is considerable. Thus, it is important to distinguish whether Faulkner uses the mask of the farmer to further his liaison with Else Jonsson or to excuse himself from attending the ceremony in which The American Academy of Arts and Letters bestowed its William Dean Howells Medal on him. In the former case, he seeks to enhance a pastoral idyll with his lady friend; in the latter, he hides his shyness of men of letters by shocking them with his rustic arrogance. In both cases, his reference is to his dabbling with work on the Greenfield Farm, which he bought as much to satisfy feudal plantation dreams as for economic reasons. In his letter to Else Jonsson, he evokes a private pastoral, while in the one to Mark Van Doren he employs the public image of the hard-driven and dumb Mississippi farmer who depends on farm work for his daily livelihood:

> . . . We are harvesting hay, for horses and cattle. It is very hot, with thunder storms about, which may descend at any time. So you watch the sky, the weather, you gamble on weather, because the hay must not become wet between cutting and the barns, risks. So you try to guess three days ahead . . . all in the hot sun, temperature about 95—all chaff and dust and sweat, until sundown, then I come back to the house, have a shower and a drink and sit in the twilight with another drink until supper. ("To Else Jonsson," *SL* 321)

> . . . I am a farmer this time of the year; up until he sells his crops, no Mississippi farmer has the time or money either to travel anywhere on. Also, I doubt if I know anything worth talking two minutes about. ("To Mark Van Doren," 302)

Fortunately, Cofield's photographs of Faulkner's farming activity give us a realistic image of the writer as a manual laborer in a blue, short-sleeved cotton workshirt, his hairy arms exposed, and a pipe in his hands ("just returned to Oxford after having spent the day working at his farm" [7]) (plate 10). Cofield mentions as characteristic of Faulkner's naturalness that "he posed in whatever clothes he happened to be wearing at the time," but he understandably does not comment further on his statement that the photo Faulkner posed for "on that hot September day in 1960" was "a passport photo for his visit to Venezuela on another State Department trip" (7). Faulkner's wearing the workshirt of a farmer to startle the diplomats at the State Department is in line with his use of his farmer persona to startle people who knew him as a writer, like the staff at Random House and Mark Van Doren of The American Academy of Arts and Letters. The motive for this role-playing is probably again very complex, deriving as much from his desire to shock by being different as from his awkwardness with people of a sophisticated cultural background.

Some of the implications of Faulkner's farmer persona can be deduced from his proposed memoirs. This work was to resemble Goethe's *Dichtung und Wahrheit* in comprising both truth and "fiction" where it "would help." The memoirs apparently were not to contain any reference to New York, Hollywood, the world of *Pylon*, or the modernist malaise. Rather, they would be selective, and thus convey to readers a stylized pastoral portrait of the writer characterized by the kind of patriarchal self-fashioning that had already informed William Byrd's (1674–1744) famous letter to the Earl of Orrery: "Like one of the patriarchs, I have my flock and herds, my bondmen and bondwomen, and every sort of trade amongst my own servants, so that I live in a kind of independence on everyone but providence."

> I am thinking about writing my memoirs. That is, it will be a book in the shape of a *biography* but actually about *half fiction*, chapters resembling essays about dogs and *horses and family niggers* and kin, chapters based on actual happenings but "improved" where fiction would help, which will probably be short stories. I would like to use some photographs. Maybe some of my drawings. It would run about novel length, it will ramble some but will mostly be confined between Rowan Oak, my home in town here, and the farm, Greenfield. What do you think of the idea? ("To Robert K. Haas, ca. 20 Aug 1951," *SL* 320–21, my emphasis)

The grotesque phrasing "dogs and horses and family niggers and kin" does indeed suggest a feudal pastoral. However, as so often with Faulkner, he apparently had ambivalent feelings about his bucolic yearnings and an equally strongly developed sense of the social realities of his time. Thus, the essay "Mississippi" (1954), apparently the only actual outcome of the memoirs project, is anything but a feudal pipe dream. Rather, with its references to the "Bilboes and Vardamans" (*ESPL* 13) and to the great changes ("altered the face of the earth itself" [*ESPL* 35]) it signals a strong sense of the sociopolitical transformation under way.[1]

In the epigraph from one of the Japanese interviews of the follow-

Plate 10: Pastoral Portrait (The Cofield Collection, Center for the Study of Southern Culture, University of Mississippi)

ing year, 1955, the social context that made Faulkner assume the countryman role but also his reinterpretation of it, for the purpose of self-fashioning, becomes apparent. Obviously, writing in north Mississippi—in contrast, for instance, to New York with its flourishing literary life—is not a respected occupation.[2] To make one's living and to be accepted, one has to be first a farmer and treat writing only as a secondary occupation. This is the situation that makes Faulkner, one of the most professional writers in American literature, who in actual life had established himself as a writer much before he played at farming and whose striving for meticulous workmanship is already recognizable in the painstaking exercises of his juvenilia, pose as a dilettante.

That the farmer role corresponding with that of the hobby writer derives as much from social chagrin as from flirtation with the ideals of the agrarians is evident from his bitter tone when he contrasts the respect for artists in Japan with their neglect in the southern desert of the "bozart": "In my country, an artist is nothing. Nobody pays attention to him . . . but in an old culture [like that of Japan] an artist is a wise man, is important" (*LiG* 193). However, there is a further connotation of the farmer image which evolves in connection with the southern lost cause mystique and Faulkner's fascination with the Scottish heritage in the South. "Yes, we are country people and we have never had too much in material possessions because 60 or 70 years ago we were invaded and we were conquered . . . We have to be clannish just like the people in the Scottish highlands, each springing to defend his own blood whether it be right or wrong . . . it is regional. It is through what we call the 'South.' It doesn't matter what the people do. They can be land people farmers, and industrialists, but there still exists the feeling of blood, of clan, blood for blood" (*LiG* 191).

In *Intruder in the Dust* he describes the offspring of the Scottish settlers of Beat 4 with grim humor and without showing any sympathy for the unsavoury racist philosophy of Thomas Dixon's *The Clansman*. But this best-seller had been of some importance in his youthful reading (*SL* 20, 33), and, in the context of the farmer persona,[3] it is resonant with regionalist affinities of a kind that recalls the period style of the thirties and its "blood and soil" ideology.[4] There is little doubt that the value of social cohesion and stability, which he sought to invoke through the mystic formula "feeling of blood, of clan, blood for blood," was closely related to his agrarian yearnings. Both these aspects of the countryman persona reflect the effort to overcome in biographical role-playing the decay of the South he had relentlessly captured in his greatest literary works, *The Sound and the Fury* and *Absalom, Absalom!*

Faulkner's role-playing as farmer, with its consequent appeal to regionalist sympathies, has inspired writers all over the world and up to our time, as is attested to by the recent example of the Chinese novelist Mo Yan, of whom his interviewer, Thomas Inge, notes: "Mo Yan indicated that he first fell in love with a portrait of Faulkner, sitting with a pipe and tweed jacket, and every other picture he has seen reminds him of the old men he knew in his native village. He felt a strong kinship with Faulkner as a fellow country man and man of the soil" ("Mo Yan" 19). However, the impression made on a leading contemporary Chinese writer by a photograph of Faulkner wearing a rustic tweed jacket and carrying a pipe has methodical implications very different from those of his role-playing through literary figures. Similarly, the role of farmer, which he played in his late life, served a purpose different from that of the persona of the young farm laborer in the visionary early prose poems "The Hill" and "Nympholepsy," which are clearly indebted to the regionalist ideals of the twenties.

Obviously, the mask of farmer and that of horseman are related, both emerging as manifestations of the pastoralism with which many contemporary writers and artists responded to the changes and challenges of modernism. However, there is also a considerable difference between the meanings of the two masks. Even in regard to the one mask of horseman there is considerable latitude among its variants. As we have seen, the social implications of Faulkner posing in his new riding habit as a recently established member of the Virginia foxhunting community are quite different from those of Faulkner as a Mississippi horseman. Furthermore, the psychoanalytical meanings of the stallion episode in *Flags in the Dust* are quite different from those in *The Hamlet*.

The photo "To Random House. Love and Kisses. Tally-ho. William Faulkner" (plate 11)[5] shows that Faulkner enjoyed presenting himself to the northern city folks at Random House as a southern aristo-

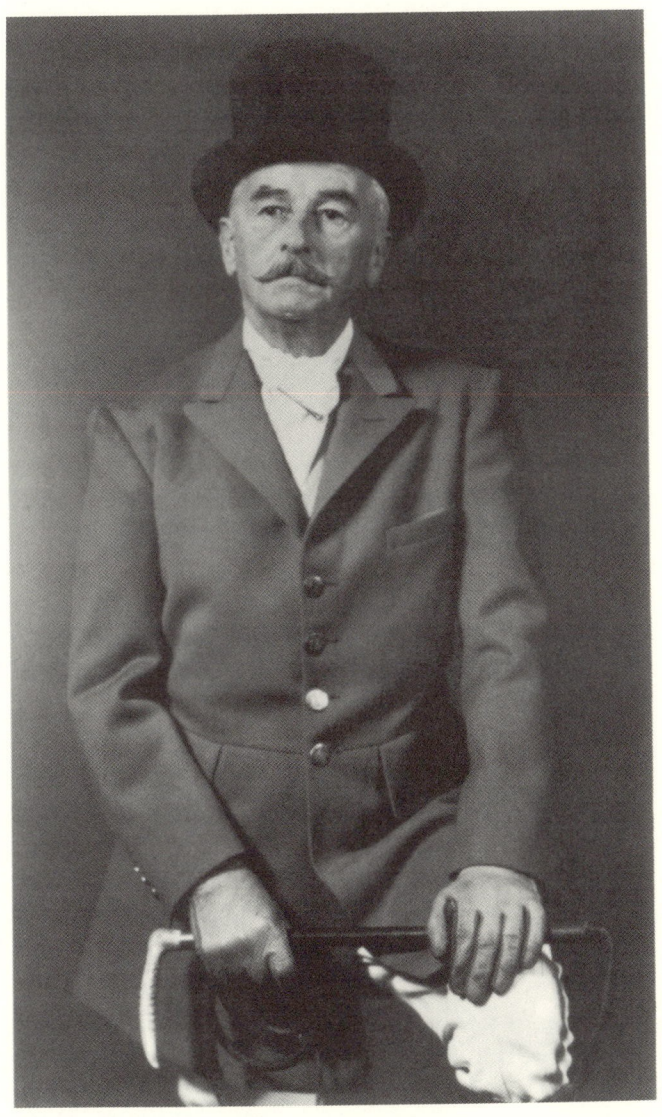

Plate 11: "To Random House. Love and Kisses. Tally-ho. William Faulkner" (The Cofield Collection, Center for the Study of Southern Culture, University of Mississippi)

crat. The three-quarter-length format of the portrait, with its clear subordination of the horizontal elements (his shoulders and powerful gloved hands which are holding the riding crop) under the vertical (the white cravat and raised white-trousered left knee functioning as foci) supports the expression of tragic awareness and relentless determination in eyes reaching far beyond the viewer's ken. What this last example and the late series of photos in 1961 by Cofield senior and Cofield junior (6–14) confirm is that the fascination with posing and assuming roles is not limited to the early Faulkner representing himself as Pierrot and marble faun.

The background to the "Tally-ho" pictures can be established from a set of photos of Faulkner in his new riding habit, which Cofield has very conveniently supplemented with some of his recollections:

> One morning Bill called me at the house and said, "Cofield, I'd like for you to take a few shots of me this morning. Some friends of mine up in Virginia are wanting some photographs of me in my riding costume" . . . His hair was all groomed and he was clean shaven. It didn't take him ten minutes to put his riding habit on. I took one look at him and said, "My god, what an outfit!" He gave me a genial smile, but he was ready to get on with the picture-making. I wanted to pose him with his foot propped on something. Bill spied this little covered stool. I told him to prop his foot up and relax. So he kind of leaned on one knee. I knew that the very first shot, *the one Bill posed himself,* was the best one . . . He was very pleased. It was an honor he was very proud of—riding to hounds in Virginia. (8)

Obviously, the important sentence here is "I knew that the very first shot, the one Bill posed himself, was the best one." The particular photograph, once more stressing the vertical from top hat to propped knee, creates the impression of a much taller man. Its diagonal arrangement, with head and glowering eyes turned over the right shoulder and with propped left knee emphasized by the riding crop held in his gloved hands and by his white breeches echoing the white cravat, culminates in penetrating and defiant eyes. They ignore viewers and are ready to face what there is to face.

While other shots of the same series show the tiredness of an old man, in this one the newness of expensive cloth and leather, the artificiality of studio lighting, and, ironically, the synthetics and aluminium leg of the all-important stool establish a major Faulkner persona, and the feudal paraphernalia of foxhunting are in line with the ruth-less determination and hauteur marking his face as it had marked that of his and the Sartoris ancestor. There is the absoluteness and seriousness of great actors about this photo, removing it from the suspicion of a snobbish Mississippian acting the part of a Virginian aristocrat. The far-seeing eyes in "Portrait of the Old Artist in a New Riding Costume" had envisioned Sutpen's belated feudal dream but had also relentlessly traced its inevitable ruin. If this set of Cofield photos displays Faulkner's posturing as foxhunting country gentle-man, it also reveals the kind of drive and courage which made him pursue his artistic career against all odds and which, in *Flags in the Dust*, he had established as a family trait and projected onto his an-cestor's sepulchral sculpture (Cofield 15): "His head was lifted a little in that gesture of haughty arrogance which repeated itself generation after generation with a fateful fidelity" (*FD* 427).

The interplay of social and psychoanalytic aspects, as well as the affinities between role-playing in writing and in life, emerges when we connect a literary motif such as the example of Bayard Sartoris's foolhardy stallion ride in *Flags in the Dust* with Faulkner's remarks on his risky horseback riding: "I can't help it, Mother, I love danger" (Blotner, "Metafiction" 13). Faulkner's many riding accidents and the photos showing him jumping his horse, Tempe, tell a horseperson all too well that he was not a great rider who cooperated with the horse and made it willingly accept the aids. As plate 12 shows, the horse is all tensed up, and consequently the rider is not firmly in the saddle. If he jumps the horse in this state, it will not react to his aids and cannot jump freely. The horse might jump somehow, but not in any controlled or effective manner, and the rider is likely to fall off. In plate 13 Faulkner stands stiffly in the stirrups and does not flexibly assist the horse in the jump by following its forward movement. In-stead of letting the horse stretch itself forward by moving his hands forward, as in this phase of the jump he must, Faulkner is reining Tempe in. His knees are not close and firmly at the saddle; he looks frightened and strained. Apparently, he belonged to the unfortunate category of riders who regard jumping less as a sport than as an op-portunity to demonstrate to the horse and themselves their superior willpower and courage. In any case, the photos corroborate both

Plates 12 and 13: The master on horseback (The Cofield Collection, Center for the Study of Southern Culture, University of Mississippi)

Faulkner's remark to his mother, "I love danger," and his description of Bayard's suicidal violence as rider, car driver, and test pilot.

He also must have found horseback riding, like farming, attractive for the reason that these roles helped him to define metaphorically his pose as nonintellectual, nonliterary person ("All my writing life I have been a poet without education" [*SL* 188]). Apart from that, there is no doubt that Faulkner not only cultivated his contacts with the Virginia foxhunting society but also took a genuine delight in the rather unpretentious Mississippi style of horsemanship. Since he grew up around the horses and hostlers of his father's transportation business, he undoubtedly enjoyed puttering about in his stable at Rowan Oak.

However, there is no doubt that country life, horses and dogs, the association of manual labor, and the aristocratic connotations of riding to hounds clearly had powerful symbolic implications for him as well. What he sought and probably did not achieve through his riding activities may have been the kind of vitalistic and heroic elevation which, in *As I Lay Dying*, Darl projects onto his brother and heroic counterself, Jewel. The metaphoric evocation in Jewel of Greek sculptures, of youthful horse tamers and demigods, and the fantastic aura of the pony rider in "Carcassonne" suggest that Faulkner's life with horses should also be regarded as part of a ritual that helped him fix an essential psychoanalytic configuration as myth. The images of hubris and untamable violence evoked by Bayard Sartoris's stallion ride in *Flags in the Dust* and the tragic killing of Lucy Pate in *The Hamlet* suggest the fatality of the male principle and demonstrate the aesthetic relevance of Faulkner's equestrian role-playing. What seems important in any attempt to come to terms with the biographic and artistic functions of horses is to allow for a wide range of possibilities. In his life, Faulkner may have continued to flirt with the horsemanship of the plantation culture, but, in his art (*Absalom, Absalom!*), he exploded its pretensions with relentless artistic acumen. Whether we think of the early novels, such as *Flags in the Dust* and *Sanctuary*, or of *The Hamlet*, his would always be a very disturbed pastoral.[6]

Faulkner's facial expression in the 1961 portrait of the aristocratic foxhunter (plate 11) is one which he had tried out, so to speak, in the 1960 series of passport photos (Cofield 7). The fact that on both occasions Cofield shot and developed a whole series of photos provides us once more with ample opportunity for studying both Faulkner's role-playing before the camera and the contribution of the photographer in the creation of Faulkner's masks. The three "pastoral photos" reproduced in Jack Cofield's volume (7) of Faulkner photos by his father and by himself are revealing in several respects. They show how Faulkner by a different expression and Cofield by different lighting and exposure produced from the same situation (Faulkner in workshirt, pipe in hand, leaning his hairy arms on what is apparently the same stool that figured in the riding costume photos) images that have totally different effects on viewers.

The full facial portrait in Cofield's 1960 series, arguably the best Faulkner photo (plate 10) (Cofield 6),[7] demonstrates even more forcefully the photographer's potential in the creation of masks. The most radical way in which the photographer can affect an image creation is, of course, in deciding which photo to blow up and put in a dominant position. Without going into all the details of the photographer's art, I note some particular strategies which strongly affect the image creation in photography. For instance, by waiting long enough for the model to settle and by narrowly focussing on the head (in the photo, even the shirt collar is slightly out of focus), the photographer avoids the impression of arrested movement, as in the two half-size photographs (*Cofield Collection* 7), and, instead, endows the picture with a lasting quality. Furthermore, by removing all paraphernalia and concentrating on the face, he makes it a more permanent representation. The unshaven chin loses its ostentatious quality as part of the iconography of the farmer persona and, together with the tragic eyes, becomes metaphoric of the *conditio humana*. All the other individual features—the crippled nose, the bushy eyebrows, the wrinkles emphasizing the dominant eyes, the straggling mustache overhanging the thin-lipped, barely opened mouth—are absorbed in this iconic quality.

If "the hero with the thousand faces" appears less fierce and aggressive here than in the photograph in the riding costume, he does not appear less resolute; he is still "intrepid" although perhaps not "unafraid." There is nothing ingratiating, compromising, or friendly, nothing smooth, elegant, or painterly about this face. It is certainly the face of someone who does not suffer fools gladly, the idealistic and weak ones included; the sculpted quality of this portrait marks a

Plate 14: Prospero's smile (The Cofield Collection, Center for the Study of Southern Culture, University of Mississippi)

stage far beyond the literary role-playing through characters like Horace, Quentin, and Gavin. Despite the fatigue around the eyes and mouth, the enormous power is still recognizable; it is the face of a writer equal to all the characters he has created. As masks are as much in the eye of the beholder as before the face of those who put them on, one should note that the lasting quality of this image also increases its metaphorizing potential, giving viewers larger scope than the more specific images of the military dandy or flyer, yeoman farmer or foxhunting squire.

Faulkner's pastoral portrait finally confirms what the study of his modernistic metaphorization of regional materials in *The Hamlet* has shown: that his regionalism is not of an escapist and provincial but of a probing and universal kind. In this regard, Robert Penn Warren has made an elucidating comparison of William Faulkner's and Robert Frost's regionalist role-play, which he sees as emerging from a specific historical situation ("one is tempted to say that the moment is the man, and that the man a role created by the moment") and as enabling both writers to take their specific critical and artistic stance vis-à-vis the modern world: "Both made a characteristic drama out of the locality and the history, and both—most important of all—created a role, a *persona*, a mask that defined a relation to the locality and the world beyond, and the mask gave the voice. Both, that is, knowing the shape and feel of life in a particular place and time, felt the story of man-in-nature and of man-in-community, and could therefore take the particular locality as a vantage point from which to criticize modernity for its defective view of man-in-nature and man-in-community" ("Introduction" 1–22).

The pastoral portrait—like one of Jack Cofield's own portraits, which he has chosen as splendid conclusion to his volume (plate 14)—suggests a remote but subtle observer. It provides powerful evidence that the role-playing artist in Faulkner was and always will be more powerful than the countryman or any other particular mask. The strong lighting emphasizing wrinkles and contours also produces a black background that intensifies the sculpted effect of the face, especially the powerful nose and the chin. Again, the format of the close-up enhances the impression that this is an essential image and will last. The light on the right cheek and the wrinkle produce the

Plate 15: The "new" vision, William Faulkner by Adelheid Bauer, 1992
(private)

effect of a smile, which is in part belied by the mouth and the pupil in the right corner.

The outcome is an ambiguous expression corresponding to the spirit of *The Reivers*, which even the more innocent critics no longer take for a harmless and inferior book. The smile in Jack Cofield's Faulkner portrait, in part because of its function as endpiece, reminds us of Prospero or of Rembrandt's final self-portrait; suggesting distance, tired irony and mournful insight, it is certainly not the smile of a benevolent grandfather. In using this close-up as grand finale of his volume, Cofield has created a powerful icon. Even so, Faulknerians all over the world will continue to make new images of their master for themselves (plate 15); however his face will remain a cryptic mask and metaphor to the last.

NOTES

Introduction
1. For a detailed discussion of the theoretical undergirding of mask and metaphor, see chapter 2.
2. See Morris; Blotner, "Metafiction" 9–26; and other contributors to the Rome session of the International Faulkner Symposium. See also Hönnighausen, "'Point of View'" 151–61 and "Metaphor" 3–19.

Chapter 1
1. See Blotner, "Metafiction" 11: "I am an artist, a sincere one and of the first class . . . I am the best in America, by God . . . what an amazing gift."
2. For a historical and biographical account of Cofield's photos, see Rankin 294–317.
3. For another cadet photo, see Sensibar 6.
4. Noel Polk has reminded me that, for many, hearing Faulkner's voice after only knowing his prose can be a curious and somewhat disconcerting experience. His prose style seems to demand a big, deep, robust voice, exactly the opposite of his own pretty "puny voice."
5. Peter Nicolaisen kindly reminded me of this passage.
6. See *The Faulkner Journal: Faulkner and Feminism* 4 (Fall 1988/Spring 1989); and Fowler and Abadie, eds., *Faulkner and Women*.
7. *Lion in the Garden* covers the period 1926–1951 (3–67) and 1952–1962 (68–286).
8. For the arts and crafts dimension, see Hönnighausen, *William Faulkner*.
9. See also Blotner, *Faulkner* (1984), 617–18.
10. Kinney, "Faulkner and Racism" 265–78; McMillen and Polk 3–14.
11. Faulkner regarded the interview with Jean Stein, the young editor of *The Paris Review*, as a "come-on," because she hoped that its publication would help increase circulation among English-speaking readers (Karl 937).

Chapter 2
1. For a detailed study, see Hönnighausen, *William Faulkner* 117–27.
2. For a recent study of the mask in comedy, see Glasgow. For the ethnological aspect, see Jonaitis.

3. See Taylor; see also Bleikasten, "The Novelist as Historian" 344–56.

4. See Hönnighausen, "'Point of View' "151–61.

5. In my reading of Nietzsche, I owe much to my friend, the Nietzsche scholar Peter Pütz (see his commentary and afterword in the several volumes of the *Goldman Klassiker* edition of Nietzsche. For an interesting—and recent—examination of this inspiration, see Pütz, ed., *Nietzsche in American Literature and Thought*.

6. Faulkner, "An Introduction to *The Sound and the Fury*," *A Faulkner Miscellany*, ed. Meriwether, 156–61. On the status of the writer in the South, see Grimwood 77–84.

7. For Bakhtinian readings of Faulkner, see McHaney, "Problems" 248–53 and Samway 254–62.

8. Hellmuth Plessner, Gesammelte Schriften, hg. von Dux, Marquard und Ströker, et al., *VII Ausdruck und menschliche Natur*, "Zur Anthropologie des Schauspielers" (1948), 399-418; *VIII Condition humana*, "Die Frage nach der Conditio humana" (1961), 136-217, particularly page 195. I became acquainted with Hellmuth Plessner's concept of the mask through one of my former doctoral students, Christoph Irmscher, who has made use of it in his fine book *Masken der Moderne*.

9. Morris quoting Foucault on the theoretical aspect of "serial representation," *Reading Faulkner* 186.

10. In regards to the problem, see Hoffmann, *"Absalom, Absalom!"* and "Historical Consciousness."

Chapter 3

1. The leading German art nouveau journal was entitled *Pan*, and, as Peter Nicolaisen has reminded me, Knut Hamsun has a novella entitled *Pan*.

2. See Sensibar 8–40 and Grimwood 40–41.

3. See Gresset, "Faulkner's Self-Portraits" 2–13 and Broughton 159–77.

4. On the biocritical aspect of "Carcassonne," see Karl 429–30; Blotner, *Faulkner* (1984) 254; *FU* 22; Grimwood 45–46; cf. Polk, "William Faulkner's 'Carcassonne' 29–43; Kreiswirth 80; and Brooks, *William Faulkner: Toward Yoknapatawpha* 60–66.

5. The continuity of this aspect of Faulkner's eschatological vision in the Noble Prize speech is striking (see Gresset, "Faulkner's Self-Portraits" 2–13). Compare particularly the shrill image of the idealistic protest against the apocalyptic end of the human race in the Noble Prize speech: "the last ding-dong of doom . . . last worthless rock . . . *puny inexhaustible voice, still talking*."

6. Critics such as Ilse Dusoir Lind, "The Mutual Relevance" 21–40, have demonstrated the applicability of Nancy Chodorow's ideas (*The Reproduction of Mothering: Psychoanalysis and the Sociology of Gender*) to Faulkner.

7. Blotner, *Faulkner* (1974): "an almost surrealist story" (I: 502); Karl: "another quasi-experimental fiction . . ." (429).

8. For the wider context, see Polk, *Children of the Dark House* 137–65.

9. In *Mosquitoes* Faulkner has sitting at Fairchild's table a man named Julius, resembling in many ways Julius Weis Friend (Blotner, *Faulkner* [1984] 183).

10. For a detailed study, see Brooks, *William Faulkner: Toward Yoknapatawpha* 100–151; Kreiswirth 70–100; Gresset, *Fascination* 67–111; Grimwood 60–62; Hönnighausen, *William Faulkner* 164–68; and Claus Daufenbach's subtle and thorough dissertation, *Ästhetizismus und Moderne*.

11. For a positive view of Charlotte Rittenmeyer's art work, see Meindl, "Romantic Idealism," and, following him, Eldred 139–58. See also McHaney, *William Faulkner's* The Wild Palms.

12. On Faulkner's unhappy Helen Baird memories, which seem to have fused with the Meta Carpenter experience and her awkward meeting with Estelle and Jill's "family visits" to Hollywood, see Blotner, *Faulkner* (1984) 372–75.

13. On the impact of Faulkner's mother-complex, see also Fowler, "Matricide" 113–25; Sass 127–38; and Rado 13–28.

14. See Hönnighausen, *The Symbolist Tradition* 201–206 and *William Faulkner* 100–101; and Daufenbach 109–116.

15. Jo sends Elmer crayons as Maud Faulkner had supported her son Bill's writing. Jo's sublimizing maternal authority is evident from the following: "He would have liked to go to his sister, to touch her, her flesh or even her dress. But he did not dare. It was this indiscriminate touching of people that she was breaking him of" (349). The motherliness of Faulkner's sister-figures is even more pronounced when the sisters are grownups, as in the case of Horace Benbow's sister, Narcissa, and Gavin Stevens's sister, Margaret.

16. For a critique of the traditional criticism concerning Temple Drake, see Moore 112–27.

17. For a metaphoric reading of this break, see Polk, "Introduction" 1–21.

18. See Bleikasten, *Faulkner's Most Splendid Failure* 46–66 and *The Ink of Melancholy* 41–55. See also Irwin, *Doubling and Incest*, 153: "Quentin's love of death incorporates his incestuous love for his sister precisely because his sister, as a substitute for Quentin's mother, is synonymous with death."

19. Characteristically, the regionalist Fairchild disapproves of attitudinizing smartness: "You know my opinion of *smartness*" (*MOS* 209).

20. *The Rubáiyát of Omar Khayyám*, trans. E. Fitzgerald (1859), was a canonical text of the British and American fin de siècle authors and artists and their American imitators in the twenties.

21. See Brooks, *William Faulkner: Toward Yoknapatawpha* 1–66.

Chapter 4

1. For a discussion of the latter aspect, see Grimwood 77ff.

2. "Spratling, whose hand has been shaped to a brush as mine has alas! not" (*NOS* 46); "So I can't write poetry any more" (*MOS* 249); "I wrote the novels because I found I couldn't write the poetry" (*FU* 4).

3. For an overview, see Lind, "The Mutual Relevance" 21–40. Cf. also the special issue of *The Faulkner Journal: Faulkner and Feminism* 4.1–2 (Fall 1988/Spring 1989).

4. The repetition of the phrase is striking, but the respective biblical text which Faulkner may have had in mind (John 20:17) reads: "Touch me not."

5. On the impact of these developments on Faulkner and other American writers, see Hönnighausen, *William Faulkner.*

6. On Faulkner's silences and his drinking as symptoms of narcissistic withdrawal and an integral part of his art, see Karl 13. In connection with these withdrawal symptoms, cf. also Bayard's—and Faulkner's—ruthless horseback riding and flying. We can better understand why Faulkner, like T. S. Eliot, William Carlos Williams, and Wallace Stevens, insisted on anonymity and privacy, rejecting the flamboyant subjectivism of romantic Byronism in favor of impersonal personae—be they marked by aristocratic reticence or the ordinariness of professional life—if we heed the following reflection on the artist in Mann's "Tonio Kröger" (1903): "because he thinks himself worthless as a living person and wants to be considered only as a creative artist; he is otherwise grey and inconspicuous, like an actor without his mask, who is nothing if he has no role to play" (*Erzählungen* 95). See also Gray, *Life* 1–12.

7. On the medical aspect of dissociation or multiple personality, see Ernest Hilgard, *Divided Consciousness: Multiple Controls in Human Thought and Action* (1977); for a literary study based on Hilgard (with an impressive chapter on Faulkner's *Absalom, Absalom!*), see Hawthorn, *Multiple Personality.* On the influential Victorian treatment of the theme, Masao Myoshi writes in *The Divided Self*: ". . . the incestuous relationship dissolves the usual familial and extrafamilial bonds between individuals it 'finally dissolves the identifying masks distinguishing one individual from another' and thus serves to fix the incestuous act as 'the moment for the self meeting with itself' " (11). While Tymm (*Doubles*) deals descriptively with respective motifs in German literature, Keppler (*Literature*) addresses issues that have a more direct bearing on Faulkner's use of the sibling and *Doppelgänger* motif, particularly pages 1–26, 147–60, and 182–210. Cf. also R. D. Laing, *The Divided Self* (1965) and Otto Rank, *The Double: A Psychoanalytic Study* (1979).

8. On the thematic complex of homoeroticism, bisexuality, and narcissism in Mann, see Renner 623–78.

Chapter 5

1. See Pitavy, *William Faulkner's* Light in August xii. Also in this volume, on Joe's hatred of femininity, see Pitavy, "Voice and Voices" 171–75; and, on imagery, Taylor, *"Light in August"* 203–24. See also Meeter 404–16; Urgo 391–401; Bleikasten, *"Light in August"* 81–102 and "In Praise of Helen" 128–43; and Fowler, "Joe Christmas" 144–61.

2. On the antifeminism in *Light in August*, see Fowler, "Joe Christmas" 144–61. She has convincingly demonstrated that Joe Christmas's sexism is that of the sexist and racist society which the novel critically explores rather than that of Faulkner.

3. On the racial aspect, see Sundquist, particularly chapters 4 and 5.

4. For a different reading of the vase as "representation" of the female body, see Roberts.

Chapter 6

1. For the psychoanalytic dimension, see Irwin, *Doubling and Incest*; on the poetic dimension, see Kinney, *Faulkner's Narrative Poetics*; Matthews, *The Play of Faulkner's Language*; and Hönnighausen, "The Novel as Poem" 127–40. Also helpful are Bernd Engler's "William Faulkner's *Absalom, Absalom!*: Five Decades of Critical Reception," *The Yearbook of Research in English and American Literature* (1987) and "Kontingenz und Kohärenz: Zur Problematik fiktionaler Sinnkonstitution in William Faulkner's *Absalom, Absalom!*," *Literaturwissenschaftliches Jahrbuch der Görres-Gesellschaft* (1988). Cf. also Judith Lokyer, *Ordered By Words: Language and Narration in the Novels of William Faulkner*, 62–71. For an appreciative approach, see Kauffman 644–70.

2. Roberts sees Rosa as wearing only the "disguise as a Daughter of the Confederacy" (30).

3. See Roberts 149–57.

4. On Faulkner and Bergson, see Kartiganer 161–63.

5. Jürgen Peper was the first to give full scholarly attention to the phenomenon in *Bewußtseinlagen des Erzählens und erzählte Wirklichkeiten* 180–207. See also Zink 258–301 and Chavkin 116–26.

6. For background, see Kirwan.

7. See Polk, *Children*; Lind, "The Mutual Relevance" 21–40, particularly page 30 on the impact of Chodorow's *The Reproduction of Mothering*; and Weinstein, " 'If I Could Say Mother' " 3–15.

8. On this aspect, see Christadler 151–80.

Chapter 7

1. Cleanth Brooks, in *Toward Yoknapatawpha and Beyond*, confines himself to the critical remark that, contrary to the assertion in the preface, mocking-

birds or the blue hills of northern Mississippi are conspicuously absent from the poems of the young Mississippian.

2. For further material on the Chapel Hill School (Howard Odum, Rupert Vance) and on the Nashville Agrarians, see Dorman; King; O'Brien; and M. Thomas Inge, "Agrarianism in Literature," *Encyclopedia of Southern Culture*, ed. Charles R. Wilson and William Ferris, 844–45. See also *Rewriting the South*, ed. Hönnighausen and Lerda; Gray, *Writing the South*; and Singal 198–231.

3. For American assessments of the problem, see Brinkmeyer 244–50 and Whiting. See also Nicolaisen, "The Southern Agrarians."

4. See Hönnighausen, "On the Uses of the Term 'Regionalism' " 41–53; Nicolaisen, "Faulkner and Hamsun" 88–101; and Inge, "Yoknapatawpha on the Don" 129–42. See also Nicolaisen, "'The dark land talking" 253–76.

5. For respective contextualizations of Faulkner, see Fowler and Abadie, eds., *Faulkner and the Southern Renaissance*; Brooks, "What Stand Did Faulkner Take?" 40–62; Rubin, "The Hound Under the Wagon" 93–119; O'Brien; King; Gray, *Writing the South*; Tindall, "Mythology: A New Frontier"; and Singal 198–231.

6. Oroszco was in the United States from 1917 to 1919 and 1927 to 1934; Siqueiros was there in 1932, and in 1934 he opened a studio in New York.

7. See Steiner and Mondale. Contemporary critics like H. W. Janson ("The International Aspects of Regionalism," *Art Journal*, 1943) were already aware that the phenomenon was not confined to American painting. See also Mecklenburg, particularly the section "Regionalismus international," 82–94, and the comparatist essay by Koppen with the programmatic title " 'Heimat' international. Literarischer Regionalismus als Gegenstand der Komparatistik" 267–74.

8. On Cather as regionalist, see Dorman 29–53 and 55–80. On the contrast between the negative metropolitan and the positive, rural west, Sherwood Anderson wrote in *Marching Men* (1917): "Chicago is one vast gulf of disorder. . . . And back of Chicago lie the long fields that are not disorderly" (113).

9. See Hönnighausen, "Landscape with Indians and Saints" 299–323.

10. "Yet just now, by reason of the *crash* of our non-regional economy, it tends to have its revival. Of the two economies, the regional is the realistic one. The industry is in sight of the natural resources of the region and of its population. The farmers support themselves and support their cities . . . perhaps it occurs to them that an interregional or world trade cannot be controlled" (294).

11. See, for instance, the exhibition catalogue *In Pursuit of Beauty: Americans and the Aesthetic Movement* (New York: The Metropolitan Museum of Art, 1987).

12. See Hönnighausen, "Faulkner Rewriting the Indian Removal" 335–43.

13. Hönnighausen, *William Faulkner* 9–81; among the plates (15) cf. also the title page of the Lantern Press edition of Sherwood Anderson's *The Modern Writer* (1925).

14. On the ambivalence of Faulkner's South, see Singal 153–97.

15. On plowing in regionalist manifestos, see Dorman 114.

16. On the emphasis on basic human relationships (mother and child) as a characteristic feature of the thirties, see Susman 206.

17. Thanks to recent feminist criticism and particularly to the psychoanalytic work inspired by Nancy Chodorow's *The Reproduction of Mothering*, we are beginning to understand that Faulkner's predilection for the madonna type or for woman as protective sister can to some extent be explained in connection with his relation to his mother and the specific erotic difficulties it entailed. For the wider context, see Michel 5–20; Roberts, especially the sections "Mothers and Motherhood" and "Dixie Madonna" 186–223; and Fowler, "Matricide" 113–25.

18. Roberts 60 (58–63), quoting and evaluating Thadious Davis ("the colors and materials of royalty") and other recent critical commentaries (Myra Jehlen, Jessie Parkhurst) on Dilsey.

19. For a discussion of criticism, see Hönnighausen, "Black as White Metaphor" 192–208.

20. Before the psychoanalytical critics, Warren ("William Faulkner," 94–109) and Straumann (462–70) had pointed out that the theme of *Light in August* and *Absalom, Absalom!* is not black reality but the complications arising from the white man's black image, and that Dilsey's character might be regarded as a "metaphor" or "symbol."

21. For different readings of the scene, see Jenkins 151–56 and Sundquist 67–68.

Chapter 8

1. See Moreland 135 and Schmitz 471–91.

2. See Houghton 361–69, Pierle 246–52, and Pilkington 217–41.

3. See Michel 5–20 and Lind, "The Mutual Relevance" 21–40, who treat the superiority of women and the relationship between Faulkner's mother, Maud, and his weak father, Murray.

4. On the thematics, structure, and content of imagery in *The Hamlet*, see Beck; Brooks, *William Faulkner: The Yoknapatawpha Country*; Morris; and Moreland 122–57. For a recent balanced overview of the major thematic aspects of the novel, see Gray, *Life* 253–71.

5. In particular, note Faulkner's metaphorizing the vocabulary through contrast and repetition: black-white, without dimension-without purpose, rigid solitude, like tears-old, sweat-old.

6. Gray, *Life*, entitles his chapter on *The Hamlet* "Let's Make a Deal" (253) and regards as major themes "two principal forms of exchange: one of them is speech, the other is goods and cash" (254).

7. On Faulkner's economic situation at the time of the writing of *The Hamlet*, see Williamson 263–65. See Williamson also on Faulkner being "at the end of the Great Depression physically among the plain white farmers of Lafayette County as never before" (428) as well as his very different view of Varner and the peasants: "a fundamentally good peasantry led by the highly effective Will Varner and the highly moral V. K. Ratliff" (428).

8. See Dorman: "Webb's concern about the deleterious effects of economic 'colonialism' and centralization were widely shared among regionalists" (161); and Williamson: "Alienation from the natural virtues continued after the war, aggravated by the reduction, the colonialization, of the South by the North" (404).

9. See *Eudora Welty Photographs*. See also Kidd's fine paper, 219–30.

10. Gray, in *Life*, rightly stresses the fact that Flem "is quite simply another if radical step in the continually unfolding of the history of the community: an agent of transformation that comes from within" (255).

11. See Wilson and Ferris 1140, Boney, and Reed.

12. See Hönnighausen, *William Faulkner*, part four.

13. See Williamson: ". . . profoundly critical of the sex roles prescribed by the Southern Social order . . ." (366). See also Fowler and Abadie, eds., *Faulkner and Women*; Mortimer 67–81; and Broughton 159–77.

14. Sass regards "the struggle between the forces of life-promoting feminine love and destructive masculine greed" as the theme of *The Hamlet* and offers a convincing thematic analysis of the Labove, Houston, and Mink plots in her essay (127–38).

15. Cf. Faulkner's turning from Hollywood and Meta to Oxford and Estelle.

16. On Faulkner's use of fin de siècle prototypes for his stylized character drawing (e.g., Mrs. Powers, Joanna Burden, and Charles Bon's mistress as "Beardsley women"), see Hönnighausen, *William Faulkner*.

17.   Bold Lover, never, never canst thou kiss,
          Though winning near the goal—yet, do not grieve;
              She cannot fade, though thou hast not thy bliss,
          For ever wilt thou love, and she be fair!

18. See also Snyder, *Earth House Hold* 117–29, especially the paragraph with the provocative title "Making Love with Animals."

19. On Ike as "the embodiment of the primordial natural love," see Watson, *The Snopes Dilemma* 48.

Conclusion

1. There are not only echoes of Quentin's ambivalence, in *Absalom, Absalom!* (378), about Mississippi ("loving it even while hating some of it" [*ESPL* 36]) but also manifestations at the time of the civil rights movement: "But most of all he hated the intolerance and injustice: the lynching of Negroes not for the crimes they committed but because their skins were black" (37).

2. "Though there is a colony of writers who gravitate toward the big cities, like New York, and their social life is a life of books but in my county that does not exist. The individual is primarily a farmer and after that he is a writer . . ."(*LiG* 191).

3. Note his insistence in the following remarks: "I am not really a writer . . . I'm a countryman. My life is farmland and horses and the raising of grain and feed" (*LiG* 169); "I am not really a literary man . . . I am a farmer, a countryman" (191).

4. For an account of the blood and soil imagery in the American regionalist tradition where it appears less negatively charged, see Dorman.

5. From the Cofield set of 1961; for the circumstances of this series of photos, see below.

6. See, for instance, the reference to foxhunting in a 1960 letter to Albert Erskine at Random House, concerning needed corrections in *The Hamlet*: "Fox hunting is fine here, country is beautiful. I have been awarded a pink coat, a splendor worthy of being photographed in" (*SL* 450).

7. For information on Colonel J. R. Cofield and his photography studio, see Rankin 300–305.

WORKS CITED

Agee, James, and Walker Evans. *Let Us Now Praise Famous Men: Three Tenant Families*. New York: Ballantine, 1978.

Barnes, Albert C. "Negro Art and America." *The New Negro: An Interpretation*. Ed. Alain Locke. New York: Arno Press 1925; *New York Times*, 1968.

Bašić, Sonja. "Parody and Metafiction: *Ulysses* and *The Hamlet*." *Faulkner, His Contemporaries, and His Posterity*. Ed. Zacharasiewicz. 41–55.

Beck, Warren. *Man in Motion: Faulkner's Trilogy*. Madison: U of Wisconsin P, 1961.

Black, Max. *Models and Metaphors*. Ithaca: Cornell UP, 1962.

Bleikasten, André. "Fathers in Faulkner." *The Fictional Father: Lacanian Readings of the Text*. Ed. Davis. 115–46.

————. *Faulkner's Most Splendid Failure: Faulkner's* The Sound and the Fury. Bloomington and London: Indiana UP, 1976.

————. *The Ink of Melancholy: Faulkner's Novels from* The Sound and the Fury *to* Light in August. Bloomington and Indianapolis: Indiana UP, 1990.

————. "In Praise of Helen." *Faulkner and Women*. Ed. Fowler and Abadie. 128–43.

————. "*Light in August*: The Closed Society and Its Subjects." *New Essays on* Light in August. Ed. Millgate. 81–102.

————. "The Novelist as Historian in *Requiem for a Nun*." *Rewriting the South: History and Fiction*. Ed. Hönnighausen and Lerda. 344–56.

Blotner, Joseph. *Faulkner: A Biography*. 2 vols. London: Chatto and Windus, 1974.

————. *Faulkner: A Biography*. New York: Random House, 1984.

————. "Metafiction and Metalife: William Faulkner's Masks as Man and Artist." *The Artist and His Masks: William Faulkner's Metafiction*. Ed. Lombardo. 9–26.

Works Cited

Bockting, Ineke. *Character and Personality in the Novels of William Faulkner: A Study in Psychostylistics*. Lanham and New York: UP of America, 1995.

Boney, F. N. *Southerners All*. Macon, GA: Mercer UP, 1990.

Brinkmeyer, Robert H., Jr. "Fascism, the Democratic Revival, and the Southern Writer." *Rewriting the South: History and Fiction*. Ed. Hönnighausen and Lerda. 244–50.

Brooks, Cleanth. *The Well Wrought Urn: Studies in the Structure of Poetry*. London: Dobson, 1949.

———. "What Stand Did Faulkner Take?" *Faulkner and the Southern Renaissance*. Ed. Fowler and Abadie. 40–62.

———. *William Faulkner: The Yoknapatawpha Country*. New Haven: Yale UP, 1963.

———. *William Faulkner: Toward Yoknapatawpha and Beyond*. New Haven: Yale UP, 1978.

Broughton, Panthea Reid. "The Economy of Desire: Faulkner's Poetics, from Eroticism to Post-Impressionism." *The Faulkner Journal: Faulkner and Feminism* 4 (Fall 1988/Spring 1989): 159–77.

Butterworth, Keen. *A Critical and Textual Study of Faulkner's* A Fable. Ann Arbor: UMI Research P, 1983.

Cather, Willa. *Death Comes for the Archbishop: The Autograph Edition of the Novels and Stories of Willa Cather*. Boston: Houghton Mifflin, 1938.

———. *My Ántonia: The Autograph Edition of the Novels and Stories of Willa Cather*. Boston: Houghton Mifflin, 1937.

Chavkin, Allen. "The Imagination as the Alternative to Sutpen's Design." *Arizona Quarterly* 37 (1981): 116–26.

Chodorow, Nancy. *The Reproduction of Mothering: Psychoanalysis and the Sociology of Gender*. Berkeley: U of California P, 1978.

Christadler, Martin. "William Faulkner's *Absalom, Absalom!*: History, Consciousness and Transcendence—The End of the Historical Novel." *Faulkner and History*. Ed. Coy and Gresset. 151–80.

Cofield, Jack. *William Faulkner: The Cofield Collection*. Oxford: Yoknapatawpha P, 1978.

Collins, R. G. "*Light in August*: Faulkner's Stained Glass Triptych." *Mosaic* 7.1 (1973): 97–157.

Coy, Javier, and Michel Gresset, eds. *Faulkner and History*. Salamanca: Ediciones Universidad de Salamanca, 1986.

Culler, Jonathan. *On Deconstruction: Theory and Criticism after Structuralism*. London: Routledge and Kegan Paul, 1983.

Daufenbach, Claus. *Ästhetizismus und Moderne. Studien zu William Faulkners früher Prosa*. Heidelberg: Carl Winter, 1990.

Davis, Robert Con, ed. *The Fictional Father: Lacanian Readings of the Text*. Amherst: U of Massachusetts P, 1981.

Works Cited

Davis, Thadious M. *Faulkner's "Negro": Art and the Southern Context*. Baton Rouge: Louisiana State UP, 1983.

Derrida, Jacques. "White Mythology." *Enclitic* 2.2 (1978): 5–33.

Dorman, Robert L. *Revolt of the Provinces: The Regionalist Movement in America, 1920–1945*. Chapel Hill and London: U of North Carolina P, 1993.

Eldred, Janet Carey. "Faulkner's Still Life: Art and Abortion in *The Wild Palms*." *The Faulker Journal: Faulkner and Feminism* 4.1–2 (Fall 1988/Spring 1989): 139–58.

Eliot, T. S. *Collected Poems, 1909–1935*. London: Faber and Faber, 1959.

Fant, Joseph L., and Robert Ashley, eds. *Faulkner at West Point*. New York: Vintage, 1969.

Fisher, Philip, ed. *The New American Studies: Essays from Representations*. Berkeley: U of California P, 1991.

Ford, Dan, ed. *Heir and Prototype: Original and Derived Characterizations in Faulkner*. Conway: U of Central Arkansas P, 1987.

Forster, E.M. *Collected Short Stories*. Middlesex: Penguin, 1965.

Foucault, Michel. *The Archeology of Knowledge*. Trans. A.M. Sheridan Smith. New York: Pantheon Books, 1972.

Fowler, Doreen. "Joe Christmas and 'Womanshenegro.' " *Faulkner and Women*. Ed. Fowler and Abadie. 144–61.

———. "Matricide and the Mother's Revenge: *As I Lay Dying*." *The Faulkner Journal: Faulkner and Feminism* 4.1–2 (Fall 1988/Spring 1989): 113–25.

Fowler, Doreen, and Ann J. Abadie, eds. *Faulkner and Race*. Jackson: UP of Mississippi, 1987.

———. *Faulkner and the Southern Renaissance: Faulkner and Yoknapatawpha, 1981*. Jackson: UP of Mississippi, 1982.

———. *Faulkner and Women*. Jackson: UP of Mississippi, 1986.

———. *New Directions in Faulkner Studies*. Jackson: UP of Mississippi, 1984.

Fowler, Roger, ed. *A Dictionary of Modern Critical Terms*. New York: Routledge, 1987.

Galinsky, Hans. "The South on Thomas Mann's Map of the United States: A Regional Aspect of Twentieth-Century German-American Literary Relations." *Yearbook of German–American Studies* 18 (1967): 125–56.

Gillen, Eckart. "Das Bild Amerikas: Ein verlorenes Paradies. Zur Malerei der Regionalisten und magischen Realisten." *Amerika: Traum und Depression, 1920–1940*. Berlin: Akademie der Künste, 1980. 236–68.

Glasgow, R. D. V. *Madness, Masks and Laughter: An Essay on Comedy*. London and Toronto: Associated Presses, 1995.

Gray, Richard. *The Life of William Faulkner: A Critical Biography*. Oxford and Cambridge, MA: Blackwell, 1994.

———. *Writing the South: Ideas of an American Region*. Cambridge: Cambridge UP, 1986.

Works Cited

Gresset, Michel. *Fascination: Faulkner's Fiction, 1919–1936*. Adapted from the French by Thomas West. Durham and London: Duke UP, 1989.

———. "Faulkner's Self–Portraits." *The Faulkner Journal* 2 (Fall 1986): 2–13.

———. "Faulkner's Voice." *Faulkner's Discourse*. Ed. Hönnighausen. 184–94.

Gresset, Michel, and Kenzaburo Ohashi, eds. *Faulkner: After the Nobel Prize*. Kyoto: Yamaguchi, 1987.

Grimwood, Michael. *Heart in Conflict: Faulkner's Struggles with Vocation*. Athens: U of Georgia P, 1987.

Gwin, Minrose C. "(Re)Reading Faulkner as Father and Daughter of His Own Text." *Refiguring the Father*. Ed. Yaeger and Kowaleski-Wallace. 238–58.

Hawthorn, Jeremy. *Multiple Personality and the Disintegration of Literary Character: From Oliver Goldsmith to Sylvia Plath*. London: Edward Arnold, 1983.

Herget, Winfried. "The Poetics of Negation in Faulkner's *Absalom, Absalom!*" *Faulkner's Discourse*. Ed. Hönnighausen. 33–37.

Hoffmann, Gerhard. "*Absalom, Absalom!*: A Postmodernist Approach." *Faulkner's Discourse*. Ed. Hönnighausen. 276–92.

———. "Historical Consciousness, Aesthetics, and the Experimental Southern Novel." *Rewriting the South: History and Fiction*. Ed. Hönnighausen and Lerda. 397–424.

Hönnighausen, Lothar. "Black as White Metaphor: A European View of Faulkner's Fiction." *Faulkner and Race*. Ed. Fowler and Abadie. 192–208.

———, ed. *Faulkner's Discourse: An International Symposium*. Tübingen: Max Niemeyer, 1989.

———. "Faulkner Rewriting the Indian Removal." *Rewriting the South: History and Fiction*. Ed. Hönnighausen and Lerda. 335–43.

———. "The Imagery in Faulkner's *A Fable*." *Faulkner: After the Nobel Prize*. Ed. Gresset and Ohashi. 147–71.

———. "Landscape with Indians and Saints: The Modernist Discovery of Native American and Hispanic Folk Culture." *Amerikastudien* 37 (1992): 299–323.

———. "Madame Bovary et le Martin-Pêcheur de Caroline: Régionalisme et modernisme dans *Sanctuaire*." Trans. André Bleikasten. *europe* 70 (Janvier/Février 1992): 45–56.

———. "Maske und Perspektive." *Englische Literatur zwischen Viktorianismus und Moderne*. Ed. Paul Goetsch. Darmstadt: Wissenschaftliche Buchgesellschaft, 1983. 339–66.

———. "Metaphor in the Twentieth-Century Novel." *Modes of Narrative: Approaches to American, Canadian and British Fiction*. Ed. Reingard M. Nischik and Barbara Korte. Würzburg: Königshausen und Neumann, 1990. 3–19.

———. "The Novel as Poem: The Place of Faulkner's *Absalom, Absalom!* in the History of Reading." *Amerikastudien* 31 (1986): 127–40.

Works Cited

———. "On the Uses of the Term *Regionalism* for the Study of Faulkner." *The United States South: Regionalism and Identity.* Ed. Valeria G. Lerda and Tjebbe Westendorp. Roma: Bulzoni Editore. 41–53.

———. " 'Point of View' and Its Background in Intellectual History." *Comparative Criticism* 2 (1980): 151–61.

———. *The Symbolist Tradition in English Literature.* Cambridge: Cambridge UP, 1988.

———. *William Faulkner: The Art of Stylization in his Early Graphic and Literary Work.* Cambridge: Cambridge UP, 1987.

Hönnighausen, Lothar, and Valeria G. Lerda, eds. *Rewriting the South: History and Fiction.* Tübingen und Basel: Francke Verlag, 1993.

Houghton, Daniel. "Whores and Horses in Faulkner's 'Spotted Horses.' " *Midwest Quarterly* 11 (1970): 361–69.

Hülser, Heike. *Die Metapher. Kommunikationssemantische Überlegungen zu einer rhetorischen Kategorie.* Münster: Nodus Verlag, 1987.

Hunt, Joel A. "Thomas Mann and Faulkner: Portrait of a Magician." *Wisconsin Studies in Contemporary Literature* 8 (1967): 431–36.

Inge, M. Thomas. "Mo Yan and William Faulkner: Influences and Confluences." *The Faulkner Journal* 6.1 (Fall 1990): 14–24.

———."Yoknapatawpha on the Don: Faulkner and Sholokhov." *Faulkner, His Contemporaries, and His Posterity.* Ed. Zacharasiewicz. 129–42.

———, ed. *William Faulkner: The Contemporary Reviews.* Cambridge: Cambridge UP, 1995.

Irmscher, Christoph. *Masken der Moderne: Literarische Selbststilisierung bei T. S. Eliot, Ezra Pound, Wallace Stevens und William Carlos Williams.* Würzburg: Königshausen und Neumann, 1992.

Irwin, John T. *Doubling and Incest/Repetition and Revenge: A Speculative Reading of Faulkner.* Baltimore: Johns Hopkins UP, 1975.

———. "The Dead Father in Faulkner." *The Fictional Father.* Ed. Davis. 147–68.

Iser, Wolfgang. *Die Appellstruktur der Texte: Unbestimmtheit als Wirkungsbedingung literarischer Prosa.* Konstanz: Universitätsverlag, 1970.

Jehlen, Myra. *Class and Character in Faulkner's South.* New York: Columbia UP, 1976.

Jenkins, Lee. *Faulkner and Black-White Relations: A Psychoanalytic Approach.* New York: Columbia UP, 1981.

Jonaitis, Aldona. *From the Land of the Totem Poles: The Northwest Coast Indian Art Collection at the American Museum of Natural History.* New York: American Museum of Natural History; Vancouver and Toronto: Douglas & McIntyre, 1988.

Karanikas, Alexander. *Tillers of a Myth: Southern Agrarians as Social and Literary Critics.* Madison: U of Wisconsin P, 1966.

Works Cited

Karl, Frederick R. *William Faulkner: American Writer*. New York: Weidenfeld & Nicolson, 1989.

Kartiganer, Donald M. *The Fragile Thread: The Meaning of Form in Faulkner's Novels*. Amherst: U of Massachussetts P, 1979.

———, and Ann J. Abadie, eds. *Faulkner and the Artist. Faulkner and Yoknapatawpha, 1993*. Jackson: UP of Mississippi, 1996.

Kauffman, Linda. "Devious Channels of Decorous Ordering: Rosa Coldfield in *Absalom, Absalom!*" *Feminisms: An Anthology of Literary Theory and Criticism*. Ed. Robyn R. Warhol and Diane Price Herndl. New Brunswick, NJ: Rutgers UP, 1991. 644–70.

Keats, John. "To Richard Woodhouse, 27 October 1818." *The Letters of John Keats 1814–1821*. Ed. Hyder E. Rollins. 2 vols. Cambridge: Harvard UP, 1958. 1: 386–87.

Kerr, Elizabeth M. *William Faulkner's Yoknapatawpha: "A Kind of Keystone in the Universe."* New York: Fordham UP, 1985.

Keppler, C. F. *The Literature of the Second Self*. Tuscon: U of Arizona P, 1972.

Kidd, Stuart. "The Farm Security Administration Photographic Projects' Reinvention of the Southern Poor White in the 1930s." *Rewriting the South: History and Fiction*. Ed. Hönnighausen and Lerda. 219–30.

King, Richard H. *A Southern Renaissance: The Cultural Awakening of the American South, 1930–1955*. Baton Rouge: Louisiana State UP, 1980.

Kinney, Arthur. "Faulkner and Racism." *Connotations: A Journal for Critical Debate* 3.3 (1993–94): 265–78.

———. *Faulkner's Narrative Poetics: Style as Vision*. Amherst: U of Massachusetts P, 1978.

Kirwan, Albert C. *Revolt of the Rednecks: Mississippi Politics, 1876–1925*. Lexington: UP of Kentucky, 1951.

Kolodny, Annette. *The Lay of the Land: Metaphor as Experience and History in American Life and Letters*. Chapel Hill: U of North Carolina P, 1975.

Koopmann, Helmut, ed. *Thomas-Mann-Handbuch*. Stuttgart: Kröner, 1990.

Koppen, Erwin. "'Heimat' international. Literarischer Regionalismus als Gegenstand der Komparatistik." *Sensus Communis: Contemporary Trends in Comparative Literature, Festschrift für Henry Remak*. Ed. J. Riesz. Tübingen: Francke Verlag, 1986. 267–74.

Kreiswirth, Martin. *William Faulkner: The Making of a Novelist*. Athens: U of Georgia P, 1983.

Kunst, Hans-Joachim. *Der Afrikaner in der Europäischen Kunst*. Bad Godesberg: Inter Nationes, 1967.

Kurzke, Hermann. *Thomas Mann. Epoche-Werk-Wirkung*. München: Beck, 1985.

Lind, Ilse Dusoir. "The Language of Stereotype in 'Death Drag.' " *Faulkner's Discourse*. Ed. Hönnighausen. 127–31.

Works Cited

———. "The Mutual Relevance of Faulkner Studies and Women's Studies: An Interdisciplinary Study." *Faulkner and Women*. Ed. Fowler and Abadie. 21–40.

Lombardo, Agostino, ed. *The Artist and His Masks: William Faulkner's Metafiction*. Roma: Bulzoni Editore, 1991.

Materassi, Mario. "Two Southern Gentlemen and Their Unsavoury Upstarts: Verga's Mazzarò and Faulkner's Flem Snopes." *Faulkner, His Contemporaries, and His Posterity*. Ed. Zacharasiewicz. 102–9.

Matthews, John. "Faulkner and the Reproduction of History." *Faulkner and History*. Ed. Coy and Gresset. 63–76.

———. *The Play of Faulkner's Language*. Ithaca: Cornell UP, 1982.

McHaney, Thomas. "The Elmer Papers: Faulkner's Comic Portrait of the Artist." *A Faulkner Miscellany*. Ed. Meriwether. 37–69.

———. "Problems of Faulkner's Poetics." *Faulkner's Discourse*. Ed. Hönnighausen. 248–53.

———. *William Faulkner's* The Wild Palms*: A Study*. Jackson: UP of Mississippi, 1975.

McMillan, Neil R., and Noel Polk. "Faulkner on Lynching." *The Faulkner Journal* 8.1 (Fall 1992; published Spring 1994): 3–14.

Mecklenburg, Norbert. *Erzählte Provinz. Regionalismus und Moderne im Roman*. Königsstein: Athenäum, 1982.

Meeter, Glenn. "Male and Female in *Light in August* and *The Hamlet*: Faulkner's Mythical Method." *Studies in the Novel* 20 (1988): 404–16.

Meindl, Dieter. *Bewusstsein als Schicksal: Zu Struktur und Entwicklung von William Faulkner's Generationenromanen*. Stuttgart: Metzler, 1974.

———. "Romantic Idealism and *The Wild Palms*." *Faulkner and Idealism*. Ed. Michel Gresset and Patrick Samway. Jackson: UP of Mississippi, 1991.

Meriwether, James B., ed. *A Faulkner Miscellany*. Jackson: UP of Mississippi, 1974.

Michel, Frann. "Faulkner as a Lesbian Author." *The Faulkner Journal: Faulkner and Feminism* 4.1–2 (Fall 1988/Spring 1989): 5–20.

Millgate, Michael. "'A Novel: Not an Anecdote': Faulkner's *Light in August*." *New Essays on* Light in August. Ed. Millgate. 31–53.

———, ed. *New Essays on* Light in August. Cambridge: Cambridge UP, 1987.

———. "Unreal Estate: Reflections on Wessex and Yoknapatawpha." *The Literature of Region and Nation*. Ed. R. P. Draper. London: Macmillan, 1989.

Minter, David, ed. *William Faulkner,* The Sound and the Fury*: An Authoritative Text, Backgrounds and Contexts, Criticism*. New York and London: Norton, 1987.

Moore, Robert R. "Desire and Despair: Temple Drake's Self-Victimization." *Faulkner and Women*. Ed. Fowler and Abadie. 112–27.

Works Cited

Moreland, Richard C. *Faulkner and Modernism: Rereading and Rewriting*. Madison: U of Wisconsin P, 1990.

Morris, Wesley, with Barbara Alverson Morris, *Reading Faulkner*. Madison: U of Wisconsin P, 1989.

Mortimer, Gail L. "The 'Masculinity' of Faulkner's Thought." *The Faulkner Journal: Faulkner and Feminism* 4 (Fall 1988/ Spring 1989): 67–81.

Myoshi, Masao. *The Divided Self: A Perspective on the Literature of the Victorians*. New York: New York UP, 1969.

Nicolaisen, Peter. "Collective Experience and Questions of Genre in *A Fable*." *The Artist and His Masks: William Faulkner's Metafiction*. Ed. Lombardo. 397–414.

———. " 'The dark land talking voiceless speech': Faulkner and 'Native Soil.' " *The Mississippi Quarterly* 45 (Summer 1992): 253–76.

———. "Faulkner and Hamsun: The Community and the Soil." *Faulkner, His Contemporaries, and His Posterity*. Ed. Zaracharasiewicz. 88–101.

———. "The Southern Agrarians and European Agrarianism." *Mississippi Quarterly* 49.4 (Fall 1996); reprinted in *Southern Landscapes*, ed. Tony Badger, Walter Edgar, and Jan Norby Gretlund. Tübingen: Stauffenburg, 1996. 85–101.

Nietzsche, Friedrich. *Beyond Good and Evil*. Trans. R. J. Hollingdale. London: Penguin Classics, 1990.

———. *The Gay Science*. Trans. W. Kaufmann. New York: Vintage, 1974.

O'Brien, Michael. *The Idea of the American South, 1920–1941*. Baltimore: Johns Hopkins UP, 1979.

Odum, Howard W., and Harry Estill Moore. *American Regionalism: A Cultural-Historical Approach to National Integration*. New York: Holt, 1938.

Page, Ralph. "John Sartoris: Friend or Foe." *Arizona Quarterly* 23 (Spring 1967): 27–33.

Peavy, Charles D. *Go Slow Now: Faulkner and the Race Question*. Eugene: U of Oregon Books, 1964.

Peper, Jürgen. *Bewußtseinslagen des Erzählens und erzählte Wirklichkeiten*. Leiden: Brill, 1966.

Percy, William Alexander. *Lanterns on the Levee: Recollections of a Planter's Son*. Intro. Walker Percy. 1941; repr. Baton Rouge: Louisiana State UP, 1978.

Perlis, Alan. "*The Sound and the Fury*: *Buddenbrooks* Reconsidered." *Heir and Prototype*. Ed. Ford. 98–112.

Pierle, Robert. "Snopesism in Faulkner's *The Hamlet*." *English Studies* 52 (1971): 246–52.

Pilkington, John. "Materialism in the Country: *The Hamlet*." *The Heart of Yoknapatawpha*. Jackson: UP of Mississippi, 1981. 217–41.

Pitavy, Francois. "Some Remarks on Negation and Denegation in William

Works Cited

Faulkner's *Absalom, Absalom!" Faulkner's Discourse.* Ed. Hönnighausen. 25–32.

———. "Voice and Voices in *Light in August." William Faulkner's* Light in August: *A Critical Casebook.* Ed. Pitavy. 171–75.

———, ed. *William Faulkner's* Light in August: *A Critical Casebook.* New York and London: Garland, 1982.

Polk, Noel. "William Faulkner's 'Carcassonne.' " *Studies in American Fiction* 12 (Spring 1984): 29–43.

———, ed. "Introduction." *New Essays on* The Sound and the Fury. Cambridge: Cambridge UP, 1993. 1–21.

———. *Children of the Dark House.* Jackson: UP of Mississippi, 1996.

Pothier, Jacques. "Negation in Faulkner: Saying No to Time and Creating One's Own Space." *Faulkner's Discourse.* Ed. Hönnighausen. 38–45.

Pütz, Heinz Peter. *Kunst und Künstlerexistenz bei Nietzsche und Thomas Mann.* Bonn: Bouvier Verlag, 1963.

Rado, Lisa. "'A Perversion That Builds Character and Invents Lear Is a Pretty Good Thing': *Mosquitoes* and Faulkner's Androgynous Imagination." *The Faulkner Journal* 9.1–2 (Fall 1993/Spring 1994): 13–28.

Rankin, Thomas. "The Ephemeral Instant: William Faulkner and the Photographic Image." *Faulkner and the Artist.* Ed. Donald M. Kartiganer and Ann J. Abadie. Jackson: UP of Mississippi, 1996. 294–317.

Ransom, John Crowe. "The Aesthetic of Regionalism." *American Review* 2 (1934): 290–310.

Reed, John Shelton. *Southern Folk, Plain and Fancy: Native White Social Types.* Athens: U of Georgia P, 1986.

Reid Broughton, Panthea. "The Economy of Desire: Faulkner's Poetics, From Eroticism to Post-Impressionism." *The Faulkner Journal: Faulkner and Feminism* 4.1–2 (Fall 1988/Spring 1989): 159–77.

Riceour, Paul. *The Rule of Metaphor: Multidisciplinary Studies of the Creation of Meaning in Language.* Trans. R. Czerny. Toronto: U of Toronto P, 1975.

Rio-Jelliffe, R. "*Absalom, Absalom!* as Self–Reflexive Novel." *The Journal of Narrative Technique* 11 (1981): 75–90.

Roberts, Diane. *Faulkner and Southern Womanhood.* Athens: U of Georgia P, 1994.

Rogin, Michael Paul. *Fathers and Children: Andrew Jackson and Subjugation of the American Indian.* New York: Alfred Knopf, 1975.

Rubin, Louis D. "The Hound Under the Wagon." *Faulkner and the Southern Renaissance.* Ed. Fowler and Abadie. 93–119.

Rubin, Louis D., and James Jackson Kilpatrick, eds. *The Lasting South: Fourteen Southerners Look at Their Home.* Chicago: Legnery, 1957.

Said, Edward W. *Orientalism: Western Conceptions of the Orient.* London: Routledge and Kegan Paul, 1978.

Works Cited

Samway, Patrick. "Narration and Naming in *The Reivers*." *Faulkner's Discourse*. Ed. Hönnighausen. 254–62.

Sass, Karen R. "Rejection of the Maternal and the Polarization of Gender in *The Hamlet*." *The Faulkner Journal: Faulkner and Feminism* 4.1–2 (Fall 1988/ Spring 1989): 127–38.

Schmitz, Neil. "Tall Tale, Tall Talk; Pursuing the Lie in Jacksonian Literature." *American Literature* 48 (1976): 471–91.

Schroeter, James. "*Buddenbrooks* and *The Sound and the Fury*." *Études de Lettres*, No.1 (1983): 43–54.

Scott, Anne Firor. *The Southern Lady: From Pedestal to Politics 1830–1930*. Chicago: U of Chicago P, 1970.

Sensibar, Judith. *The Origins of Faulkner's Art*. Austin: U of Texas P, 1984.

Singal, Daniel Joseph. *The War Within: From Victorian to Modernist Thought in the South, 1919–1945*. Chapel Hill: U of North Carolina P, 1982.

Singer, Alan. *A Metaphorics of Fiction: Discontinuity and Discourse in the Modern Novel*. Tallahassee: UP of Florida, 1983.

Smith, Henry Nash. "Three Southern Novels." *Southwestern Review* 15 (Autumn 1929): iii–iv; rpt. in M. Thomas Inge, ed., *William Faulkner: The Contemporary Reviews*.

Snead, James. *Figures of Division: William Faulkner's Major Novels*. New York: Methuen, 1986.

———. "Litotes and Chiasm: Cloaking Tropes in *Absalom, Absalom!*" *Faulkner's Discourse*. Ed. Hönnighausen. 16–24.

Snyder, Gary. *Earth House Hold: Technical Notes to Fellow Dharma Revolutionaries*. New York: New Directions, 1969.

———. *The Real Work: Interviews and Talks, 1964*. Ed. Scott McLean. New York: New Directions, 1980.

Steiner, Michael, and Clarence Mondale. *Region and Regionalism in the United States: A Source Book for the Humanities and Social Sciences*. New York: Garland, 1988.

Stetsenko, Katerina. "W. Faulkner and V. Astafiev: The Problems of Nature and Civilization." *Faulkner, His Contemporaries, and His Posterity*. Ed. Zacharasiewicz. 143–51.

Straumann, Heinrich. "Black and White in Faulkner's Fiction." *English Studies* 60 (1979): 462–70.

Sundquist, Eric. *Faulkner: The House Divided*. Baltimore: Johns Hopkins UP, 1983.

Susman, Warren I. *Culture as History: The Transformation of American Society in the Twentieth Century*. 1973; New York: Pantheon Books, 1984.

Taylor, Carole Anne. "*Light in August*: The Epistemology of Tragic Paradox." *William Faulkner's* Light in August: *A Critical Casebook*. Ed. Pitavy. 203–24.

Works Cited

Taylor, Walter. *Faulkner's Search for a South*. Chicago: U of Illinois P, 1983.

Tindall, George Brown. *The Ethnic Southerners*. Baton Rouge: Louisiana State UP, 1976.

———. "Mythology: A New Frontier in Southern History." *The Idea of the South*. Ed. Vandiver. Chicago: U of Chicago P, 1964.

Tymm, Ralph. *Doubles in Literary Psychology*. Cambridge: Bowes & Bowes, 1949.

Urgo, Joseph R. "Menstrual Blood and Nigger Blood: Joe Christmas and the Ideology of Sex and Race." *Mississippi Quarterly* 41 (1987/1988): 391–401.

Vandiver, Frank, ed. *The Idea of the South: Pursuit of a Central Theme*. Chicago: U of Chicago P, 1964.

Vechten, Carl Van. *Nigger Heaven*. New York: Octagon Books, 1926.

Vickery, Olga. *The Novels of William Faulkner*. Baton Rouge: Louisiana State UP, 1964.

Warren, Robert Penn., ed. "Introduction: Faulkner: Past and Future." *Faulkner: A Collection of Critical Essays*. Englewood Cliffs, NJ: Prentice Hall, 1966. 1–22.

———, "William Faulkner." *William Faulkner: Four Decades of Criticism*. Ed. Linda Welshimer Wagner. East Lansing: Michigan State UP, 1973. 94–109.

Watson, James G. *The Snopes Dilemma: Faulkner's Trilogy*. Coral Gables, FL: U of Miami P, 1968.

———, ed. *Thinking of Home: William Faulkner's Letters to his Mother and Father, 1918–1925*. New York: Norton, 1992.

Weinstein, Philip M. "'If I Could Say Mother': Constructing the Unsayable About Faulknerian Maternity." *Faulkner's Discourse*. Ed. Hönnighausen. 3–15.

Welty, Eurdora. *Eudora Welty Photographs*. Foreword by Reynolds Price. Jackson and London: UP of Mississippi, 1989.

White, Hayden. *Metahistory: The Historical Imagination in Nineteenth Century Europe*. Baltimore: Johns Hopkins UP, 1973.

Whiting, Cecile. *Antifascism in American Art*. New Haven: Yale UP, 1989.

Williamson, Joel. *William Faulkner and Southern History*. New York and Oxford: Oxford UP, 1993.

Wilson, Charles R., and William Ferris, eds. *Encyclopedia of Southern Culture*. Durham: U of North Carolina P, 1989.

Wilson, Edmund. *Patriotic Gore: Studies in the Literature of the American Civil War*. New York: Oxford UP, 1966.

Wittenberg, Judith Bryant. "Faulkner and Women Writers." *The Faulkner Journal: Faulkner and Feminism* 4.1–2 (Fall 1988/Spring 1989).

———. *The Transfiguration of Biography*. Lincoln: U of Nebraska P, 1979.

———. "The Women of *Light in August*." *New Essays on* Light in August. Ed. Millgate. 103–122.

Works Cited

Wright, Elizabeth. *Psychoanalytic Criticism: Theory in Practice*. London and New York: Methuen, 1984.

Yaeger, Patricia and Beth Kowaleski-Wallace, eds. *Refiguring the Father: New Feminist Readings of Patriarchy*. Carbondale: U of Illinois P, 1989.

Zacharasiewicz, Waldemar, ed. *Faulkner, His Contemporaries, and His Posterity. Transatlantic Perspectives*. Vol. 2. Tübingen: Francke, 1993.

Zender, Karl F. *The Crossing of the Ways: William Faulkner, the South, and the Modern World*. New Brunswick: Rutgers UP, 1989.

Ziegler, Heide. *Existenzielles Erleben und kurzes Erzählen: Das Komische, Tragische, Groteske und Mythische in William Faulkner's Short Stories*. Stuttgart: Metzler, 1977.

Zink, Karl E. "Flux and the Frozen Moment: The Imagery of Stasis in Faulkner's Prose." *PMLA* 71 (1956): 258–301.

INDEX

Index

Index

Index

Index

Index

motif
of mother and child, 213
of vase, urn/woman, 101
populist ideals of the thirties in, 207
references to Beardsley in, 79
regionalist and modernist features in, 150, 188
Rev. Hightower, 56
role of readers, 215
Simon McEachern, 37, 148
social drama of race and gender, 145
Lion in the Garden, 31, 42, 46
"Lo!," Indian theme in, 203

Mann, Thomas, 32, 33, 103, 125, 128
Buddenbrooks, 127
theme of decadence in, 124
twin brothers, 128
Mansion, The, 85
Faulkner's regionalist sympathies in, 188
Mink Snopes, 195
Marble Faun, The, 7, 60, 80, 109, 182
preface
organicist metaphors in, 194
role of southern regionalist in, 185, 188
Marionettes, The, 25, 33, 61, 79
repetition effects in, 167
Masks. *See also* Faulkner, William; Masks and metaphors
cognitive aspect of, 71
creating process, 38
different thematic aspects of, 18
discursive status of the biographical "I," 58
impact of cultural patterns, 43
impact on readers, 33
intertextual aspects, 37
not one artistic identity, 59
and role-play, 169, 172
self-castigating, 114
in the theater, 62
theory of, 50
use of the term, 73
Masks and metaphors
Faulkner's concepts of, ix, 11, 21
"I" vs. "not I," 73
as performances, 73
psychological patterns, 114
Masquerade, use of the term, 72
Mayday
echoes of Dante's Beatrice in, 100
illustration of faun in, 80

Melville, Herman, 3, 49, 176, 193, 244
allegories of moral consciousness, 152
Moby-Dick, 56, 58
Metaphor, x, 64. *See also* Metaphorics; Metaphoricity; Metaphorization
as aesthetic principle, 72
black
as cultural *m.*, 221
as white *m.*, 217
of the cage, 117
categorical boundaries of, x
cognitive aspect of, 71
discussion of, 70
distortive, 260
dramatization of, 120
experience of, 148, 163
interaction with narration, 167, 178
interplay
of modernist and regionalist *m.*, 189
with narration, 74
of masks and disguise, 36
of mirroring, 260
organicist *m.*, 110, 190
vs. sophisticated narration, 39
photographic *m.* in, 239
precedence over image, 74
regionalistic ("postage stamp of native soil"), 186
as rhetorical figure, 71
rituals of male mythicization of woman, 148
"simplicity, earth, and land," 197
sociopolitical and psychological dimensions of, 72
as substitution of the truth, 65, 168
totality of, 66
transcendence in, 138, 163, 263
transfer of, 71, 141, 218
use of term, 232
vase/urn, 102
Metaphor-narration
conjectural narration and dynamic structure of metaphor, 168
in *The Hamlet*, 229
Metaphoricity, x, 141
concept of, 71
contextuality and intertextuality, 138
in *A Fable*, ix
modes and contexts of, 225
of narrative contexts, 141
structural aspect of, 139
Metaphorics, 173, 257. *See also* Reader
of actor, role-playing, and mask, 68
complex and synergic effect of, 162

307

Index

elements in character drawing, 217
forms of, x, 58, 149
modernist *m.* and regional material, 227
narrative communication between characters and readers, 224
processes of, 141
of racial communication, 218
and the reader, 238, 249
reflection of social experience in, 225
role of memory in, 143
study of, in *Absalom, Absalom!*, 176
and tall tale, 230
and transformations, 37, 121, 138
Metaphorization, x, 6, 11, 88, 145, 147, 260, 276
of language, 177
of the narrative, 119
process of, 215, 251
of reality, 139
ritualization of banal occurrences, 154
as a syntactical event, 70
transference of meaning, 73
"translation," 179
use of the term, 72–73
"Mississippi," 265
Faulkner's stand on the race question, 206
politicized regionalist outlook in, 204
Modernism, 207
definition of, 191
and regionalism, 181, 184, 190, 223
Modernist features, ix. *See also* Regionalist features
rootlessness, 21
Mosquitoes, 3, 22, 28, 33, 79–110, 220
artist personae, 57, 104
and role models in, 93
caricature of fellow artists, 90
echoes of Dante's Beatrice in, 100
Fairchild's aesthetics, 108
Faulkner's participation in the *Zeitgeist*, 89
faun motif in, 81
Freudian readings of Swinburne, 103
Gordon, 97
hermaphrodite motif, 95
importance of place in, 186
ironic self-portrait, 23
Josh, 56
organicist tendencies, 109
Prufrock persona in, 104, 113
"ready-mades" in, 97
regionalist element in, 188

role of Gordon and Fairchild, 102
sadistic spider image, 131
Talliaferro as a recast of Prufrock, 111
virginal torso, 98

Native American culture, 184, 190, 202
and nature, 203
New Deal, 183
New historicism, 184, 190, 205, 236
New Orleans Sketches
experimenting with poetic roles and literary styles, 92
Faulkner's regionalist role-play in, 200
Faulkner's regionalist sympathies in, 188
organicism and anti-intellectualism in, 197
"Out of Nazareth," 185, 193, 199
regionalist aspects of, 110
sketches of artists, 90
"Wealthy Jew," 110
Nietzsche, Friedrich, 56, 66
and the artist, ix
Beyond Good and Evil, 64, 69
The Gay Science, 67
mask concept, 66
on metaphor, masks, "perspectivism-mask-metaphor," 65, 66
"Nympholepsy," 87, 186, 268
functions of regionalism in, 188, 193
peasant heroes in, 200

O'Keeffe, Georgia, 202
O'Neill, Eugene, 61
"On Fear: Deep South in Labor: Mississippi," 182
myth of the land, 187
"On Privacy: The American Dream and What Happened to It," 51, 65

Perspective
to assimilate materials, 27
in Faulkner's narrative, 64
Pilots
as impersonations, 18, 20
as modernist artists, 21
Poe, Edgar Allan, 193, 212
Pound, Ezra, 62, 103
Primitivism, 207
connotations of the term, 222
definition of, 191
and regionalism, 184, 190, 214
Pylon, 20, 48, 265
reporter as persona in, 21

Index

Readers, 212. *See also* Metaphorics
  analogy to role-playing artist, 138
  and boundaries between author and
    character, 173
  connotative perceptions, 146
  effect of forms on, 144
  enhanced role of, 71
  experience of leitmotifs, 142
  impact of ironic perspective on, 42, 117
  and interview partners, 40
  metaphorical guidance of, 58, 140
  metaphorization processes of, 139, 143,
    215, 227, 237, 261
  moving between several contexts, 72,
    151, 168, 214
  reaction
    imagery, 152, 224, 248
    psychoanalytic theme, 95, 147
  reenacting the metaphorizing of the
    writer, 138, 215
  role of, 37, 87, 155
  and role-playing author, 223
  transfer in metaphor, 138, 254
"Red Leaves," Indian theme in, 203
Rednecks, 179
  and racism, 177
  rise of, 173, 204, 212, 240
Region
  concept of, 190
  sociocultural, psychological context of,
    190
  transformation of *r.* into symbolic
    space, 186
  and the universality of aesthetic shape,
    92
Regional
  characteristics, 213, 216
  connotations of the term, 222
  Faulkner's appreciation of *r.* architec-
    ture, 203
  Faulkner's handling of guilty *r.* past,
    212
  as integral part of the national, 197
  as mythic gut feeling, 187
  and national, 193
  reality, 255
  settings as basic human values, 207
  similes, 216
  symbolist effect of Faulkner's *r.* inspi-
    ration, 217
  and the universal, 186, 200
Regionalism, 179, 183, 207, 276
  and agrarianism, 190
  artist colonies, 202

  and cultural nationalism, 196, 199
  definition, 191
  emphasis on concrete and general, 225
  and influence
    of Sherwood Anderson, 110
    of Robert Frost, 195
    of A. E. Housman, 110, 195
  international context of, 192
  and modernism, 181, 184, 190, 223
  and naturalism, 185
  old vs. new, 190
  and organicism, 109, 192
  and pastoralism, 263, 268
  poetics of, 186
  political and cultural motives of Faulk-
    ner's, 187
  and primitivist elements, 184, 190, 214
  southern, 212
  spirit of, 11
  as style of the thirties, 188
  and universality, 180, 196
Regionalist features, ix. *See also* Modernist
    features
  affinity with socialist and fascist art of
    the thirties, 210
  of art, 188
  and decadence movement, 186
  and Faulkner's antimodernist stance,
    194
  vs. Faulkner's international character-
    istics, 185
  and Faulkner's rural preoccupations,
    185
  and motifs, 208, 213
  mythicizing of country folks, 209
  nationalist-populist-organicist tenden-
    cies, 110
  of realism, 7
  vs. regionalist idealism, 208
Reivers, The, 278
Requiem for a Nun, mythicizing history in,
    203
Role-play, ix, 3, 11, 26, 69, 253. *See also*
    Faulkner, William; Masks;
    Readers
  aesthetics of, x
  art in life, 20
  concept of, 66
  encounter with the nonself, 62
  of impostors and actors, 22, 67
  literary, 7
  photographic, 7
  psychological and sociological
    aspects of, 67

Index